Schizophrenia: the epigenetic puzzle

Dedicated to

ELIOT SLATER, CBE, MD, FRCP, FRC Psych, LLD (Hon)

Our Friend and Mentor

Schizophrenia

The epigenetic puzzle

IRVING I. GOTTESMAN
Washington University School of Medicine

JAMES SHIELDS
The Institute of Psychiatry, London

With the assistance of **DANIEL R. HANSON**
University of Minnesota School of Medicine

450044

CAMBRIDGE UNIVERSITY PRESS

Cambridge
London   New York   New Rochelle
Melbourne   Sydney

Published by the Press Syndicate of the University of Cambridge
The Pitt Building, Trumpington Street, Cambridge CB2 1RP
32 East 57th Street, New York, NY 10022, USA
296 Beaconsfield Parade, Middle Park, Melbourne 3206, Australia

First published 1982

Printed in the United States of America

Library of Congress Cataloging in Publication Data
Gottesman, Irving I.
Schizophrenia, the epigenetic puzzle.
Includes bibliographical references and index.
1. Schizophrenia. 2. Schizophrenia –
Genetic aspects. 3. Nature and nurture.
I. Shields, James. II. Hanson, Daniel R.
III. Title.
RC514.G675   616.89′82071   81–18181
ISBN 0 521 22573 6 hard covers   AACR2
ISBN 0 521 29559 9 paperback

Contents

Contents

Tables and figures

Figures

Preface

There are many different ways to "lose one's mind." The best-known form of "madness," which today goes by the name (diagnosis) of schizophrenia, fascinated scientists, philosophers, novelists, and laymen even before it was called dementia praecox by Kraepelin near the turn of this century. If we are ever to have a science of schizophrenia, it must be distinguished as clearly as possible from the other varieties of mental illness, disease, and dis-ease that are depicted with varying accuracy in films and on television. What causes schizophrenia? Can anyone get it? Is it inherited? If so, how is it transmitted? Are there distinct genetic and environmentally produced types, or could the amazing range of clinical phenomena be explained as variations on a single underlying theme? Can children unrelated or even related to a schizophrenic who are at risk of becoming affected be detected in advance? What are the relationships among infantile autism, childhood schizophrenia, and adult schizophrenia, if any? What genetic counseling services, if any, should be made available to schizophrenics and their relatives?

These questions and related issues are dealt with in the pages that follow. It will be our goal to adduce the scattered facts generated by research in the growing field of behavioral (psychiatric) genetics and to attempt to integrate them within a broad framework called diathesis–stressor theory. We hold that the genes are necessary as a predisposing diathesis but that they are not sufficient by themselves for the development of schizophrenia.

Some of the new work in behavioral genetics is referred to in passing in introductory and advanced textbooks for students of psychology, psychiatry, child development, education, human genetics, sociology, and "allied health fields" (e.g., nursing); but the task of those seeking an overview, researchers as well as students, has been a difficult one. Our hope is that this book will be a useful resource for anyone seriously interested in the problem of schizophrenia.

For us, schizophrenia is a gigantic jigsaw puzzle and its etiology defies simplistic explanations. We reflect our bias, background, and research when we say that the genetical pieces in the puzzle are more central and more important clues to its solution than the environmental pieces. In other words, the genetical pieces provide more of the figure; the environmental ones provide the ground, sky and other scenery. To repeat a truism, genes and environment are both essential for the development of any human characteristic; the puzzle is epigenetic. The task ahead is to discover how genes and environment interact to produce schizophrenia. Of course, it is much easier to talk about such epigenetic interactions than to design experiments that will elucidate them! Despite brilliant advances in the "harder" sciences of molecular biology, neurochemistry, computerized and positron emission tomography, and psychopharmacology, we cannot yet detect a particular biological defect in all or most schizophrenics. Despite selfless expenditures of time and energy by psychotherapists and sophisticated efforts in the "softer" sciences, we cannot implicate any specific life experience that is common to all or most schizophrenics. And, despite advances in analytic power and in model building by population geneticists, we have no grand systems model that integrates or predicts the diverse facts about schizophrenia.

We believe that schizophrenia is the kind of common genetic disorder that makes research on it more like research on diabetes, heart disease, and mental retardation. Such rare but familiar, clear-cut genetic disorders as phenylketonuria, a simple recessive, or Huntington disease, a simple dominant, are much less useful as models. The evidence for the important contribution of genetic factors to the etiology of schizophrenia comes from the simultaneous consideration of data from family, twin, and adoption studies. Naïve environmental theories that assume that unspecifiable stressors are sufficient to cause schizophrenia either have been refuted or are phrased in ways to make them untestable. It is essential to merge the wisdom of experienced clinicians about the roles of environment in the pathogenesis of schizophrenia with enlightened genetic suggestions that focus on etiology.

All data sources and designs in this area have their faults and limitations, and we have no wish to engage in a shouting match with those who are more genetical than we are or with those who are much more environmentally minded than we are. Our wish is to provide a set of leads about the probable roles of genetic factors in mental illness as well as the necessary references for those colleagues and students who wish to pursue the ideas in more depth. Impatience in the face of complexity may lead to an unwarranted confidence that one has one's hands on the "truth"; we deplore such attitudes because they will delay the process of understanding this disorder, which brings so much suffering to victims and their families. We are skeptical about received wisdom from *all* quarters, but we hope that our skepticism will not be confused with pessimism about the solution to the schizophrenia puzzle. It will be solved, undoubtedly before the twentieth century ends.

We have dedicated this book to Eliot Slater, our friend and mentor. He more than anyone else, by his generosity and example, has shaped our interest in schizophrenia. In addition, we are indebted to the following colleagues for either their comments on drafts of this book or their contributions to our continual learning about schizophrenia: E. Essen-Möller, S. E. Nicol, K. L. Moreland, P. E. Meehl, L. L. Heston, L. Erlenmeyer-Kimling, Ø. Ødegaard, E. Zerbin-Rüdin, M. Bleuler, J. K. Wing, D. Rosenthal, and J. Welner. Any errors are our responsibility. We thank J. Hoffman and M. E. Peters for their secretarial and bibliographic assistance and S. Buchsbaum, L. R. Mosher, T. Reich, and S. B. Guze for their encouragement; this project was also supported in part by USPHS grants MH-31302 and AA-03539. James Shields died June 20, 1978 – a tragic loss to his colleagues and to the field of psychiatric genetics.

Irving I. Gottesman
Daniel R. Hanson

Wetterberg, L. *A neuropsychiatric and clinical investigation of acute intermittent porphyria.* Lund, Sweden: Scandinavian University Books, 1967.

Wyatt, R. J., Murphy, D. L., Belmaker, R., Cohen, S., Donelly, C. H., & Pollin, W. Reduced monoamine oxidase activity in platelets: A possible genetic marker for vulnerability to schizophrenia. *Science,* 1973, *179,* 916–918.

Wyatt, R. J., Potkin, S. G., Bridge, T. P., Phelps, B. H., & Wise, C. D. Monoamine oxidase in schizophrenia: An overview. *Schizophrenia Bulletin,* 1980, *6,* 199–207.

Wyatt, R. J., Saavedra, J. M., Belmaker, R., Cohen, S., & Pollin, W. The dimethyltryptamine-forming enzyme in blood platelets: A study in monozygotic twins discordant for schizophrenia. *American Journal of Psychiatry,* 1973, *130,* 1359–1361.

5   Genetical puzzle pieces: family studies

In the past 50 years a large number of family studies of the relatives of schizophrenics have come out of Germany, Switzerland, the Scandinavian countries, and the United Kingdom that use similar, conservative diagnostic standards for schizophrenia. A few of the earlier studies were reviewed in Chapter 3. The European researchers, unlike those in the United States, had better access to their relatively unmobile populations, often using special or national registers of the mentally disordered. Such factors, together with the relative homogeneity for race, religion, and social class within the studies and a high degree of cooperation from the relatives have led us to emphasize the European data in our assembling of puzzle pieces. The advantages of family-based genetic research include ease of collecting a large and representative sample, freedom from the special problems associated with twins and with adoptees, and a rich heritage of comparison studies for other traits in the human genetics literature.

We have selected well-done studies to highlight some of the points we shall make and have pooled the results from systematically conducted studies for the different degrees of genetic relationship. We have pooled despite the hazards of possible lack of comparability because the advantages here outweigh the risks. We have followed in the footsteps of Zerbin-Rüdin (1967) and Slater and Cowie (1971) in compiling the family studies and have added two comprehensive family studies by Kay and Lindelius (1970) in Sweden and by Manfred Bleuler (1978) in Switzerland; we have deleted data that added noise.[1] The Swedish work started with 270 schizophrenic probands admitted to hospitals in 1900–1910 and examined data on some 4,000 of their relatives; data on some of their relatives were old and difficult

---

[1] Brugger, in the 1920s, used schizophrenic probands who were mentally retarded; Galatschjan worked in isolation in Moscow in the 1930s and seemed to generate results ("outliers") that should not be pooled with West European studies. (See Zerbin-Rüdin, 1967, p. 507, for a description of Brugger's and Galatschjan's work.)

to differentiate, leading to many diagnoses of "undiagnosed psychoses."[2] The Swiss work, by the son of Eugen Bleuler, began with 208 schizophrenics admitted to the Burghölzli Hospital in 1942–1943; it focused on the longitudinal development of their disorders and also provided information on the statuses of some 3,000 relatives. Our discussion will emphasize the related problems of what disorders affected relatives of schizophrenics have, the genetic relationship of schizophrenia to other psychiatric disorders, and, always a problem, clues to etiological heterogeneity within the "schizophrenias."

Table 5.1 presents an overview of the risks for definite plus probable schizophrenia in the various kinds of first-, second-, and third-degree relatives of schizophrenic probands. It also includes the risks from the five studies of the offspring of dual-mating schizophrenics from Table 3.3 and the risks in genetically unrelated persons, spouses. All the risks are to be evaluated with the previous chapter and Figure 4.7 in mind, as well as the lifetime morbid risk in the general population of about 1%. The pooled sample sizes (risk lives or BZ) in most categories are sufficiently large to make for quite small standard errors. *It should be noted as a source of hope that the overwhelming majority of all relatives of schizophrenics are not themselves schizophrenic.*

Within the category of first-degree relatives, parents and children of probands share exactly half their genes in common whereas siblings of probands average 50% gene overlap; sampling fluctuations in small samples of sibs may lead to greater- or less-than-expected genetic similarity with consequent "irregular" results. The tabled value of a 5.6% risk of schizophrenia in the parents of probands is important for a number of reasons. It makes clear why the *absence* of a parental history of schizophrenia is an unacceptable *ex*clusion criterion for diagnosing schizophrenia in a patient. However, why is the risk for parents so out of line and reduced compared to other first-degree relatives? Does the fact embarrass a genetic argument? The process of marriage and reproduction leads to a positive "selection" for mental health compared to those who remain unmarried. Not only is the rate of mental retardation significantly less in married persons but so is the rate of schizophrenia. From data provided by M. Bleuler and by Mednick, who looked at adults who were parents, we can estimate the risk of schizophrenia as about half that in the general population of adults that combines parents and nonparents. Even the schizophrenias experienced by those parents of schizophrenics who were schizophrenic themselves are compatible with this

---

[2] We have converted these diagnoses to schizophrenia in our pooling because it made the results more consistent with the literature.

Table 5.1. *Risks of schizophrenia for relatives of schizophrenics*

Relationship	Number of studies	Total relatives (BZ)	Schizophrenic (incl. probable)	Morbid risk (%)
First degree				
Parents	14	8,020	447	5.6
Siblings				
All	13	9,920.7	1,002	10.1
Parents not Sc	9	7,264	698	9.6
One parent Sc	5	623.5	104	16.7
Children	7	1,577.3	202	12.8
Children of two Sc	5	134	62	46.3
Second degree				
Half siblings	5	499.5	21	4.2
Uncles/aunts	3	2,421	57	2.4
Nephews/nieces	6	3,965.5	120	3.0
Grandchildren	5	739.5	27	3.7
Third degree				
First cousins	3	1,600.5	39	2.4
Genetically unrelated				
Spouses	4	399	9	2.3

picture of selection against severe mental pathology (see also the discussion on fertility in Chapter 10). Only 5 of 28 such schizophrenic parents of schizophrenics had their onsets before age 30 and 19 of them had mild end states or recoveries, quite unlike the run-of-the-mill schizophrenic (Bleuler, 1978). Furthermore, Essen-Möller has argued that the risk in parents could be corrected upward because they do not enter observation for risk until the proband is born; such a correction will reduce the BZ for parents considerably, in fact enough for the "adjusted" MR to rise to about 11%. We are unsure of the validity of the pooled MR in parents – "other" psychoses in parents were omitted in some studies, senile psychoses (Heston et al., 1981) are quite common and may have been diagnosed as schizophrenic, and some BZs cannot be calculated. It is reassuring that the MR in Bleuler's clearly presented study is 6.9% ± 1.3%.

While we are talking about schizophrenics who become parents, we shall mention that the sex ratio among them is 2 females to 1 male. This results from the combination of earlier onsets of schizophrenia in males than in females (thus reducing their eligibility for marriage or mating) together with

earlier marriages/childbearing in females than in males (thus their schizophrenia appears after they have reproduced). The net result is that twice as
many children are born to schizophrenic mothers as to schizophrenic fathers.
Such a situation has led to the mistaken notion that mothers are somehow
more "schizophrenogenic" than fathers. No compelling evidence exists,
however, to show a higher risk of schizophrenia to the offspring of female
probands than to the offspring of male probands. The risks were symmetrical
in the older work by Kallmann and in the latest work by Bleuler in
Switzerland. This "null" from family studies is as important to constructing
theories of etiology as are the positive findings on risks as a function of gene
overlap. The higher risks to the offspring of female psychotics in the Warren
State Hospital (Pennsylvania) study by Reed et al. (1973) can be resolved
by limiting the analysis to only the schizophrenics among them and by
attending to the higher prevalence of psychopathology among their male
partners.

One fact on which almost all European family studies agree is that the age-
corrected risk for schizophrenia in the sibs of probands, ignoring information
about the parents, is about 10%. With the exception of Ødegaard (see Table
5.5), the studies have found no excess of affective psychoses in the sibs of
schizophrenics. Similar conclusions apply to the recent studies on parents
and children. In those studies that we pooled for the sib risk in which the
parental status was given, risks could be calculated for sibs with and without
an affected parent. The difference was considerable – 9.6% versus 16.7%.
The exact meaning of this finding is uncertain. It is compatible with polygenic
theory expectations; it is not compatible with a dominant rare gene
theory where the risks should have been the same; it is compatible with
common-sense environmental contributions in that two schizophrenics in the
house, one a parent, are worse than one who is a sib. The latter inference is
undermined by the fact that in what must be an almost equally disturbed
environment – one parent schizophrenic and the other psychopathic – the
risk to sibs of schizophrenics was still only 15% (Kallmann, 1938). Are not
the more than 500 nonschizophrenic sibs in the indicated families difficult to
reconcile with exposure-to-chaos as a sufficient cause?

The pooled risk to the children of schizophrenics is another of the major
puzzle pieces. The tabled value of 12.8% is without regard to the psychiatric
status of the other parent. For example, 16 (a further 10 had a co-parent who
was suspected of being schizophrenic) of the tabled 202 schizophrenic
children with a schizophrenic parent actually came from Kallmann's subsample of children with both parents definitely schizophrenic (and also
appear in the next line of the table). Few have remarked on the contribution
of such cases to the higher risk reported in children than in sibs of

schizophrenics. Recent studies have reported equal risks in sibs and in children of probands; if confirmed, such a fact makes genetic theorizing less complex and is compatible with both incomplete dominance and with polygenic theory. If the risk is in fact higher for children, it could be taken as evidence of the environmental contribution from schizophrenic rearing.

We can unpack the various contributors to the combined risk figure of 12.9% in offspring by expanding on the information derivable from the 1938 Kallmann study summarized in Table 3.2. We return to his data because only he among the investigators had a large enough sample of offspring ($BZ = 678.5$) to permit subclassification by status of parent. No other study of offspring comes close to his number of affected cases. We must first note that Kallmann's diagnostic selection criteria artificially restricted his probands on the dimension of severity; he required his cases to have their onsets before age 40 thus guaranteeing that his paranoid schizophrenics would be more severely ill than a sample without an age cutoff. Table 5.2 shows the risks to offspring of schizophrenics differentiated according to the status of the other parent (co-parent). The lowest risk was only 1.8% when the schizophrenic parent was subtyped as simple (their average duration of hospitalization was only 0.8 year versus the total sample average of 9.5 years) and the parents were married, and the co-parent was psychiatrically normal. The illegitimate matings were between schizophrenic females and unknown but probably psychiatrically abnormal males; they yielded a risk of 26.7%. We can infer abnormality in these unknown males from the similarity in risk, 21.0%, from matings between schizophrenics as a whole with abnormal but married co-parents. The risk figure of 16.4% overall is the one usually cited in connection with Kallmann's research; its value is given more weight in pooled risks simply because of his sample size. The differentiated results of Table 5.2 are well worth keeping in mind for a more accurate perspective on the issues involved. The data easily lend themselves to the interpretation that there is a relationship between the severity of illness in parent *and* co-parent and the risk of schizophrenia to their offspring.

Conventional wisdom about the psychopathology of schizophrenia leads to the belief that a substantial proportion of the children of schizophrenics are conspicuously abnormal even after the overt schizophrenics among them are removed. We challenge that belief, with data. The dogma, if true, would support either a dominant gene theory wherein the trait transmitted was "schizoidia," or a psychogenesis theory of the kind preferred by Lidz. Three German studies (of the total of seven on children of schizophrenics in Table 5.1) by Hoffmann, Oppler, and Kallmann are the sources of the belief; Kallmann believed that fully 2/3 of the offspring were "eugenically doubtful," owing, we believe, to his too vague and elastic definition of "schizoi-

Table 5.2. *Risk of schizophrenia in offspring as a joint function of severity-subtype and co-parent status*

Schizophrenic parent × Mate	BZ	Offspring risk (%)
Hebephrenic × Combined	265.5	20.7
Catatonic × Combined	106.5	21.6
Paranoid × Combined	212.0	10.4
Simple × Combined	94.5	11.6
Combined schizophrenic × Combined	687.5	16.4
Combined *female* Sc × Illegimate	37.5	26.7
Combined schizophrenic × Abnormal & legitimate	271.5	21.0
Hebephrenic × Normal & legitimate	144.5	17.3
Catatonic × Normal & legitimate	49.5	16.2
Paranoid × Normal & legitimate	118.0	8.5
Simple × Normal & legitimate	57.0	1.8
Combined schizophrenic × Combined normal	369.0	11.9

dia," which added more noise than signal to the schizophrenia data sets. Let us examine the total array of psychopathology and normality displayed in the longitudinally observed Swiss offspring of Bleuler's schizophrenics. Table 5.3 shows the kinds of pathology as a function of age at last observation. First, in accordance with the literature, the 10 schizophrenic offspring led to a typical age-corrected risk of 8.7% ± 2.6%. If we limit our view to those children over age 20, no more than 8[3] of the 148 or 5.4% would be called schizoid by Bleuler; fully 72% of these children were considered normal, and 78% of all 184 children. At the conclusion of Bleuler's study he found that 5 of the 10 schizophrenic offspring had "fully recovered." How can the differences between Bleuler and the older studies be reconciled given that all were accurate observers and, as was customary, operating without a blindfold?

We cannot improve on Bleuler's own efforts to reconcile the very different expectations (both senses of the word) for the children born to schizophrenic parents.

In the course of their purely scientific interest, the earlier investigators aimed specifically at deviant personality characteristics. I searched for these, too, but I saw primarily also the good and normal aspects. . . . In short, it was inevitable that I should find considerably more mentally sound and fewer psychopaths than I would have, if I had seen my probands' children in but a single interview and only for the purpose of scientific inquiry. . . .

If the hitherto prevailing dogma . . . is to be retained, to the effect that over half the

---

[3] In Table 5.3 they are the 3 schizoid psychopaths plus only 5 of the 22 "other eccentricities."

Table 5.3. *Psychopathology among the offspring of Bleuler's schizophrenics*

Status	Age at last information					
	<20	20–29	30–39	40–59	>60	Total
Normal limits	39	22	32	48	2	143
Schizophrenic		1	4	5		10
Schizoid psychopaths		1	1	1		3
Other eccentricities[a]	1	7	6	8		22
Suicide	1			1		2
Alcoholic			1			1
Epilepsy		1				1
Mental retardation		1	1			2
Total	41	33	45	63	2	184

[a]E.g., a schizoid, a schizoid eccentric, a schizothymic, an embezzler, a deaf-mute, a postpartum depression, etc.
Source: Data from Bleuler (1978, p. 376).

children of schizophrenics are in some way abnormal (and therefore basically "undesirable"), it is in serious need of more exacting definitions. These children can only fit that classification if "abnormal," "pathological," or "undesirable" are terms to be applied even to those whose behavior becomes different from and more difficult than that of their basic nature because of an added stressful situation. They will not fit that classification if the normal person is permitted to exhibit behavior traits in stressful situations that might be difficult to distinguish from abnormal or psycho-pathic behavior patterns. (1978, p. 381)

The points are well made and can serve as a warning about reading too much into the sources of a "state" by assuming you are dealing with a "trait." In our terms, Bleuler is underscoring the difference between pathology that may be transmitted genetically versus that which may be reactive *and* adaptive to the presence of a sick and demanding parent in one's environment. Only twin and adoption studies can help sort out these difficulties in interpretation. We shall return to these issues in the next two chapters.

Clinical resemblance within families

One of the major uses of family data has been to shed light on some aspects of etiological heterogeneity. It is especially important to note that clinical or phenotypic heterogeneity (e.g., symptoms, course, outcome, or onset age) does not necessarily imply nor guarantee etiological heterogeneity, the classical example being general paresis or syphilis of the central nervous system. Another confusion is the use of the term "heterogeneity" to refer to different points on a continuum when the points are associated with verbally defined nodes, for example, process or reactive, and severe, moderate, and mild. Of course, at some point a quantitative difference becomes large enough to be handled as if it were qualitative. Early attempts to compare the schizophrenic subtypes did not support the notion that they represented genetically distinct, qualitatively different diseases. The risk for schizophrenia of *any* Kraepelinian type was increased for the relatives of probands of *each* type. Table 5.4 shows the subtype resemblance for affected parent–offspring pairs from Kallmann's Berlin study. The resemblance in subtype is striking, but the amount of overlap is equally important for the point we are making here about the lack of evidence for a hypothesis of qualitatively distinct subtypes. The overall chi square for the table is 15.32 for 4 *df* significant at less than the .01 level. Because all types of schizophrenia appear in the children of each of the parental types, it is clear that the Kraepelinian subtypes do not "breed true" and cannot be genetically discontinuous. Earlier we discussed one important quantitative difference, namely, the greater risk of schizophrenia in the offspring of the "nuclear" cases, that is, the hebephrenic and catatonic (see Table 5.2).

There is further evidence against the popular conclusion that the phenotypic heterogeneity of schizophrenia is derived from qualitative genetic heterogeneity. Achté, in Finland, compared schizophrenics with schizophreniform psychotics, carefully diagnosed, and found that the parents of both groups were equally often schizophrenic. Using a division into good- and poor-prognosis Swedish probands and the same strategy, Larson and Nyman (1974) found no differences between first-degree relatives. A. K. Nyman (1978), also in Sweden, contrasted regressive and nonregressive schizophrenics' (defined in terms of good social functioning) "near relatives" and found them to be equally often hospitalized for mental symptoms. In Bleuler's hands the type of onset, acute versus others, did not lead to differences in the incidence of families with a positive history of schizophrenia. Of his 208 probands, 22% had an acute onset ending in recovery; 32% of their families contrasted with 38% of the others had a positive history for schizophrenia. When he used hard data on prognosis, namely, outcome at follow-up (*Endzustand*), to detect familial resemblance, he found only a slight tendency for similarity. It is significant that Bleuler did not bother to use the hebephrenic-catatonic-paranoid groupings in his study because he had found that his results would be redundant with those of Kallmann and Schulz: "The family studies thus confirm the theory that all these clinical subtypes have some kind of close genetic relationship. Despite this, the

Table 5.4. *Similarity/dissimilarity in subtype for Kallmann's affected parent–offspring pairs*

Parental subtype	Offspring subtype			
	H	C	P + S	Total
Hebephrenic	34	8	14	56
Catatonic	6	18	10	34
Paranoid + Simple	5	9	7	21
Total	45	35	31	111

tendency persists to combine one and the same subtype in the relatives of schizophrenics" (1978, p. 274).

After reviewing his own data on 228 pairs of schizophrenic sibs and those on the illnesses in the 77 probands with a positive family history and the 131 with a negative family history (i.e., in first-degree relatives or nephews or nieces), Bleuler reached the following conclusion, which withstands the criticisms of the splitters against the lumpers: " ... Among the schizophrenias occurring in two schizophrenic relatives, frequent combinations occur in which the 'end states' and the course types are totally different. This lends renewed impetus to the need for summarizing the psychoses of schizophrenic symptomatology under one all-inclusive concept – that of schizophrenias in general – despite the variety of their courses" (p. 331). Arguing by authority even when accompanied by data is not likely to diminish the controversies among those with firm opinions on these matters. We shall return to the problem of heterogeneity in Chapters 11 and 12.

By now some readers would be suspecting a cover up if we were to ignore the evidence about between-psychiatric-syndrome heterogeneity as opposed to the within-schizophrenia-heterogeneity issue discussed so far. Family studies that deal with consecutive admissions or total hospital populations as their probands rather than with "textbook cases" of schizophrenia remind us of the true complexity of "speciation" in psychopathology. Kraepelin was well aware of the complexity of the conditions that determine psychiatric symptomatology: "No experienced psychiatrist will deny that there is an alarmingly large number of cases in which it seems impossible, in spite of the most careful observation, to make a firm diagnosis" (1974, p. 28). He knew that schizophrenic symptoms were by no means limited to dementia praecox (cf. Chapters 1 and 3). Recall that Rüdin found almost equal numbers of schizophrenics and affectively ill relatives in the families of schizophrenics.

Although disciples of the Munich school thought that by selecting clinically homogeneous probands (today we hear cries about Research Diagnostic Criteria) they could minimize the occurrence of psychoses of different types in the same family, the problem would not disappear. Although Bleuler found no excess of manic-depressives among the sibs of his schizophrenics and only 2% among the parents, Slater (see Chapter 3) found that the sibs of schizophrenics found within a total psychiatric population of twin index cases had affective disorders as often as they had schizophrenia. He actually found more parents of schizophrenics with affective psychoses than with schizophrenia (16 vs. 12). When Ødegaard took 1,678 consecutive admissions to the Norwegian national register of psychoses (1972) and examined the register information about their 824 psychotic first- and second-degree relatives, he found a disquieting mixture. Table 5.5 presents data derived from his findings about what went with what. The percentage figures given for relatives cannot be taken as equivalents to the risk figures in Table 5.1 because the nonpsychotic relatives involved in the pedigrees were neither examined nor counted in the denominator. The focus here is on the taxonomic issues.

Although there is a significant degree of resemblance as to type of psychosis in pairs of affected relatives, it is important to recognize that neither schizophrenia with severe defect nor typical manic-depressive psychoses breed true to type. The findings in Table 5.5 do not fit easily into Leonhardian views about a multiplicity of distinct disease entities (Leonhard, 1979) nor into that of a unitary *Einheitspsychose* (e.g., an ego weakness dimension). The Norwegian data certainly refute the notion that manic-depressive psychoses and schizophrenia cannot appear in the same sibship. Clinical, symptom-based diagnoses in the absence of pathognomic biological markers, as yet undiscovered, lead to an inherent uncertainty for schizophrenia puzzle solvers.

Dual-mating studies

Because prospective studies of the offspring of schizophrenic parents have come to be called high-risk studies, it is useful to designate studies in which both the mother and the father are schizophrenic as "super high risk." Table 5.1 shows that whereas the average risk for schizophrenia to the children of one schizophrenic is about 12.8%, dual-mating schizophrenics produced 46.3% definite or probable schizophrenics. These findings, although very important to theories about etiology, are based on a rather small number of offspring (BZ = 134) – the smallest data set of any in Table 5.1. Even so, the 99% confidence interval for the risk lies between 35% and 58%.

Table 5.5. *Diagnostic distribution of Norwegian index patients and their psychotic relatives*

Proband diagnosis	No. of psychotic relatives	Percentage of psychotic relatives diagnosed as:		
		Schizophrenia	Reactive psychosis	Affective psychosis
Schizophrenia, severe defect	109	78.0	7.3	14.7
Schizophrenia, slight defect	368	70.5	15.7	13.8
Schizophrenia, no defect (schizoaffective, etc.)	179	45.8	22.9	31.3
Reactive psychoses	82	28.0	47.6	24.4
Atypical affective psychoses	39	35.9	28.2	35.9
Manic-depressive psychoses	47	19.1	10.6	70.2

Source: After Ødegaard (1972).

The strategy of studying offspring where both parents are severely mentally disordered need not be restricted to the schizophrenia by schizophrenia ($S \times S$) matings, which are extremely rare; information relevant to the heterogeneity of schizophrenia and on the specificity of the alleged components of a schizophrenia spectrum can be generated by looking at the offspring born to any pairing of diagnoses. Using this less restrictive technique, one can search for differential maternal effects because both mother S and father, say manic-depressive, and the reciprocal "cross" father S and mother manic-depressive would be examined to see whether the sex of the schizophrenic parent made a difference in offspring risks. Elsässer (Chapter 3) used the wider strategy, and recent work by Kringlen in Norway and by Fischer and Gottesman in Denmark has used the method to advantage. A classical illustration of the use of dual matings to elucidate the modes of transmission of a syndrome was research on the "group of deafnesses": An unforeseen increase in assortative matings was an unintended side effect of special schools for the deaf. Conventional wisdom had it that most cases were recessive and some were dominant, but no one suspected the large amount of heterogeneity within both modes that was revealed by the lack of deafness in the offspring of two deaf spouses. Briefly, matings between spouses with an apparently recessive form of deafness led to no affected offspring, whereas the expectation had been 100% (see Chapter 4). Such results mean that two different loci are involved, each under different recessive gene control. Similar findings emerge from studies of genetic blindness.

Elsässer's 1952 monograph (see Chapter 3) was based on research done before World War II but delayed by the war. A follow-up study of the children in 30 out of 38 of his rare dual-mating families was finished by 1959 and reported in 1971. The 11 S × S families are described in detail; the other mating types receive shorter treatment. Depending on the age-correction procedure used, his earlier 39% risk of schizophrenia was lowered to 36%. The psychosis risks for the other mating types do not differ much from this. Earlier, 20 MD × MD matings yielded 14 psychotics, but only 1 of them was a schizophrenic, and 19 S × MD produced an even split of 8 schizophrenics and 8 manic-depressive offspring. One difficulty in accepting these results at face value is that no diagnoses were made blindfolded, that is, the researcher knew the parental diagnoses at the time he was diagnosing one of their children. Nevertheless, Elsässer concluded that at least 1/3 of the offspring born to S × S matings become schizophrenic, that conflict situations and frustrations act as releasers of endogenous psychoses, and that particularly good or bad family environments appear to have no (!) influence.

Among the 48 dual-mating psychotic parents examined by Kringlen (1978) in Norway with offspring over age 20, 8 were S × S and a further 26 had 1 mate schizophrenic. Schizophrenic offspring were only produced by those matings involving a schizophrenic. Seven of the 25 (28%) offspring of the S × S matings were psychotic, 5 schizophrenic and 2 "borderline," 40% were neurotic, and 28% were normal. Because the mean age of the unaffected offspring was 36, Kringlen considered an age-corrected risk of 29% for schizophrenia to be a maximum one. He made the important observation that risk of schizophrenia from matings of S × another psychosis was not higher than the risks in the literature for the offspring of schizophrenics generally (9.3%) but the risk of any psychosis was raised to 17%. Such a finding speaks to the specificity of schizophrenia transmission. Fully 51% of the offspring from the dual matings were normal and only 17% (no age correction) were psychotic.

Although Bleuler had only 3 S × S matings in his sample with a total of 5 children age 30 to 54, his case histories and comments are valuable. None was schizophrenic, 1 a schizoid psychopath, 1 extremely neurotic, 1 mildly schizoid, and 2 were perfectly normal despite rearing by their parents.

A normal development can prevail in spite of total neglect, of copious teaching of irrationality, and of the complete degeneration of the imaginative world of the parents. Nothing in these statements is directed against the true pathogenic significance of all these adverse influences; on the contrary, I am quite convinced of their pathogenic validity. But on the other hand, I cannot assert that these psychopathological influences (individually or combined) would be a decisive cause by themselves. (Bleuler, 1978, p. 388)

Elsässer had also found that 70% of the nonpsychotic offspring of S × S pairings were perfectly healthy. Because we do not obviously have a situation of matings between homozygous recessives, we can expect a great deal of genotypic variation among the offspring of dual matings. The high proportion of normality found in the recent studies can be taken as evidence against assigning too strong a role to within-family environmental events such as communication deviances and neglect as uniform causes of schizophrenia.

A dual-mating study conducted in the Soviet Union by Moskalenko (1972) made possible the clinical observation of a large number of offspring within the framework of Russian psychiatry. Because Moscow was one of the WHO centers for the IPSS (see Chapter 1), we can translate some of their terms, for example, "shiftlike schizophrenia," to our framework. Thirty S × S families and 44 S × not-S formed two groups of study children. Of the 57 children from dual matings, 78.9% (no age correction!) were called definite or probable schizophrenics and only 5 were considered within normal limits. In the singly loaded families 50.7% were affected. Such impossibly high rates cannot be pooled with the literature so far reviewed because many of the families were ascertained through their already affected children and the latter were not excluded when the risks for offspring were calculated. Nevertheless the technique would be useful for finding cases to study in their own right for possible genetic polymorphisms or biological markers, using neurochemistry and tomography strategically.

In 1968 Erlenmeyer-Kimling reported on a study that had been launched with Kallmann and Falek to collect a statewide sample of the offspring of S × S matings. Although the results are still quite preliminary and combine different sampling strategies, 77 S × S matings have produced 201 offspring. The diagnoses of the parent couples have yet to be reviewed (see Chapter 1) so as to correct for New York State hospital chart diagnoses. The crude percentage already hospitalized psychiatrically amounts to 19% (32/167); a preliminary age-corrected risk for "psychosis" with hospitalization comes to 32% (32/100). We look forward to the results of this study as it develops within the context of Erlenmeyer-Kimling's prospective high-risk research and its emphasis on psycho/neurophysiology (Watt et al., in press).

Fischer and Gottesman (1980, preliminary results) have collected a sample of all dual-mating psychiatric inpatients from the Danish national psychiatric register and have identified and followed up all their children surviving to age 15. Of the 198 couples, 158 had surviving offspring, 452 of them to be exact. The couples were the total yield from a register containing 150,000 psychiatric inpatients. Only 6 couples were S × S matings but 45 matings were S × some kind of diagnosis with a total of 111 offspring. In the total sample of 452 offspring, 121 or 27% had already been psychiatrically hospitalized at some point in their lives and the vast majority were over age 35. Of the 9 children from the S × S matings, only 3 have been hospitalized but all were diagnosed as schizophrenic. Of the total of 111 children from S × — matings, 27 have been hospitalized, 11 with diagnoses of schizophrenia; the 4 offspring who had diagnoses of bipolar affective disorder all had 1 parent with an affective psychosis.

The studies from Norway and Denmark are important for the taxonomic problems. They shed light on what goes with what, which schizophrenics can be produced without a schizophrenic parent, what could be included in a valid schizophrenic spectrum, and whether there are any "antischizophrenia" genes detectable by a *lowered* risk from S × ? matings. Further information will come when the data from the nonhospitalized offspring in the Danish study, all of whom have been interviewed in the field as part of a "health survey" without mentioning their parents, are analyzed. More than half of those offspring appear to deserve a diagnosis, usually from the personality disorder or neurosis categories.

Spouses of schizophrenics

At the bottom of Table 5.1 you will see the risk of schizophrenia in the spouses of schizophrenics from the four systematic studies in the literature reported as 2.3%. If social class controls had been available they might not be different from this value. In other words, there does not appear to be any marked evidence for assortative mating for overt schizophrenia in these samples. Halfway houses and self-help groups could change this picture in the future with important consequences for psychiatric genetic researchers. The study of such strategic populations as dual-mating and single-mating offspring, whether cross-sectional or prospective, has much to offer us at this stage of our ignorance about the genetics of schizophrenia. The studies we have reviewed so far seldom examine or spell out the characteristics of the other spouse. Tables 5.1 and 5.2 show how critical this information can be for comparing studies with one another. Rosenthal (1975) with his interest in schizophrenia spectrum disorders has provided information on the co-parents in the Danish adoption study to be discussed in Chapter 7. He has reported that 13/40 of interviewed spouses of schizophrenics had a "soft-spectrum" diagnosis and a further 9 (all male) were psychopathic. When the co-parent

psychiatric disorders. In L. Robins, P. Clayton, & J. Wing (Eds.), *The social consequences of psychiatric illness.* New York: Brunner/Mazel, 1980, pp. 75–90.

Hanson, D. R., Gottesman, I. I., & Meehl, P. E. Genetic theories and the validation of psychiatric diagnosis: Implications for the study of children of schizophrenics. *Journal of Abnormal Psychology*, 1977, *6*, 575–588.

Heston, L. L., Mastri, A. R., Anderson, V. E., & White, J. Dementia of the Alzheimer type. *Archives of General Psychiatry*, 1981, *38*, 1085–1090.

Hoffmann, H. *Die Nachkommenschaft bei endogenen Psychosen.* Berlin: Springer-Verlag, 1921.

Holland, J., & Shakhmatova-Pavlova, I. V. Concept and classification of schizophrenia in the Soviet Union. *Schizophrenia Bulletin*, 1977, *3*, 277–287.

Kallmann, F. J. *The genetics of schizophrenia.* New York: Augustin, 1938.

Kay, D. W. K., & Lindelius, R. Morbidity risks for schizophrenia among parents, siblings, probands' children, and siblings' children. In R. Lindelius (Ed.), A study of schizophrenia: A clinical, prognostic, and family investigation. *Acta Psychiatrica Scandinavica*, 1970, Suppl. 216, 86–88.

Kay, D. W. K., Roth, M., Atkinson, M. W., Stephens, D. A., & Garside, R. F. Genetic hypotheses and environmental factors in the light of psychiatric morbidity in the families of schizophrenics. *British Journal of Psychiatry*, 1975, *127*, 109–118.

Kraepelin, E. [*Patterns of mental disorder.*] In S. R. Hirsch & M. Shepherd (Eds.), *Themes and variations in European psychiatry.* Bristol, England: John Wright, 1974, pp. 7–30. (Originally published 1920.)

Kringlen, E. Adult offspring of two psychotic parents, with special reference to schizophrenia. In L. C. Wynne, R. L. Cromwell, & S. Matthysse (Eds.), *The nature of schizophrenia.* New York: Wiley, 1978, pp. 9–24.

Larson, C. A., & Nyman, G. E. Schizophrenia: Outcome in a birth cohort. *Psychiatria Clinica*, 1974, *7*, 50–55.

Leonhard, K. *The classification of endogenous psychoses* (5th ed.). New York: Irvington, 1979.

Lidz, T. *The origin and treatment of schizophrenic disorders.* New York: Basic Books, 1973.

Lidz, T., Fleck, S., & Cornelison, A. R. *Schizophrenia and the family.* New York: International Universities Press, 1965.

Lindelius, R. (Ed.). A study of schizophrenia: A clinical, prognostic, and family investigation. *Acta Psychiatrica Scandinavica*, 1970, Suppl. 216.

McCabe, M. A., Fowler, R. C., Cadoret, R. J., & Winokur, G. F. Familial differences in schizophrenia with good and poor prognosis. *Psychological Medicine*, 1971, *1*, 326–332.

Mednick, S., Mura, E., Schulsinger, F., & Mednick, B. Perinatal conditions and infant development in children with schizophrenic parents. In I. I. Gottesman & L. Erlenmeyer-Kimling (Eds.), Fertility and reproduction in physically and mentally disordered individuals. *Social Biology*, 1971, Suppl.

Modrzewska, K. The offspring of schizophrenic parents in a North Swedish isolate. *Clinical Genetics*, 1980, *17*, 191–201.

Moskalenko, V. D. A. [A comparative study of families with one and two schizophrenic parents.] *Zhurnal Nevropatologii i Psikhiatrii*, 1972, *72*, 86–92.

Nyman, A. K. Non-regressive schizophrenia: Clinical course and outcome. *Acta Psychiatrica Scandinavica*, 1978, Suppl. 272.

Ødegaard, Ø. The multifactorial theory of inheritance in predisposition to schizophrenia. In A. R. Kaplan (Ed.), *Genetic factors in "schizophrenia."* Springfield, Ill.: Charles C Thomas, 1972, pp. 256–275.

Oppler, W. Zum Problem der Erbprognosebestimmung. *Zeitschrift für die Gesamte Neurologie und psychiatrie*, 1932, *141*, 549–616.

Reed, S. C., Hartley, C., Anderson, V. E., Phillips, V. P., & Johnson, N. A. *The psychoses: Family studies*. Philadelphia: W. B. Saunders, 1973.

Reisby, N. Psychoses in the children of schizophrenic mothers. *Acta Psychiatrica Scandinavica*, 1967, *43*, 8–20.

Reider, R. O., & Nichols, P. L. Offspring of schizophrenics. III. Hyperactivity and neurological soft signs. *Archives of General Psychiatry*, 1979, *36*, 665–674.

Rosenthal, D. Discussion: The concept of subschizophrenic disorders. In R. R. Fieve, D. Rosenthal, & H. Brill (Eds.), *Genetic research in psychiatry*. Baltimore: Johns Hopkins University Press, 1975, pp. 199–208.

Rüdin, E. *Zur Vererbung und Neuentstehung der Dementia Praecox*. Berlin: Springer, 1916.

Scharfetter, C. On the hereditary aspects of symbiontic psychoses: A contribution towards the understanding of the schizophrenia-like psychoses. *Psychiatria Clinica*, 1970, *3*, 145–152.

Scharfetter, C. Studies of heredity in symbiontic psychoses. *International Journal of Mental Health*, 1972, *1*, 116–123.

Scharfetter, C., & Nüsperli, M. The group of schizophrenias, schizoaffective psychoses, and affective disorders. *Schizophrenia Bulletin*, 1980, *6*, 586–591.

Slater, E., & Cowie, V. *The genetics of mental disorders*. London: Oxford University Press, 1971.

Tsuang, M., Winokur, G., & Crowe, R. Morbidity risks of schizophrenia and affective disorders among first degree relatives of patients with schizophrenia, mania, depression and surgical conditions. *British Journal of Psychiatry*, 1980, *137*, 497–504.

Welner, J., & Strömgren, E. Clinical and genetic studies on benign schizophreniform psychoses based on a follow-up. *Acta Psychiatrica Scandinavica*, 1958, *33*, 377–399.

World Health Organization. *Schizophrenia: An international follow-up study*. Chichester, England: Wiley, 1979.

Wittermans, A. W., & Schulz, B. Genealogischer Beitrag zur Frage der geheilten Schizophrenien. *Arkiv für Psychiatrie und Nervenkrankheiten*, 1950, *185*, 211–232.

Zerbin-Rüdin, E. Endogene Psychosen. In P. E. Becker (Ed.), *Humangenetik* (Vol. 2). Stuttgart: Thieme, 1967, pp. 446–577.

Zerbin-Rüdin, E. Psychiatrische genetik. In K. P. Kisker, J.-E Meyer, Ch. Müller, & E. Strömgren (Eds.), *Psychiatrie der Gegenwart* (Vol. 1) (2nd ed.). Berlin: Springer, 1980, pp. 545–618.

6   Genetical puzzle pieces: twin studies

The family studies reviewed in the previous chapter support the hypothesis that genetic factors are importantly involved in the etiology of schizophrenia even given the uncertainties that will continue to exist. Still, some will argue that family environment rather than the families' genes accounts for the findings. We would remind them that no environmental factors have been identified that will predictably produce a rate of schizophrenia of 10% in persons not already known to be genetically related to a schizophrenic. Furthermore, the nature of the shared environments for parent–offspring pairs is quite different from that shared by two siblings, yet the risk of schizophrenia is the same, as is the degree of genetic relatedness. To disprove the genetic hypothesis it would be necessary to show that samples known to differ genetically such as the MZ and DZ co-twins of schizophrenics (100% vs. 50% gene overlap) do *not* differ in their rates of schizophrenia when exposed to the same family environments. This chapter will review the twin studies completed since those reviewed in Chapter 3 as well as variations on the twin method such as discordant MZ pairs, MZ twins reared apart, and the offspring of discordant MZ twins followed into adulthood. Like family methods, the twin methods can be criticized methodologically and for their apparent inconsistencies; some of the criticisms were discussed in Chapter 4 and we shall take up some others later in this chapter.

Despite the critical scrutiny (informed as well as uninformed) to which twin studies of schizophrenia have been subjected, their major conclusions have held up remarkably well. They no longer have to bear the burden of advancing genetic interpretations by themselves but can be seen as part of a nomological network that includes family and adoption studies together with more molecular information from the neurosciences.

Since the studies of twins conducted prior to World War II (some not reported until the postwar period) and described in Chapter 3, further advances responsive to criticism have been made. Inouye has updated his

1961 report with a final sample[1] (1972) (see Table 6.1). Five newer studies have been reported since 1963, three from Scandinavia, one from the United States based on chart reviews of U.S. veterans, and one from the United Kingdom. The 11 older and newer studies of adult twins comprise some 1,300 pairs of same-sex twins from eight countries; in each study the MZ concordance rate has been considerably higher than the DZ rate except for the Finnish work by Tienari (1975).

An overview of where we have been and where we are going can be gotten by comparing summaries of the older and newer studies in Tables 6.1 and 6.2. The rates reported in the older studies are simple pairwise ones; they are less satisfactory than probandwise rates for comparison with the risks reported for other relatives and for the general population, but the information available often does not permit other calculations. Data in Table 6.2 are presented both with the pairwise range of rates reported by the investigators as well as with probandwise rates calculated by us at the level corresponding to a hospitalized functional schizophreniclike psychosis, one not likely to be an affective one. No age corrections have been applied to these tables because we are not sure how to age correct the concordance rates. Because age of onset is highly correlated in MZ twins (perhaps 0.5 or higher), the usual age-correcting procedures are inappropriate in that they assume no correlation. We shall comment on the age of the different samples where appropriate, but the longer the co-twin has been observed since the proband became schizophrenic, the less is the concern over age correction, even when the co-twin is still rather young by absolute standards.

Tienari in Finland

A once-over-lightly glance at the reported concordance rates for schizophrenia in identical twins in current textbooks reveals the remarkable range of 0% to 86% (Kallmann, 1946). The value of zero comes from the first report of his sample by Pekka Tienari; the 86% rate is the inappropriately age-corrected value that is reduced to 69% in Table 6.1 by removal of the correction. Tienari's study is based on a birth register of only male twins born from 1920 to 1929. Fully half the starting sample of some 3,000 pairs were lost by age 16 by death (ordinary and war related) in one or both male twins. Tienari was able to determine the presence of psychoses in some 1,000 intact surviving pairs by use of the national health insurance and hospital records for inpatient and outpatient contacts. In 1969 he followed up the twins that

---

[1] The proportion of the Inouye sample that are MZ differs from the non-Japanese samples but is not an indicator of unrepresentative sampling. In Japan, about 2/3 of twin births are MZ.

Table 6.1. *Simple pairwise concordance in older schizophrenic twin series*

Investigator	MZ pairs		SS DZ pairs	
	Total	% concordant	Total	% concordant
Luxenburger	19	58	13	0
Rosanoff	41	61	53	13
Essen-Möller	11	64	27	15
Kallmann	174	69	296	11
Slater	37	65	58	14
Inouye[a]	58	59	20	15
Total	340	65	467	12

[a]Updated with 1972a final report and using schizophrenic plus schizophreniclike psychotic disorders in co-twins.

had been interviewed and reported on in 1963, as well as new psychotic pairs. To the surprise of the schizophrenia-watching world, none of the 16 MZ co-twins of schizophrenics found initially was psychotic. Three, according to Tienari, exhibited borderline features but none of them would be regarded as borderline schizophrenics, and a further nine were called schizoid. Although one might have expected a low concordance rate from a small sample of male twins with a range of severity, one would not, on *any* theory, have expected a 0% concordance rate in 16 MZ pairs and about 10% in 20 DZ pairs. The findings were mitigated by the fact that some of the pairs seemed to us to be organic psychoses from the detailed case histories Tienari provided. By 1968 one pair was concordant for schizoaffective psychosis and four co-twins were called borderline. The maximum pairwise concordance rate of 36% for the MZ pairs comes from Tienari's omitting two organic phenocopies and his counting five co-twins as affected with schizophrenia-related illnesses (see Table 6.2).

The young age of Tienari's birth cohort is highlighted by the fact that it begins in 1920, the year the Danish work of Fischer ended (see the section on Fischer). The Norwegian study by Kringlen samples from twin births in the period 1901–1930. The final results of the Finnish twin research have yet to be written as it is still in progress with an expanded sample. By 1971 a search of the registers of mental hospitals uncovered a second schizophrenic MZ co-twin as well as three new MZ pairs, one concordant and two discordant for a pairwise rate of 3/19 or 16%. We tabled a provisional value of 4/17, which becomes a probandwise rate of 7/20 independently ascertained co-twins being affected at the level in which we are interested. The 35% concordance rate is a long way from the 0% of Tienari's earliest provisional report.

Table 6.2. Concordances[a] in newer schizophrenic twin series

Investigator/locus	MZ pairs			SS DZ pairs		
	Total	Pairwise % concordance[b]	Probandwise % concordance	Total	Pairwise % concordance[b]	Probandwise % concordance
Tienari[c]/Finland	17	0–36	35	20	5–14	13
Kringlen/Norway	55	25–38	45	90	4–10	15
Fischer/Denmark	21	24–48	56	41	10–19	27
Pollin et al.[c]/U.S.A.	95	14–27	43	125	4–8	9
Gottesman & Shields/U.K.	22	40–50	58	33	9–19	12
Weighted total			46			14

[a]At the level of functional schizophreniclike psychoses in co-twins.
[b]Value or range reported by investigators.
[c]Only male twins were studied. Results for 1971 tabled for Tienari because 1975 summary data adding 3 MZ and 22 DZ new pairs lack details; he reports MZ rate 15%, DZ 7%.

Obviously, we could not defend this value as a definitive one in this sample, and in a brief summary of work-in-progress in 1975 Tienari reports that 3 of 20 MZ pairs with schizophrenic or paranoid psychoses are concordant and so are 3 of 42 DZ pairs. The possible use of some kind of age correction together with the probandwise method of calculating rates makes the Finnish study no longer so much of an odd man out in the literature. It is unfortunate that female pairs were not studied so as to provide a check on consistency of the findings.

Kringlen in Norway

The availability of a central register for psychosis initiated by Ødegaard in 1936 in Norway together with a twin birth register made it natural for Einar Kringlen to conduct a careful study with an excellent sample and personal investigation in the field. All functional psychoses were included in addition to schizophrenia; his two-volume work (1967) includes case history, pedigree, clinical analysis, and rating scale data. Kringlen found 55 pairs of MZ twins registered for schizophrenic (45) or schizophreniform psychosis (10). In 14 of these pairs both were registered and would be independently ascertained probands for the calculation of probandwise rates. After extensive fieldwork throughout the length of Norway, 3 unregistered MZ co-twins were added for a total of 17 (31%) found to be schizophrenic or schizophreniform and a further 4 to have borderline states yielding a pairwise concordance he reported as 38% (see Table 6.2). To convert the 31% rate to a probandwise one, we add the 14 MZ pairs where both are registered (and confirmed) as schizophrenic to both the numerator and denominator to obtain a new fraction: $(14 + 14 + 3)/(14 + 55) = 31/69 = 45\%$. This figure, tabled in 6.2, tells us how many of the independently ascertained (central psychosis register) twins with schizophrenia or a schizophreniform psychosis (69 probands) had an affected partner. (If we had included cases that Kringlen diagnosed as borderline on interview, the probandwise rate would have risen to 51%, 35/69, putting him, ironically, within shouting distance of Kallmann's 69%.) In 90 same-sex DZ pairs the concordance rate ranged from 4% to 10%. The concordance rate in opposite-sex DZ pairs was not different from the latter range, a fact that is strong evidence against the relevance of sex identification to a theory of schizophrenia. As in the U.K. and the Danish studies to be described shortly, the concordance rate was as high in male pairs as in female pairs, unlike the results in the older studies. We shall return to this important point in the subsection on Sex and Concordance.

Kringlen concluded that the genetic factors in schizophrenia were weaker

than previously thought and were not specific to schizophrenia. The first part
of his conclusion must refer to lack of support for a monogenic theory such as
put forward by Kallmann. The recessive theory he advocated required very
high MZ rates and he had reported an age-corrected pairwise rate of 86%,
more than twice as high as the one calculated by Kringlen on his Norwegian
sample. A different perspective is possible on the "weakness" claim when a
dimension of severity of illness is used to analyze Kringlen's MZ twins. The
concordance rate ranged from 60% for the most severe part of the sample to
25% for the most benign. The question of specificity is best left to repeating
Kringlen's findings. For schizophrenia, not yet including schizophreniform
psychoses, 14 co-twins had the same type of psychosis and 13 were even
concordant for the same subtype, for example, in seven pairs both had a
catatonic–paranoid form of the disorder. Each of the three concordant pairs
for schizophreniform psychosis consisted of pairs where both have schizophreniform psychoses. For the reactive and manic-depressive proband twins
in the total sample, none of the co-twins had an illness with schizophrenic
features but the pattern of specificity continued. Treating Kringlen's 21
psychotically concordant pairs as a group (the four categories combined), the
degree of specificity is amazing in that 20 co-twins had the same form of
psychosis as the proband; the findings are difficult to reconcile with his claim
that genetic factors are nonspecific.

Fischer in Denmark

By matching up the national psychiatric register started in 1938 by Kemp
with the national twin register listing all same-sex twins born in Denmark
from 1870 to 1920, Margit Fischer, a psychiatrist, in concert with the
medical geneticists Bent Harvald and Mogens Hauge, created a national
psychiatric twin register. The final report they published in 1973 supersedes
the scanty early returns from 1965 that still appear in some reviews. From a
starting sample of almost 7,000 same-sex pairs surviving to age 6 they found
70 schizophrenic probands belonging to 62 pairs, 21 MZ and 41 DZ. The
representativeness of the sample is reflected in the proportion of twin types
and in the balance of sexes – 32 males, 38 females. Only probands who met
Fischer's conservative criteria (she is one of the collaborators in the WHO
IPSS study mentioned in Chapter 1) for chronic or process schizophrenia
were included, but co-twins turned out to include schizophreniform, paranoid, and atypical psychoses. The age of the sample together with the fact
that she followed all discordant pairs for an average of more than 24 years
eliminates the need for any age correcting in this sample.

The use of a Kraepelinian orientation to the co-twins' disorders resulted in an MZ concordance rate of 24% (5/21) and a rate of 10% (4/41) for the SS DZ pairs, as shown in the table. Converting these rates in the standard appropriate manner to probandwise ones gives 36% and 18%, respectively. The Danish investigators broadened the concept of concordance in a reasonable, heuristic way and those results, probandwise, have been put into Table 6.2 for comparison with similar standards applied to the other recent twin studies. Their "Grade 2" probandwise rates were 56% (14/25) for MZ pairs and 27% (12/45) for DZ pairs. The rate in fraternal twins does look rather high but is easily reconciled with sampling fluctuations; the 95% confidence interval on the 27% concordance rate runs from 15% to 42%. Recall also that this sample is the least in need of age correcting because the subjects were born from 1870 to 1920. One undesirable consequence of the age of the sample was the high proportion who were dead (35%) by the time of follow-up and could not be interviewed. The 56% MZ probandwise rate suggests that unthinking application of Weinberg abridged or other methods for age correcting by twin researchers is unwise at best and distorting at worst. On the other hand, although most concordant MZ pairs became so within a brief span (hence the source of the correlation-in-onset culprit), Fischer's long follow-up uncovered two pairs with differences in onset of 29 years and 17 years.

When attention was shifted to any kind of psychiatrically noteworthy abnormalities in co-twins (neurotic, nervous, or odd), 64% of MZ co-twins and 41% of DZ co-twins had accumulated, ranging from schizophrenic to odd. As in the Norwegian and U.K. studies, there were no conspicuous sex differences in concordance rates. Using age at first admission or outcome status on a 7-point scale, Fischer found no relation between severity and concordance. She suggests that the difference here between the Danish findings and those we and Kringlen report in support of such a relationship stems from heterogeneity of environmental influences that may affect onset ages and outcomes. We would suggest in addition that a restriction in range for severity, that is, selecting only clear process cases as probands, may also have prevented finding a relationship. It must be noted that, as in other twin studies, the schizophrenias found in the concordant pairs did not differ qualitatively from those seen in the discordant pairs – again an argument in favor of the essential unity of the underlying processes and genotypes (see Bleuler, 1978).

A careful consideration of the role of environmental factors led the Danish workers to conclude that a variety of different factors may be partly responsible for the development of schizophrenia, but no one factor deserved to be singled out as especially contributory. Childbirth had precipitated some cases, but, importantly, the childless MZ co-twins were as concordant for schizophrenia as the remainder of the sample. Interesting facts came to light when the rate of emigration in her twin sample proved higher than that in the general Danish population. Eight MZ twins had emigrated, mostly to the United States. Six of them became schizophrenic within 5 years and were inhospitably returned to their homeland (in accord with U.S. immigration policies). We are not suggesting a causal relationship, that is, that American society caused schizophrenia in Danish immigrants. Fischer did compare her findings with Ødegaard's classical study of Norwegian immigrants to Minnesota and asked how far the selective emigration of predisposed misfitting persons contributed to the findings. Because Kringlen's twentieth-century twins were not tempted to emigrate like their earlier relatives, elegant designs to test hypotheses using MZ co-twins who remain behind as controls will have to remain fantasies. Perhaps someone will make use of the large samples of Vietnamese boat people or other contemporary involuntary and voluntary colonizers to test the hypothesized relationships.

Offspring of discordant identical twins

One more unique feature of the Danish twin study of schizophrenia deserves close attention. The mental status of all 71 children born to identical twins in the sample was examined as a function of their parents' statuses – schizophrenic versus nonschizophrenic. After age correcting to obtain the BZs, Fischer found that 3 out of 31.2 offspring of the schizophrenic MZ twins compared with 3 out of 23.1 offspring of the genetically matched but nonschizophrenic MZ co-twins had schizophrenia or schizophrenialike psychoses. Thus the risks of 9.6% and 12.9% were not only not different from each other, but they are well in line with the risks for the children of schizophrenics reviewed in the previous chapter. Note the peculiar relationship of the children of two MZ twins: Legally they are nephews and nieces (2° relatives) of their mother's sister but genetically they are her first-degree relatives, and their legal first cousins (3° relatives) are their genetic half sibs (2° relatives). A variation on the analysis just described was performed by dividing the parental sample of MZ twins into concordant and discordant pairs and examining the risks in the two groups of their offspring. The risk to the offspring of the concordant schizophrenic pairs was 6% (1/17.5) and the risk to the offspring of discordant pairs was 13.6% (5/36.8), a nonsignificant difference with samples of these sizes. Thus both analyses suggest that the predisposition to schizophrenia is transmitted genetically and with no appreciable heterogeneity given the similar risks to offspring from concordant versus discordant pairs. The first part of the conclusion assumes that aunts and uncles will have little influence on their nieces and nephews compared to their own parents. Interestingly, these approaches have been tried in a large sample of twins with manic-depressive disorders from the same twin register used by Fischer. Aksel Bertelsen found that the risk to the children of the affected MZ twin partner was not higher than the risk to the children of the nonaffected member of the pair – 15.3% versus 15.2%. For the discordant fraternal twins, however, the risks were markedly different as might be expected from the twins sharing only 50%, on average, of their genes in common. The risk to the offspring of the affected DZ twin was 28.9%, whereas it was only 4.9% in the offspring of their nonpsychotic partners. The BZs ranged from 13 to 20 for the four groups just described.

Pollin and co-workers: United States Veterans Panel

In 1969 William Pollin at the National Institute of Mental Health and a team of psychiatrists reported the preliminary results of a twin study of mental disorders found among 15,909 pairs where *both* men had passed the military induction processes for physical and mental health. They had served in the armed forces during the period spanning World War II and the Korean War (1941–1955). Although the sample is neither representative nor cross-sectional, it is a well-defined epidemiological sample with the virtues of a twin register. Zygosity was diagnosed from mailed questionnaires obtaining the opinions of the twins plus backup information about fingerprints and physical features; 31% of the twins could not be assigned a zygosity because of insufficient information. The information about their mental health/illness is based entirely on chart diagnoses available from Veterans Administration records and whatever was volunteered in response to a mailed questionnaire when the twins were aged 38 to 48. The investigators have not themselves seen or interviewed the twins. The yield from the vast number of pairs was 420 pairs with a computer-listed diagnosis of psychosis. A total of 313 schizophrenics was found among the 31,818 twin individuals, a prevalence of 0.98% in this cohort of men in their forties.

When the information was used to calculate zygosity-specific concordance rates in 1972 after a chart review that combined schizophrenic and schizo-affective cases, 27% (26/95) of the pairs known to be MZ were concordant as were 5% (6/125) of the DZ pairs. Converting these rates into proband-wise ones results in the findings seen in Table 6.2 of 43% in MZ (52/121) and 9% in DZ (12/131) pairs, not very different from the other samples but quite different from the very first reports of these data by the investigators. Given the age of the sample at follow-up together with the initial screening for mental health, little age correcting appears necessary.

Because we are dealing with a large particular population of twins from which the probands were selected, we can calculate the prevalence of schizophrenia in twins per se and use that information to state how much greater "risk" a co-twin of a schizophrenic has of falling ill than a twin selected at random from this population. The prevalence of 0.98% for the entire sample did not require zygosity information; the zygosity-specific prevalences were 1.28% in MZ, 1.05% in DZ, and 0.62% in the unknown-zygosity pairs. It does not appear that MZ twins as such are appreciably more prone to becoming schizophrenic than are DZ twins. Such rates are not lifetime risks and cannot be compared directly with the risk of 1% we have been using for the general population of singletons up to now. We need an age-specific prevalence in nontwin veterans to reach a conclusion about the difference if any between twins and nontwins in schizophrenia risks. In the absence of such data we use instead an age-specific prevalence in male New York State nontwin, nonveterans provided by Deming (1968) using hospital chart diagnoses that may be roughly comparable to the data base used in the Veterans Twin Panel. For living males age 35 to 44 Deming calculated a prevalence for a first admission with schizophrenia to be 2.18%; if we are correct in this kind of extrapolation, the prevalence of 0.98% in twin veterans reveals the success of selecting out individuals with obvious psychopathology at the time of induction. Using the calculated zygosity-specific prevalences, we can see that the "risk" in MZ co-twins of schizophrenics here is 33.6 times the risk of an unselected veteran monozygotic twin and the risk in DZ co-twins is 8.7 times that of an unselected dizygotic twin. The evidence and inference about the importance of genetic factors, 100% versus 50% gene overlap, is impressive.

Gottesman and Shields: Maudsley Hospital, United Kingdom

Our sample of schizophrenic twins was selected from the Maudsley twin register maintained in a Psychiatric Genetics Research Unit at the Hospital. The unit was directed by Eliot Slater, who started the twin register in 1948 recognizing its value for systematic ascertainment of cases in an unbiased manner. After 16 years of continuous registration of all twins admitted to either the inpatient or outpatient or children's units, 479 twins with various psychiatric diagnoses were identified among some 45,000 consecutive admissions from 1948 to 1964. Twins did not appear in excess but were proportional to their numbers in the general population. The proportion diagnosed as schizophrenic among the adult patients was equal to the proportion of nontwins with that diagnosis. Using the follow-up information in the twin register we were able to select probands who had received a diagnosis of schizophrenia at the Maudsley or at some other hospital, and later refined the sample by using the blindfolded diagnoses of a panel of six judges. The starting series consisted of 62 probands from 57 pairs because in 5 pairs both twins were independently ascertained as schizophrenic through the register. Unlike most schizophrenic samples ours has a higher representation of cases with a good prognosis because we sampled consecutive admissions to an outpatient service. As it turned out, on follow-up all the probands had been admitted for some time even if only for a few weeks. Further evidence of the representativeness of the twin sample comes from the even split for sex among the probands. At last information the median age was 37 with a range from 19 to 64. Zygosity was determined by blood-grouping and fingerprinting in most pairs; we saw and interviewed all but 14 twins, 4 of whom were dead by follow-up in 1963–1965.

After losing two MZ pairs from the sample who did not meet the criteria of the six-judge diagnostic panel, we had pairwise concordance rates of 50% (11/22) in MZ and 9% (3/33) in DZ pairs for definite or probable schizophrenia. Stricter criteria led to rates at the lower end of the ranges in Table 6.2 of 40% and 10%. When the six-judge consensus at the broader level is converted in probandwise fashion we obtain the concordance rates that best express our results without age correcting, 58% (15/26) in MZ and 12% (4/34) in DZ pairs.

We have already presented in Table 1.3 the consequences for concordance rates of too broad or too narrow an orientation to the diagnosis of schizophrenia. It bears repeating that either extreme eroded the MZ : DZ contrasts: Too narrow lowered the MZ rate to the value of the DZ rate and reduced the sample size unmercifully; too broad raised both the MZ and DZ rates to dilute an indicator of "biological specificity," the ratio of the rates. We can now briefly address the issue of age correcting the probandwise rates. Conventional and standard procedures would have raised the MZ rate to 77% and the DZ to 17%, but neither figure is satisfactory because no provision is made for the correlation in age of onset nor for the long follow-up times on the discordant twins, a minimum of 13 years. When we finished our intensive follow-up in 1965 we considered two MZ co-twins to be at especially high risk of decompensating, but the rest were clinically "out of the woods." Neither high-risk twin was ever hospitalized but one was by consensus an unhospitalized schizophrenic and enters into our final figure of 58%. Therefore, although many of the co-twins are still *formally* within the risk period for developing schizophrenia, we see no reason to adjust any further the rates of 58% in MZ and 12% in DZ pairs. In order to be on safer ground, we began another systematic follow-up in 1980.

One of the ways we used the data was to explore the relationship between severity of illness, assessed in numerous ways, and the risk of the co-twin falling ill. For example, inability of the probands to work or being in the hospital within the past 6 months at follow-up as indicators of severity led to strikingly different concordance rates in the two resulting classes of *MZ* pairs: Concordance in the severe group was 75% (no age correction) whereas in the mild MZ group it was only 17%. Using Slater's subtype diagnoses of nuclear versus nonnuclear probands led to two MZ concordance rates of 91% and 33%. Consistent with these findings was an analysis showing that concordance was higher when the premorbid personality of the proband was judged to be conspicuously schizoid; it was 9/11 versus 2/8 for MZ pairs with and without a schizoid premorbid personality in the proband.

No one or two concordance rates from Tables 6.1 and 6.2 provide *the* definitive concordance rates from the twin method. We prefer an informed pooling of the newer studies because their sampling was more representative, at least in those operating with accurate twin and psychiatric registers. The pooled data giving an MZ rate of 46% and a DZ rate of 14% are useful points for orientation and important puzzle pieces in their own right. The fact that persons sharing all of their genes and much of their formative environment have considerably higher schizophrenia rates than do persons sharing only half their genes and much of their formative environment cannot be explained away or denied. Diagnostic or sampling errors or biases do not destroy the orderliness of the findings by different investigators who provide much of their raw data. Of course, the fact that only half of the identical twin pairs are concordant for recognizable schizophrenia highlights the importance of environmental or cultural factors that are yet unknown.

Older and newer twin studies compared

It is apparent from Table 6.2 that there is reasonably good agreement among the recent twin studies of schizophrenia. No bizarre findings such as an MZ concordance rate of 0%, a result incompatible with either a genetical or environmental argument, are evident for the probandwise rates. Even a 14% rate (e.g., the veterans sample) "disappears," although we can construct a part of our Maudsley sample of MZ pairs, using severity to stratify, to yield a valid, very low concordance rate. Such a picture is partly the consequence of using the proband method, partly the result of more thorough sample investigation or longer follow-up times since the first published results, but largely it is caused by our use of a diagnostic criterion cutoff that was as similar as possible to the consensus diagnoses we had found so useful in our Maudsley twin study. That is, we called co-twins concordant if they were schizophrenic or probably schizophrenic, virtually all having been hospitalized for a functional psychosis, one not likely to be an affective psychosis. We were not constrained to lean toward calling schizoaffective cases an affective illness and, wherever possible, we eliminated probands where marked brain disease or injury confounded the diagnostic picture.

The differences between the classical studies summarized in Table 6.1 and the recent studies are less marked than was supposed during the 1960s. In Table 6.3 we set out some of the main reasons why MZ concordance rates could be too high as well as why they could be *too low*. Only a few of the reasons will be discussed in this section.

Sex and concordance

Perhaps enough has been said about the rationale for calculating a probandwise rate in addition to a pairwise one. We would merely repeat that it is only the former that can be contrasted with the population lifetime risk of 1% so as to gain perspective about how much more likely the co-twin of a proband is to become schizophrenic than is some other relative or member of the general population. Contrary to received wisdom, Kallmann did not use the proband method; his high rates come from other flaws, mainly the inappropriate age correcting of his data. Only Luxenburger and Slater (Table 6.1) did use the proband method in their twin studies and it had very little effect on the magnitude of their concordance rates.

Because female pairs tended to be concordant more often than male pairs, and because the older studies were unbalanced in this regard, it is reasonable to conclude that this fact contributes importantly to the higher rates. Recall also that two of the recent studies, those with the lowest rates, only sampled male twin pairs. A complete evaluation of this source of variation is difficult because it is so closely linked with other problems of sampling such as chronicity of illness. In all studies but Kringlen's the female concordance rates were numerically higher. Kallmann did not break down his results by sex but simply said there had been no difference.

Table 6.4 divides the relevant twin studies into two strata, one where sampling was based on consecutive admissions to hospitals or to a psychiatric twin register, and the remainder where sampling was mainly based on resident (standing) hospital populations containing an excess of severe and female cases. We have divided the Slater sample into a resident and a consecutive part based on unpublished information our mentor has kindly supplied.

The concordance rates generated by this procedure show that there is no sex difference in concordance for schizophrenia and no difference in the

Table 6.3. *Possible reasons for the magnitude of MZ concordance rates*

Too high?	Too low?
1. Illegitimate use of proband method	1. Proband method not used
2. Unrealistic correction for age	2. No allowance made for age
3. Preferential reporting of concordant pairs	3. Potentially concordant co-twins missed through mortality, etc.
4. Discordant MZ pairs diagnosed as DZ	4. Inclusion of nongenetic varieties among probands
5. Too loose a criterion of schizophrenia, especially for MZ co-twins	5. Relevant phenotype may be unrecognized precursor of schizophrenia; too strict a criterion used for co-twin
6. Female schizophrenia concordant largely for psychogenic or environmental reasons; samples overweighted with females	6. Division of role in twins makes MZ pairs less alike than they would otherwise have been
7. Concordance in co-twin related to severity of proband; samples overweighted with severe cases	7. Environmental and genetic heterogeneity of populations

representation by sex in those samples with more complete and thorough sampling. The higher concordance in females is accounted for entirely by the use of samples with biases introduced through the loss of certain cases. The fact that opposite-sex twins, when studied, are no *less* concordant than same-sex fraternal twin pairs further reinforces this line of evidence. Hypotheses about a decreasing risk of schizophrenia to females in the post-Ibsen world, as put forward by Einar Kringlen, may not be necessary; their increased risk of alcoholism, unipolar depression, and of carcinoma of the lungs, however, may well fit an environmental hypothesis implicating emancipation in behavioral variation.

Severity and concordance

Our preferred main reason for the higher MZ concordance rates in the earlier studies is that those samples, unlike the recent ones, were heavily weighted with chronic, unremitting cases of schizophrenia; such cases are much more likely than others to have schizophrenic partners. In this and the preceding chapter we presented much of the evidence for a relationship between severity of illness and risk of schizophrenia in relatives. It was David Rosenthal who first put the various pieces together and formulated the important general hypothesis Luxenburger noted in the very first twin study

Table 6.4. *Sex, sampling, and concordance*

Studies investigating both sexes and reporting results separately	Concordance for schizophrenia in MZ twins by sex and source		
	Male	Female	
Based on consecutive admissions, twinship checked[a]	27/59 (46%)	25/53 (47%)	n.s.
Not so based[b]	28/55 (51%)	60/84 (71%)	$p < 0.02$
All studies	55/114 (48%)	85/137 (62%)	

[a]Essen-Möller, Slater (consecutive sample), Kringlen, Gottesman and Shields, Fischer.
[b]Luxenburger, Rosanoff et al., Slater (resident sample), Inouye.

that early hebephrenic and catatonic twins were the most concordant, whereas paranoid forms were more variable within pairs. Kallmann also noted the frequent pairing of nonschizophrenic co-twins with nondeteriorating probands. Although our own series confirms this line of reasoning, other series do not. Differences in severity need not reflect differences in "genetic loading" in a one-to-one manner. It is clear that environmental factors, including treatment or its absence, also play an important role in the various indicators of severity.

Reprise

Allowing as we have for the small sample sizes in some of the twin studies and for certain key dimensions, many of the alleged discrepancies among all the twin studies are attenuated. We feel quite comfortable in concluding that the twin studies of schizophrenia as a whole represent variations on the same theme and are, in effect, sound replications of the same experiment. No doubt critics will feel less comfortable with such a conclusion. We had the great advantage of having two of the contributors to the classical literature, Eliot Slater and Erik Essen-Möller, serve as blindfolded judges/diagnosticians for our twin sample (Gottesman & Shields, 1972). Their results with our sample are very close indeed to their results with their own samples studied some 30 years earlier.

The nonschizophrenic co-twins of MZ schizophrenics

What about the "clones" of schizophrenics who are not themselves diagnosed as schizophrenics? It may seem that the co-twins of identical twin schizophrenics should provide direct information about what constitutes the range of phenotypes that indicate the presence of the unseen schizophrenic genotype. But such a belief would be naïve even if we were to ignore the part played by nongenetic phenocopies such as the symptomatic schizophrenias associated with epilepsy or head injury. Uncontrolled environmental forces in the lives of the co-twins from the moment of fertilization lead to the *effective* genotypes of MZ twins being different at any point in time; we have not yet learned to cope with the complexities introduced in our research lives by the facts of molecular biology and the turning on and off of genes (see Chapter 4). We shall pursue the reasons behind complete discordance in the next section. Here we can ask what proportion of MZ co-twins of schizo-phrenics across studies were seen as normal, and what kinds of abnormalities existed when they were noted. Table 6.5 shows the pairwise rates for normality, other psychiatric conditions (schizoid as well as neurotic), and for definite plus probable schizophrenia. In the seven studies where we could make the determination from published information, the proportion normal ranged from 5% in Kallmann to 43% in Fischer (despite her long follow-up).

In our study as well as others, normal co-twins could be found paired with severe cases of schizophrenia. Such pairs lend support to the importance of such concepts as ontogenesis and epigenesis and make us wish for more understanding of the effects of gene regulation on complex human pheno-types. We can understand the diversity of interpretations and observations in the light of such complications. On the one hand, Inouye concluded that no classically schizophrenic MZ twin had a co-twin without a distinctively deviant personality, and Essen-Möller's own MZ co-twins were said all to have a characterological trait (genetically) related to schizophrenia. On the other hand, the specially selected NIMH sample of discordant identicals led Mosher, Pollin, and colleagues to use the frequent presence of normality as evidence against a genetic stance. Some of the twin researchers did not try to assess schizoid abnormalities in twins, and those who did so did not agree with one another. At any rate it cannot be claimed, even when using liberal or loose criteria, either that 100% of MZ co-twins are schizophrenic or schizoid, or that all co-twins are abnormal. The "other disorders" in Table 6.5 were mostly neurotic and character disordered. We shall defer questions about the schizophrenic spectrum concept until later in this book. Our own experience, however, can make the disorders in MZ co-twins less abstract.

Six of the 11 nonschizophrenic co-twins had some psychiatric diagnosis. However, only two of them had disorders resembling schizophrenia clinically and deserving of the term "schizoid" as it has been used clinically or in the spectrum sense of Rosenthal and Kety. MZ 14B was 20 at the first follow-up and has not yet been admitted for psychiatric reasons in the ensuing 16 years.

Table 6.5. *Pairwise MZ rates for schizophrenia, schizoid, and other psychiatric conditions, and normality in some schizophrenic twin studies*

Study	Numbers of pairs	% schizophrenia & ? schizophrenia	% schizoid[a]	% other disorders[b]	% normal
Luxenburger[c]	14	72	14	—	14
Rosanoff et al.	41	61	—	7	32
Kallmann	174	69	21	5	5
Slater	37	64	—	14	22
Kringlen	45	38	—	29	33
Fischer	21	48	5	5	43
Gottesman & Shields	22	50	9	18	23

[a]So diagnosed by investigators.
[b]Includes as examples: alcoholic, psychopath (Kallmann); psychopathic, suicide (Slater); alcoholic, character neurosis (Kringlen).
[c]Only includes co-twins of certain schizophrenics.

His consensus diagnosis was personality disorder (inadequate personality, hypochondriacal). Individual judges called him pseudoneurotic schizophrenia or schizophrenia-related personality. His personality test (MMPI) would have been read blindly as psychotic, nearest to schizophrenia. He had fixed ideas about having ulcers for which he treated himself and made frequent outpatient visits; repeated tests found nothing of significance. When his verbatim language from a recorded interview was content analyzed for schizophrenicity by the methods of Gottschalk and Gleser, he scored very much like our overt schizophrenic twins. Another male twin, MZ 16B, 44 at last information, refused to be tested or tape-recorded and was quite litigious. He was clearly suspicious, resentful, humorless, irritable, and showed little capacity for warmth (unlike his schizophrenic brother!). He was married, successful in a profession, and had one child. He had never sought psychological help; one judge called him a schizotype and another, a schizophrenia-related personality. The diagnoses of the other four co-twins were neurotic depression with anxiety (she also had a high score on her language sample); hysterical personality disorder and hospitalized for 51 weeks at age 20 for neurosis (called pseudoneurotic schizophrenia by one judge); neurotic depression with anxiety (normal-limits personality test at age 47); and a brief postpartum depression requiring hospitalization at age 31 (completely normal on tests and interview at age 40). We may well have underestimated the prevalence of schizoidia in the 11 co-twins, but contaminated diagnosis is a special danger without an objective means of making such a determination. Some of the abnormalities may be explained largely on traditional psychodynamic lines (cf. the quotations from Manfred Bleuler in Chapter 5). Others may develop on a constitutional basis but not one specially connected to a schizophrenic diathesis. After all, schizophrenics have many genetically conditioned potentialities besides the one for schizophrenia.

Discordant MZ twins as pointers to specific stressors

Although the study of discordant identical twins tends to be associated with the work at the NIMH of Pollin, Stabenau, and Mosher, it is a fact that all the systematic studies of MZ and DZ twins from Luxenburger on paid special attention to discordant identicals for the value they had in highlighting environmental contributors to schizophrenia and for the suggestions they held in regard to etiological heterogeneity. The NIMH series has grown to 17 MZ pairs at first thought to be discordant and who have now been followed up (Belmaker et al., 1974). It would be a meaningless task to calculate the concordance rate for schizophrenia in such a series at any point in time because they were selected especially to be discordant. Discordant MZ pairs are ideal for revelations about specific stressors that precipitate schizo-phrenia and they can be used to indicate endophenotypes that are not the *result* of the disease but that may be necessary for the disease.

In the earlier reports on the NIMH series (Pollin et al., 1969), intrapair submissiveness, birthweight, identification with parents, and a few other variables studied were so intercorrelated that it was not possible to treat information on the variables separately. In the first 11 pairs the future schizophrenic was lighter at birth in every instance, if only by .5 ounce in one. Of the current 17 pairs (including Pair 9 with suicide in the co-twin), 2 had the proband *heavier* at birth. One pair has become concordant and 3, including a borderline case, possibly concordant. Of the 12 discordant pairs with available birthweight information, 10 probands were lighter at birth. An unusual feature in an already unusual sample was the frequency of triplets (treated as if they were simply twins): Much the biggest weight differences were attributable to the "triplet-twins" whereas in the 8 discordant ordinary pairs where the proband was lighter, the mean difference was 205 grams (less than half a pound). Systematically ascertained twin samples do not support the hypothesized role of birthweight differences in discordant pairs. Further-more, the idea that either weight or other perinatal difficulties have a *specific* role in the etiology of schizophrenia in those at risk for it now seems unlikely (Hanson, Gottesman, & Heston, 1976; McNeil & Kaij, 1978).

Intrapair submissiveness was more consistently related to discordance in both the NIMH and other studies. Table 6.6 contrasts the data on both birthweight and submissiveness in regard to (pooled) discordant MZ pairs. It is clear from Table 6.6 that *within-pair* submissiveness is indeed associated with which of two genetically identical individuals became schizophrenic, and that lower birthweight occurs as often in the nonschizophrenic as in the schizophrenic member of such matched pairs. The first fact, however, does not lend itself to easy interpretation along the lines of therapeutic interven-tion. One reason is the difficulty of distinguishing between cause and effect; the submissiveness could merely be an early sign of the schizophrenic process having started. Second, the entire discussion of submissiveness in the context of the dyadic relationship of twins makes use only of *relative* status on this trait vis à vis the other twin and may have no relationship to *absolute* levels.

In principle the study of discordant MZ pairs should be useful for detecting the role of neurological dysfunction in causing or precipitating schizophrenia, even if it means using so-called soft signs. The Pollin team made use of two blindfolded neurologist raters and came up with admittedly inconsistent findings. Partly because of necessarily different standards for the presence of soft signs, only random agreement was reached between the two raters;

Table 6.6. *Differential association of submissiveness and lower birthweight with schizophrenia in discordant MZ pairs*

More submissive twin is schizophrenic	Lower-birthweight twin is schizophrenic
84/100 (84%)	43/87 (49%)

Note: MZ pairs from studies by Slater, Inouye, Tienari, Kringlen, and Gottesman and Shields (as analyzed by Gottesman & Shields, 1972), and from Fischer (1973).

because follow-up showed 4/17 possibly concordant pairs, the task of the neurologists was even more difficult than thought. It is worth recalling that the other recent twin studies did not detect any differences in the quality of the schizophrenias in concordant as opposed to discordant MZ pairs, nor did selected social factors distinguish the two classes.

Despite high hopes, the study of discordant MZ pairs has not yet led to a big payoff in the identification of crucial environmental factors in schizophrenia. The problem is simply more difficult than we can cope with: Environmental variation within twin pairs is limited to a relatively narrow range, sample sizes are small, the data needed are subject to retrospective distortions, and the culprits may be nonspecific, time-limited in their effectiveness, and idiosyncratic. Sophisticated efforts that take into account individual differences in genetic background yield heuristic suggestions for further analyses of twin data (see Chapter 9).

We can summarize the kinds of questions that may be asked heuristically about MZ twin pairs discordant for schizophrenia. The answers could cast light both on the etiological heterogeneity of schizophrenia and on the environmental contributors to its exacerbation and amelioration.

1. Has the proband been misdiagnosed, or is his illness mild, schizophreniform, psychogenic, or reactive, or symptomatic of organic disease? We would not expect phenocopies of schizophrenia to be genetically related to the predominant varieties of the disorder.

2. Should the co-twin, because he is not overtly schizophrenic, be considered a compensated schizotype? Where information about the co-twin is vague or unreliable, this possibility may have been overlooked.

3. Is the co-twin still within the period of risk for developing the disorder, and for how long since the onset of schizophrenia in the proband has the pair been followed?

4. What unique factors in the life, including prenatal, of the proband might

have elicited the illness, or what unique factors in the life of the co-twin might have insulated him against it?

A few examples from our unselected series of discordant MZ pairs can illustrate some of these points.

In one pair, A, the proband, probably has an organic psychosis with schizophreniclike features and a deteriorating course. His illness was called paranoid state at the Maudsley. The etiology of his psychosis is probably nutritional brain damage sustained as a Japanese prisoner of war. He is completely deaf, and has an abnormal electroencephalograph ("brain waves") recording suggesting a brain lesion. B, the co-twin, is married, has a stable job history, and an MMPI within normal limits (but he refuses to be interviewed).

In another pair, A was diagnosed as an acute schizophrenic reaction after her thyroid was removed at age 43. Shortly before this surgery she had had a hysterectomy and was involved in divorce proceedings from an abusive, bullying husband. On her most recent admission she was called a depressive. B, however, had neither surgical procedure although she also had a thyroid disorder. Her husband was an unusually kind and understanding man. B at age 46 is one of the pillars of her community.

Another proband has had only one hospitalization and that for 6 weeks. He was an unusual boy with longstanding interests in Oriental religion. At 20 he joined a messianic cult and 2 years later left his second wife to go for special training at the cult's London headquarters. There he underwent "psychic realignment" and was given training in telepathy. Within a month he reported that he was radiating his thoughts and felt that other members knew the details of his sex life. On follow-up 4 years later he was working, back with his wife and child, not on medication, but freely described feelings of depersonalization and auditory hallucinations. He called himself a "radiating telepath," and his keen interest in the occult continued. B, in his middle twenties, is married, has children, and has a responsible position. He reported that things were "disinturbulated." Like A he is an enthusiast for the occult; on last information he had left his job to go to headquarters for special training. He told us that "Paul of Tarsus started off in many respects a similar way to what I did." He considers himself too careful to become "insane," more self-reliant than A, and stronger all around. Their MMPI profiles show that both twins have their highest scores on the clinical scales labeled *Paranoia, Psychopathic deviate,* and *Schizophrenia.* B is not a consensus "hit" according to our judges although he has never been diagnosed as a case.

One final example again involves our youngest discordant proband MZ 14. A has had three hospitalizations, the first at age 16 when he was diagnosed (out of concern for his future employability) as an adolescent depression. He is in the sample by virtue of a diagnosis of schizoaffective psychosis from an area psychiatric hospital. When treated with electroshock therapy his depression cleared but his thinking disorder remained. When treated with phenothiazines (antipsychotic medication), he showed enough improvement to be discharged to outpatient status. His brother has had no contact with the psychiatric world but has hospitalized himself twice for physical complaints with no detectable organic basis. He has put himself on an ulcer diet although no physician has verified this self-diagnosis. B has a very poor work history, never staying long. B was heavier at birth (4.5 lbs. vs. A's 3.25) but the poorer in school achievement; they attended different schools after the qualifying (at about age 11) examination. For the past 4 years A has lived mostly with the kindly maternal grandmother, uncle, and aunt, whereas B has been more exposed to the "schizophrenogenic" mother and cold, harsh stepfather. At the time of follow-up B was clinically free of marked schizophrenic symptomatology, but his MMPI profile was grossly abnormal and clearly of a psychotic shape. Because B was only in his early twenties, the labeling of this pair as discordant seemed premature in 1963. Now, still discordant in 1980, we are forced to face the complexity of the whole problem of inferring genotypes.

The last two cases in particular illustrate some of the reasons for dissatisfaction with the concept of concordance: It imposes an artificial dichotomy on behavior that is more fruitfully measured on a continuum.

We found no striking differences between the ages at first hospitalization or ages at first diagnosis of schizophrenia when contrasting the concordant with the discordant MZ pairs; in 6/10 of the concordant and 6/14 of the discordant MZ pairs the proband was first hospitalized and diagnosed schizophrenic after age 30. This finding further weakens Rosenthal's conclusion (1959) that the schizophrenia observed in Slater's discordant identicals represented a nongenetic variety with a later appearance, no family history, and an overrepresentation of paranoid types. None of the first-degree relatives of our MZ pairs, concordant or discordant, has been diagnosed as schizophrenic and there does not appear to be a predominance of paranoid types in the discordant MZs.

Although it is clearly important to account for differences within the MZ pairs, the task is difficult. The environmental reasons suggested in the studies we have reviewed are not sufficient as causes of schizophrenia. Not many premature babies, or children tied to the apronstrings of constricting, inconsistent mothers, or twins who have difficulties in fending for themselves because of their close relationship, actually develop schizophrenia. Given the genetic predisposition, however, features such as these may make a crucial difference in determining which twin becomes schizophrenic. The same features, differing in degree between members of concordant pairs, may also be important determiners of within-pair differences in the severity of the illness.

MZ twins with schizophrenia reared apart

Identical twins reared apart from birth and placed into uncorrelated environments and where one of the twins has become a schizophrenic proband constitute an ideal experiment of nature that combines the virtues of genetic control and adoption studies. Alas, the "experiment" is exceedingly rare in practice and fraught with unforeseen difficulties. After all, what kinds of parents have to put both twins out for adoption, and what kinds of circumstances require that they be placed separately? Quite unlike the 75 cases of identical twins reared apart who have been studied by those interested in intellectual ability, only some dozen authenticated pairs of MZ twins reared more or less apart with one a schizophrenic proband are known. The expected probability of finding a pair of identical twins reared apart with one a schizophrenic requires the multiplication of three probabilities: .006, (the probability of being an identical twin), .0085 (the probability of being schizophrenic), and some unknown but very small probability of separate-home adoptions for a pair of twins. The first two figures alone yield a probability of .000053, or 53 per million.

Up to now no accurate count has been available about the real number of relevant pairs identified in the course of systematic twin research. We omit isolated case studies from this count because they are not representative and will have been selected for their sensational value in "proving" *or* "disproving" opposing points of view. We and others have erred in the past, through ignorance, in reporting some 25 or 26 pairs of identical twins reared apart with schizophrenia in a proband. Eight pairs identified in the studies from European and American sources we reviewed earlier in this chapter can still be counted.[1] The source of error in the literature on such pairs comes from the adding of cases reported in Japan by two different investigators, 10 pairs from Inouye (1972b) and 8 pairs from Mitsuda (1967). The details of the original work were only available in Japanese. We are now able to straighten out the confusion through the courtesy of Professor Eiji Inouye's help in describing to us the overlap between the two reports and the clinical features and diagnostic orientation involved. Another problem that has been

[1] We omit from this count the pair from the special case study report of Craike and Slater (1945), who were not from Slater's 1953 series, and we include a pair of preadolescent schizophrenics from Kallmann and Roth (see Chapter 8).

highlighted by our personal correspondence is the definition of the term "separated." Most of the Japanese pairs were reunited before age 5 even though they had been separated before that age for a period of more than 2 years. The logic and utility of the MZ-reared-apart strategy require a much more prolonged separation of rearing ecologies. Four of the nine pairs reported by Inouye were not reunited and two of them were concordant for schizophrenia; these two were separated at 7 days and at 2 years, 8 months. By 1972 Mitsuda's sample of eight pairs was reduced to five (two were no longer considered "proper" schizophrenics and one no longer MZ), and three more must be subtracted because they were already studied and reported by Professor Inouye. The two remaining pairs are both concordant for schizophrenia, but we lack details about their age at separation and whether they were reunited.

Thus the yield from the worldwide literature on systematically ascertained pairs of identical twins reared apart with schizophrenia is 12 or 14 pairs of whom 7 or 9 are concordant for schizophrenia.[2] The more conservative yield gives a pairwise concordance rate for these rare birds of 58% (7/12).

We regard the data on identical twins reared apart as a precious curiosity to be studied in its own right for the unique lessons each case history can teach. The data are not the kinds one would choose to use in building a solid foundation for either a genetical or an environmental theory about the etiology of schizophrenia. The fact that the concordance rate is not numerically lower than the rates we reported in Tables 6.1 and 6.2 for identicals reared together is no genuine embarrassment of environmental views about the weakness of genetic factors in schizophrenia. It is the kind of datum about which we can merely say, Lo and behold! and then get on with the work of filling in the puzzle as best we can.

Because one of the eight Western pairs comes from our own study at the Maudsley Hospital, we offer a brief summary that may shed light on the attitude we have expressed toward such material.

Herbert and Nick (not their real names) were the illegitimate children of a 19-year-old, half-Chinese girl impregnated by a pinball machine repairman whom she never saw again. Separated at birth in 1934 to two different series of foster homes, they were reunited during the evacuation of London to avoid the German blitz (for less than a year), and separated again with Herbert being reared by his maternal grandmother. They were reunited after the war (age 7½) but only briefly, because the grandmother did not want to raise Nick, whom she gave away to a 41-year-old married but childless woman

---

[2] Using a broad definition of "separated" in his sample, Inouye considered 3/9 pairs to be completely concordant and 6/9 to be completely or partly concordant.

(Mrs. M., the foster mother of the twins' aunt). This narrative will become even more like a daytime soap opera. Mrs. M.'s husband, a building contractor, was not consulted but acquiesced. A year later, at 42, Mrs. M. became pregnant. Herbert continued to live in the East End of London (Limehouse) with his grandmother and her second husband, also a Chinese immigrant who spoke little English; neither payed much attention to Herbert. Nick lived comfortably in suburban London with caring, warm parents and a compatible younger stepsibling.

After 2 days' labor, only Herbert had a forceps delivery and he was described as smaller and more delicate; he had probable head concussions at ages 10 and 12. Nick did poorly in a private school and from ages 10 to 14 was put into classes for slow learners; he wet the bed until 14; he was brought to police attention for setting fires at ages 9 and 10, and was twice convicted of theft (scrapmetal) at 17 and sent to a hostel on probation. He was drafted into the army and was found illiterate with an IQ of 75; he served honorably, doing menial tasks. After discharge he worked briefly for his stepfather but quit because "fellows were spying on me." Herbert was also a bedwetter until 12, and in addition a firesetter including dog torture because "the devil told me to." After thievery at 15 he was committed to a school for delinquents for a year. He was drafted into the army, and was also found illiterate with an IQ of 87; he served honorably, doing menial tasks (he never met his twin during this period).

Both held various unskilled jobs as delivery boys until age 22. Herbert then behaved oddly, staring silently into space, sitting in awkward positions for long periods, neglecting himself, grimacing and laughing to himself; he interpreted passing automobiles as the sound of enemy aircraft (Christmas 1956). Nick's family heard that Herbert was not well and thought a visit might help; they had rarely seen each other since age 7½ but were aware of each other. The visit took place on December 22 at which time Nick learned that their biological mother had visited Herbert and their grandmother briefly in October while visiting the country from her home in the United States. On January 8 Herbert was admitted to hospital and became a proband; "You feel people are deceiving you . . . I'd be reading people's thoughts when I concentrate . . . Some people talk backwards and some people you have to get along on top of their talk. [later] I'm sure an interdiscrete society could help you. Communist aggression mixed with racial intolerance . . . " He was committed to long-term care in a mental hospital and has been there for more than 20 years. Unknown to us at the time, Nick was admitted to a different hospital on January 5 after running across a plowed field with arms outstretched as if in prayer. The night of his visit to Herbert he was found crying and the next day he seemed lost in thought and was making clicking sounds with his tongue. After New Year, he amazed his father with unintelligible talk; he felt he had special powers but that they left him when a cigarette pack was thrown away; he smashed a window with a porcelain dog – "The devil was there and it was either him or me"; he saw a mass of flames and heard voices singing "Hark, the Herald Angels Sing." He was admitted to mental hospital the next day in a confused and agitated state. Like his twin he has been virtually continuously in hospital for over 20 years with no contact with his twin. Both do better on different phenothiazines than without them, but neither improves enough for discharge. During our follow-up in 1963 a maternal aunt was admitted with paranoid schizophrenia.

Only part of the fascinating story has been told here but it is enough to illustrate how unusual these kinds of cases can be. The similarity and time of onset may have been due to both twins experiencing similar stresses at the same time despite their having been reared apart in two very different sets of circumstances. Curiosities, yes, but not any kind of a definitive, crucial experiment or puzzle piece. We must press on with our search for more puzzle pieces by turning next to the studies that use variations of adoption strategies.

BIBLIOGRAPHY

Abe, K., & Coppen, A. Personality and body composition in monozygotic twins with an affective disorder. *British Journal of Psychiatry*, 1969, *115*, 777–780.

Allen, M. G., Cohen, S., & Pollin, W. Schizophrenia in veteran twins: A diagnostic review. *American Journal of Psychiatry*, 1972, *128*, 939–945.

Belmaker, R., Pollin, W., Wyatt, R. J., & Cohen, S. A follow-up of monozygotic twins discordant for schizophrenia. *Archives of General Psychiatry*, 1974, *30*, 219–222.

Bertelsen, A. A Danish twin study of manic-depressive disorders. In M. Schou & E. Strömgren (Eds.), *Origin, prevention and treatment of affective disorders.* London: Academic Press, 1979, pp. 227–239.

Bleuler, M. *The schizophrenic disorders: Long-term patient and family studies* (Siegfried M. Clemens, trans.). New Haven: Yale University Press, 1978.

Carey, G., & Gottesman, I. I. Reliability and validity in binary ratings: Areas of common misunderstanding in diagnosis and symptom rating. *Archives of General Psychiatry*, 1978, *35*, 1454–1459.

Craike, W. H., & Slater, E. Folie à deux in uniovular twins reared apart. *Brain*, 1945, *68*, 213–221.

Deming, W. E. A recursion formula for the proportion of persons having a first admission as schizophrenics. *Behavioral Science*, 1968, *13*, 467–476.

Essen-Möller, E. Twenty-one psychiatric cases and their MZ cotwins: A thirty years' follow-up. *Acta Geneticae Medicae et Gemellologiae*, 1970, *19*, 315–317.

Essen-Möller, E. Aspects of continuity in the aetiology of mental disorders. In M. Roth & V. Cowie (Eds.), *Psychiatry, genetics and pathography: A tribute to Eliot Slater.* London: Gaskell Press, 1979, pp. 45–61.

Essen-Möller, E., & Fischer M. Do the partners of dizygotic schizophrenic twins run a greater risk of schizophrenia than ordinary siblings? *Human Heredity*, 1979, *29*, 161–165.

Fischer, M. Psychoses in the offspring of schizophrenic monozygotic twins and their normal co-twins. *British Journal of Psychiatry*, 1971, *118*, 43–52.

Fischer, M. Genetic and environmental factors in schizophrenia. *Acta Psychiatrica Scandinavica*, 1973, Suppl. 238.

Fischer, M., Harvald, B., & Hauge, M. A Danish twin study of schizophrenia. *British Journal of Psychiatry*, 1969, *115*, 981–990.

Gottesman, I. I., & Shields, J. *Schizophrenia and genetics: A twin study vantage point.* New York: Academic Press, 1972.

Gottesman, I. I., Shields, J., & Heston, L. L. Schizoid phenotypes in the co-twins of schizophrenics: The signals and the noises. In M. Roth & V. Cowie (Eds.), *Psychiatry, genetics and pathography: A tribute to Eliot Slater.* London: Gaskell Press, 1979, pp. 3–21.

Gottschalk, L. A., & Gleser, G. C. *The measurement of psychological states through the content analysis of verbal behaviour.* Berkeley: University of California Press, 1969.

Hanson, D., Gottesman, I. I., & Heston, L. L. Some possible childhood indicators of adult schizophrenia inferred from children of schizophrenics. *British Journal of Psychiatry*, 1976, *129*, 142–154.

Inouye, E. Personality deviation seen in monozygotic co-twins of the index cases with classical schizophrenia. *Acta Psychiatrica Scandinavica*, 1970, Suppl. 219, 90–96.

Inouye, E. A search for research framework of schizophrenia in twins and chromosomes. In A. R. Kaplan (Ed.), *Genetic factors in schizophrenia.* Springfield, Ill: Charles C Thomas, 1972, pp. 495–503. (a)

Inouye, E. Monozygotic twins with schizophrenia reared apart in infancy. *Japanese Journal of Human Genetics*, 1972, *16*, 182–190. (b)

Kallmann, F. J. The genetic theory of schizophrenia: An analysis of 691 schizophrenic twin index families. *American Journal of Psychiatry*, 1946, *103*, 309–322.

Kallmann, F. J., & Roth, B. Genetic aspects of preadolescent schizophrenia. *American Journal of Psychiatry*, 1956, *112*, 599–606.

Kringlen, E. *Heredity and environment in the functional psychoses.* London: Heinemann, 1967.

Kringlen, E. Twins – still our best method. *Schizophrenia Bulletin*, 1976, *2*, 429–433.

McNeil, T. F., & Kaij, L. Obstetric factors in the development of schizophrenia: Complications in the births of preschizophrenics and in reproduction by schizophrenic parents. In L. C. Wynne, R. L. Cromwell, & S. Matthysse (Eds.), *The nature of schizophrenia: New approaches to research and treatment.* New York: Wiley, 1978, pp. 401–429.

Mitsuda, H. *Clinical genetics in psychiatry.* Tokyo: Igaku Shoin, 1967.

Mosher, L. R., Pollin, W., & Stabenau, J. R. Identical twins discordant for schizophrenia: Some relationships between identification, thinking styles, psychopathology and dominance submissiveness. *British Journal of Psychiatry,* 1971, *118,* 29–42. (a)

Mosher, L. R., Pollin, W., & Stabenau, J. R. Identical twins discordant for schizophrenia: Neurologic findings. *Archives of General Psychiatry,* 1971, *24,* 422–430. (b)

Mosher, L. R., Stabenau, J. R., & Pollin, W. Schizoidness in the non-schizophrenic co-twins of schizophrenics. In *Proceedings of the Fifth World Congress of Psychiatry.* Amsterdam: Excerpta Medica Foundation, 1973, pp. 1164–1175.

Ødegaard, Ø. Immigration and insanity: A study of mental disease among the Norwegian-born population of Minnesota. *Acta Psychiatrica et Neurologica Scandinavica,* 1932, Suppl. 4.

Pollin, W., Allen, M. G., Hoffer, A., Stabenau, J. R., & Hrubec, Z. Psychopathology in 15,909 pairs of veteran twins. *American Journal of Psychiatry,* 1969, *7,* 597–609.

Rosanoff, A. J., Handy, L. M., Plesset, I. R., & Brush, S. The etiology of so-called schizophrenic psychoses with special reference to their occurrence in twins. *American Journal of Psychiatry,* 1934, 91, 247–286.

Rosenthal, D. Some factors associated with concordance and discordance with respect to schizophrenia in monozygotic twins. *Journal of Nervous and Mental Disease,* 1959, *129,* 1–10.

Rosenthal, D., & Van Dyke, J. The use of monozygotic twins discordant as to schizophrenia in the search for an inherited characterological defect. *Acta Psychiatrica Scandinavica,* 1970, Suppl. 219, 183–189.

Shields, J., & Gottesman, I. I. Cross-national diagnosis of schizophrenia in twins. *Archives of General Psychiatry,* 1972, *27,* 725–730.

Shields, J., Gottesman, I. I., & Slater, E. Kallmann's 1946 schizophrenic twin study in the light of new information. *Acta Psychiatrica Scandinavica,* 1967, *43,* 385–396.

Slater, E., & Shields, J. *Psychotic and neurotic illnesses in twins* (Medical Research Council Special Report Series No. 278). London: Her Majesty's Stationery Office, 1953.

Tienari, P. Psychiatric illnesses in identical twins. *Acta Psychiatrica Scandinavica,* 1963, Suppl. 171.

Tienari, P. Schizophrenia and monozygotic twins. *Psychiatria Fennica,* 1971, 97–104.

Tienari, P. Schizophrenia in Finnish male twins. In M. H. Lader (Ed.), *Studies of schizophrenia.* Ashford, England: Headley Brothers, 1975, pp. 29–35.

Genetical puzzle pieces: adoption studies

The logic and design of various adoption strategies were discussed in Chapter 4. In this chapter we shall illustrate and discuss the kinds of data collected with these techniques. In adoption studies the adoptee of interest receives his or her genes (and prenatal environment) from one family and his or her rearing environment from another family not related genetically. It is in this sense that it has been said that adoption strategies permit the disentangling of genetical and environmental influences. It is important to "disentangle" because such confounding has been a source of criticism of the family and twin studies already discussed and presented in previous chapters.

Adoption studies, wherein individuals with genotypes assumed to be similar in respect of their predisposition to schizophrenia are then exposed to kinds of rearing by adoptive parents screened so as to be low on anyone's continuum of schizophrenicity, can be used to test specific environmental and interactional hypotheses. Adoption studies wherein the biological child of a schizophrenic does *not* become a schizophrenic cannot be used to rule out genetic factors. Thus an adoption study of favism, a hemolytic anemia known to be dependent on an X-linked mutant gene leading to an enzyme deficiency, could easily obscure the genetic basis of this disease. We must mention that the disease does not express itself unless the genotype is exposed to the fava bean (or to pollen from its plant) which is used as food in the Mediterranean region (Kirkman, 1971). An adoption study of favism (before its etiology was known) in which offspring of probands were placed in a nonbean-eating family and compared to controls reared by their own parents would find a zero prevalence of the hemolytic anemia in the adoptees. Such findings could not rule out the necessity of a specific genotype, which could only be discovered by means of studies in a bean-ridden environment.

Many people are taken aback by our claim that the major accomplishment of the adoption strategies applied to schizophrenia that we shall review in this chapter was to rule out *some* alleged environmental factors as *either* necessary or sufficient for the development of schizophrenia in the offspring of schizophrenic parents. Such factors had been proposed as ad hoc alternatives to the conclusions concerning the role of genetic factors in the etiology of schizophrenia that had been drawn from ordinary family and twin studies. We see the role of adoption strategies as one of revealing important, specific triggering/releasing environmental factors or specific protective/insulating environmental factors for children separated from their "natural" rearing experiences at the hands of a schizophrenic parent.

The fact, as we shall see, that adopted-away children of schizophrenics still grew up to become schizophrenics at an increased rate compared to control adoptees strengthened the genetic hypothesis. Adoption studies, better than any other, sort out a family's genes from that family's rearing environment. Of course some adoptive homes will turn out to be poorly suited to particular adoptees; this even happens with natural families where it may be confused with the "generation gap." It is unreasonable, however, to assume that even the mismatches as a group are as schizophrenogenic as a schizophrenic parent would be, or as schizophrenogenic as the vast majority of parents who have produced a child with schizophrenia without themselves being diagnosable. Thus we might expect that adoptive homes would somehow be *anti*schizophrenogenic and serve to protect or insulate a predisposed genotype. The trouble is that "schizophrenogenic" cannot be defined reliably except circularly and after the fact. If we could obtain a definition, we could define a sample for a new high-risk prospective study so as to test the power of a construct that was free of the genetic bias in the usual high-risk studies.

Heston in Oregon

Once in a while results are obtained in the nonlaboratory study of psychopathology that have a major impact on thinking in the field. Such was the case with the 1966 publication of the adoption-fostering study conducted by Leonard Heston, then a young resident in psychiatry. The study dealt with children removed from their chronically schizophrenic mothers within the first 3 days of life and reared by nonmaternal relatives. Of the 74 offspring born to such mothers, 15 died in infancy or childhood and others had had contact with their maternal relatives, leaving a final sample of 47 children (30 males and 17 females) who were followed up and interviewed in 14 states and Canada when they were at a mean age of 36. A control group was selected of offspring born to normal mothers over the same period, 1915–1945, who had been placed in the same foundling homes as half of the "experimental" children. Those children who went directly into foster or adopting families were matched with controls who had spent a maximum of 3 months in the foundling homes. The control mothers were "normal" in the sense that they had no record of psychiatric hospitalization; the most frequent reasons for their children being in the foundling homes were maternal death or desertion. The 50 control children were also followed up at a mean age of 36 and had been matched to the others for sex, age, type of final placement, and quality of early care. The major findings are shown in Table 7.1. None of the fathers of either group was known to be a psychiatric patient, but it is unlikely that they represented a desirable segment of society. Regrettably, no further hard data are available on the fathers.

Five of the 47 fostered-away children of schizophrenic mothers were found schizophrenic themselves at follow-up, whereas none of the 50 controls was even psychotic. The raw prevalence of 10.6% in these offspring becomes 16.6% with standard Weinberg-abridged age correcting; both rates are close to those reported for the offspring of schizophrenics reared by their own parents in Tables 5.1 and 5.2. If more information were available, we would be able to make an informed guess as to whether the offspring rates are so high and apparently unmodified by normal rearing because the "dementia praecox" biological mothers had transmitted a maximum dose of schizophrenia-related genes, or because of the narrow reaction range (Figure 4.2) of the schizophrenic genotype, or because of the absence of a specific antischizophrenic rearing experience. Table 7.1 also shows that there were considerably more abnormalities such as sociopath personality and other personality disorders or neurosis in the experimentals than in the controls. A major question facing the field is whether or which of these other conditions are relevant to the search for a schizophrenia-related genotype. It is important to note that diagnoses were made blindly by two psychiatrists in addition to the author. Psychosocial disability on a global basis was rated objectively with the 100-point Menninger Mental Health-Sickness Scale (MHSRS). The experimentals obtained a mean score of 65.2 and the controls, 80.1; scores lower than 75 represent the point where psychiatric symptoms become disabling (mean for the entire sample was 72.8 with an SD of 18.4). When the entire sample was divided according to whether subjects had been reared in institutional situations versus in families, disregarding biological mothers' schizophrenia, it made no difference to their MHSRS ratings in that both were relatively disabled with scores of 73.0 and 72.7. Heston observed that the low score of 65.2 was not due to a general

Table 7.1. *Follow-up status of children separated at 3 days old from schizophrenic mothers*

	Mother schizophrenic	Mother not psychiatric
Number studied	47	50
Males:females	30:17	33:17
Mean age	35.8	36.3
Schizophrenic at follow-up	5	0
Morbid risk	16.6%	0%
Sociopathic personality	9	2
Other than honorable discharge	8/21	1/17
Other personality disorder or neurotic	13	7
Mental retardation (only)	2	0
MHSRS	65.2	80.1
Mean IQ	94.0	103.7
Mean education (yrs)	11.6	12.4

lowering but was instead associated with the scores of 26 out of 47 of the schizophrenics' offspring.

In anticipation of an important reported difference between Heston's findings and those of the Danish adoption study to be reported next, we must call attention to the prevalence of antisocial personality and criminality in the Oregon study. Fully 8/30 of the male offspring of schizophrenics in Heston's sample were sociopathic personalities, were felons, and had prison records. None of 35 similar males in the Danish study as of a 1973 report (Wender et al.) had a criminal history. Thus Rosenthal (1975) could make the point that because 9/43 of the males who were co-parents to the female schizophrenic probands in his adoption study were sociopaths, sociopathy could well be transmitted independently to some adopted-away offspring of schizophrenics. Only one of the male schizophrenic probands in Rosenthal's study was known to have mated with a psychopathic female co-parent; there may not have been enough parental sociopathy to show up in the Danish adoption study. Such a line of reasoning could account for this particular difference between the results, but we shall examine this point again later in the chapter. Other contributors to the high rate of antisocial activities in the Heston offspring include the fact that only their mothers were in a mental hospital at the time of their birth, and, because they were in a state hospital rather than a private one, they are likely to be of a lower socioeconomic class (as a group) than the proband parents in Denmark with its unified social welfare system of mental health care.

Rosenthal and colleagues in Denmark

David Rosenthal, Paul Wender, and Seymour Kety of the NIMH and Fini Schulsinger and Joseph Welner of Kommunehospitalet Copenhagen capitalized on the existence of two nationwide registers, one for all psychiatric inpatients and another for all residents, and then created a nationwide adoption register, enabling them to produce an elegant study of the adopted-away children of male and female schizophrenics. They were working at the same time as Heston but did not report their initial findings until 1968. The starting point for the research was the pool of 5,500 children put up for formal, nonfamilial adoption in the Greater Copenhagen metropolitan area from 1924 to 1947. The 10,000 identifiable biological parents of these adoptees (the biological father could not be identified for 25% of the adoptees) were then matched against the national psychiatric register so as to pick the psychotic parents who became the probands in this design. Seventy-nine mothers and fathers (in the ratio 2 : 1) were found who had been judged psychotic by the Americans from English summaries of hospital chart information. Ten of them were manic-depressive, leaving 69 schizophrenic probands who had one adopted-away child; these became the focus of intense interest. From the remaining adoptees, a total of 79 controls were picked with neither parent known to the psychiatric register and were matched for sex, age, age at adoption, and social class of adoptive home. The mean ages at the time of study of the adopted index (AI) and the adopted control (AC) were 32.5 and 32.7 with a range of 20 to 52. These adoptees and others yet to be described for a total of 258 volunteers were brought in to the Psykologisk Institut (S. Mednick and F. Schulsinger, directors) for 2 days of psychological and psychophysiological tests and a 3- to 5-hour psychiatric interview by Joseph Welner, a senior Danish clinician.

The study is extremely rich in detail and far from its final form; no complete report giving such details as the histories of the parent probands or of the index adoptees is yet available. We have culled from the various published reports some of the relevant highlights now available. Table 7.2 shows the proportions of the AI and AC offspring who were judged to be in the upper quartile of a psychopathology rating scale when all 258 subjects were ranked by four judges after reading a summarizing paragraph prepared by Welner. The upper quartile corresponds to borderline schizophrenia or more severe, that is, what the group calls the "hard spectrum" of definite (B)

Table 7.2. *Danish adoption studies ("Rosenthal strategy"): interim prevalences of hard- and soft-spectrum disorders in adopted-away offspring of male and female schizophrenics*

Group	N	% hard spectrum[a]	95% confidence intervals[b]	% hard + soft[c] spectrum
NA: children of schizophrenics, not adopted	42	not available	—	31
AI: children of schizophrenics, adopted-away index	69	18.8	10.4–30.1	32
AC: children of normals, adopted-away controls	79	10.1[d]	4.5–19.0	16[d]

[a]Upper quartile of psychopathology rankings equivalent to B or D (see text).

[b]With repeated measures from similarly derived samples we would expect the true percentage of cases to be within these intervals 95% of the time; too wide an interval lowers our confidence.

[c]Taken from Paikin et al. (1974), p. 313, Table 14. Ns: NA, 42; AI, 79; AC, 97.

[d]May be used as population prevalences of hard and soft spectrum.

or doubtful (D) schizophrenia. These data are taken from the article by Wender et al. (1974). The wealth of information in the interviews covering 26 different areas of personal–social functioning and a psychodynamic formulation has yet to appear in print. Another report on the research, concentrating on the status of 76 additional subjects who had refused to come in for interviews of whom 37 were nevertheless seen in the field, gives further information about the 258 formally tested and interviewed subjects. From the paper by Paikin et al. (1974) we can see the proportion of AI and AC as well as of a group of 42 offspring of schizophrenics *not adopted away* (NA) who fell into either the hard or the "soft" spectrum. The latter includes nonrecurrent acute schizophrenic episodes and "schizophrenic personalities such as undifferentiated inadequate and subparanoid, and schizoid personalities" (Rosenthal, 1975, p. 202). The Paikin et al. findings are based on somewhat different samples from the Wender et al. report and are not strictly comparable; still, they form the only basis for examining the entire spectrum concept of the Danish–American team. The 95% confidence intervals are provided for the B or D levels of pathology as a caution about the effects of small sample sizes on our results in the field of psychiatric genetics.

Some points need to be made before we proceed further with the Danish adoption studies. First, the interviewer and the judges at different stages of the project are completely blindfolded as to the group membership of the subjects. The vast amount of psychopathology reported for the AI group is largely the result of nonhospitalized illness; only 1 of the AI has been hospitalized with a diagnosis of schizophrenia, and 10 others have had admissions to psychiatric facilities as have 7 of the AC. The age of the samples is such that more hospitalizations may be expected in the future, changing the results. Of the 69 AI proband parents, 42 were considered chronic or process cases, 8 borderline, 9 doubtful schizophrenic or schizoid, and 10 acute schizophrenic or schizoaffective. Thus the Rosenthal et al. sample is less severely ill as a group than the Heston mothers, all of whom were chronic cases. This study answers questions left over from the Heston study in a number of ways. Criticisms about the role of prenatal and perinatal contributors are less relevant here because 1/3 of the schizophrenic parents were fathers. Furthermore, the children were born much before the first psychiatric admission of their parents, only 9/76 parents (5 mothers) being hospitalized before the birth of an index child. These facts weaken roles attributed to birth factors associated with psychosis or its treatment as well as any alleged contributions from self-fulfilling prophecies that might have come from adopting families knowing about the biological parents' mental disorders.

The difference shown in Table 7.2 between the percentage of AI and AC offspring who are in the definite or doubtful schizophrenic category, 18.8% versus 10.1%, just misses formal statistical significance (p < .06). The too generous use of the definite and doubtful categories may have been at fault in raising the prevalence among the control group.

We saw in Chapter 1 that either too narrow or too broad a view of what constitutes schizophrenia-relevant psychopathology can erode a view of genetic specificity for schizophrenia-related genes. We can ask whether the use of the soft spectrum or the boundaries of the hard spectrum could have obscured results more strongly supportive of a genetic interpretation of the Danish adoption data of Rosenthal et al. They have provided information in a number of their papers on the kinds of pathology found in offspring as a function of parental proband grouping for severity (1968, 1971, 1975). In the judgment of the American clinicians 44 of 69 parents were chronic or probably chronic cases; the only 3 unqualified schizophrenic offspring, a prevalence of 6.8%, appear among *their* adopted-away children. The finding of 10.1% of definite or doubtful schizophrenia in the AC, adopted-away children of normals suggests the need to use a narrower set of criteria.

Returning now to the question whether sociopathy has a place in the schizophrenia spectrum, we can at least resolve one discrepancy with the Heston findings. Although none of 35 male AI offspring in the Rosenthal study initially had a record of sociopathy, unlike 30% of Heston's males, Paikin's follow-up made use of the central police register. That source of national information revealed that (Paikin et al., 1974, p. 305) 46% of the total number of males interviewed by Welner for the adoption projects had been registered as criminals and 14% of them had actually been imprisoned at some time. It is highly probable that some of these sociopaths/felons were in the AI group, thus making the results of the Heston and Rosenthal studies more congruent. However, there are possible qualitative differences among the varieties of behavior called psychopathy. American usage has coincided with the terms sociopathy and/or antisocial personality whereas European usage (following Kurt Schneider) of the term psychopathy is much broader, subsuming American sociopathy/antisocial personality as a fraction of the phenotypes described. Heston considered his sociopaths to be close, clinically, to what Kallmann and Schneider would have called *schizoid psychopathy* and thus deserving of inclusion in *a* schizophrenic spectrum. Kallmann did not consider ordinary criminals relevant to the schizophrenia story, and in this view we find ourselves in agreement with Rosenthal and Heston, as we understand them. It is primarily Mednick (1978) among contemporary writers who sees a direct connection with the schizophrenia-relevant genotype, a connection that comes via the characteristics of the autonomic nervous system as indexed by psychophysiological measures. It is a fact that adoptees

Table 7.3. *Cross-fostering designs ("Wender strategy"): normal genotypes in schizophrenic environments and schizophrenic genotypes in normal environments*

Group	N	% hard spectrum[a]	95% confidence intervals	% hard + soft[b] spectrum
CF: children of normals, adopted by future schizophrenics	28	10.7	2.3–28.2	26
AI: children of schizophrenics, adopted by normals	69	18.8	10.4–30.1	32

[a]Upper quartile of psychopathology rankings.
[b]Taken from Paikin et al. (1974). Ns: CF, 28; AI, 79.

are much more likely than nonadoptees to have police records themselves and to have biological fathers with police records. The rates are so high as to call for caution in attempting a final answer to this vexing problem of correlation versus contributory cause; Hutchings and Mednick (1975) reported a 16.2% rate of registration with the police for felonies among a representative sample of 1,145 Danish male adoptees, the rate rising to 51% if misdemeanors were included. (Comparable rates among nonadoptees matched to adoptees were 9% for felonies and 37% for the inclusive category. The felony rate among the biological fathers of adoptees was 31% versus 11% among the fathers of the matched nonadoptees.) Similar confounding problems would arise if we were to consider the issue of alcoholism as a candidate for one or another schizophrenia spectrum. We shall spare the reader the anguish, but the issue is open for pursuit (cf. Bleuler, 1978).

Wender and colleagues in Denmark

The completion of the 2 × 2 adoption design described in Chapter 4 requires information about the offspring of normal parents who, through no fault of their own or of the adoption authorities, were reared by parents who later became schizophrenic. So far only Paul Wender and his colleagues (1974) have been able to manage this unusual strategy, analogous to the cross-fostering studies performed in animal genetics. Table 7.3 shows the results of the research using the same criteria as reported in Table 7.2, the work being done at the same time in a blindfolded manner. We also show the much higher prevalences for hard- plus soft-spectrum disorders reported by Paikin for these groups. All the data for the cross-fostered (CF) group should also be compared with that for the adopted controls (AC), who are the children of normals reared by normals and who control for the factors associated with adoption per se. Looked at from this point of view the CF group has no more schizophrenia-related pathology than does the AC (10.7% vs. 10.1%), and one might be tempted to conclude that these kinds of "schizophrenogenic" environments are ineffective in producing schizophrenia among those without the genetic predisposition for it. However, the rate in the adopted-away children of schizophrenics reared by normals, although numerically higher than the CF (18.8% vs. 10.7%) and the AC (10.1%), *is not statistically significantly higher than either.* It did not help to remove from the three groups children who may have been deviant prior to the adoption process (i.e., abnormal enough to be rejected by a number of prospective adoptive parents), although the value for the "purified" CF group did drop to 4.8%. Once again some combination of small sample sizes and the criteria for hard and soft spectrum as used here frustrated efforts to provide definitive findings. In mitigation, Wender et al. observed that the control group of biological parents had significant pathology not listed by the national psychiatric register; in fact about half of all the AC group biological parent couples fell into their definition of spectrum disorders after they had been interviewed. Clearly, this would make the control group *not* a control group, and clearly the utility of the concept is eroded by "conceptual inflation." The last column of Table 7.3 also highlights this problem because fully 26% of the CF group and 32% of the AI group fell into the broadest definition of the schizophrenia spectrum.

We can ask whether the design gave a fair chance for the schizophreno-genic factor, admittedly vague, to show itself in the CF group. The CF parents were not deviant enough at the time of adoption to be dropped from consideration, thus guaranteeing a much shorter exposure time to the constellation of possibly relevant intrafamilial factors emphasized by Lidz, Laing, Wynne, and Singer. Furthermore, the severity of eventual schizo-phrenia was not comparable in the CF adoptive parents and the AI biological parents; only 32% of the former versus 61% of the latter were called chronic schizophrenics (chi square 5.49, a statistically reliable difference even with a small sample). Taken at face value and looking at the internal contrasts of the entire 2×2 design, the cross-fostering results do not directly strengthen a genetic argument so much as they weaken environmental ones. We turn now to the third variation on the adoption theme, the adoptees' family design, uniquely pioneered by Kety and the same set of colleagues.

Kety and colleagues in Denmark

The starting point for this unique variation of the adoption strategies is the *nationwide* pool of nonfamilial adoptees, which numbers 14,500 and includes as a subsample the Greater Copenhagen pool of 5,500 used as the foundation for the Rosenthal and Wender strategies we have described. Those adoptees among the 14,500 who had been hospitalized for psychiatric reasons had English summaries prepared of their charts; those summaries were independently diagnosed by the three Americans and F. Schulsinger to obtain 74 definitely schizophrenic adoptees, who became the probands for this strategy. Most of the reports in the literature about this project have been based on the probands first identified from the Copenhagen pool, a total of 33 schizophrenic adoptees (Kety et al., 1968, 1975). More recent data are available (Kety et al., 1978) for the enlarged national sample of 74. Controls were matched from the remaining adoptees who were not in the psychiatric register. These probands were all definite or B cases, none of them doubtful or D, and comprised 37 chronics, 24 latent or borderline schizophrenics, and 13 acute schizophrenic reactions. It then became important to focus on the biological and the adoptive relatives of the probands and of the controls. They consist of the two groups of biological parents (probands' and controls'), the two groups of adoptive parents, the biological half sibs of the probands (there being few full sibs), and the adoptive sibs of control adoptees (plus their full and half sibs). In the national sample Kety et al. located 405 biological relatives of their schizophrenic probands (combining first- and second-degree relatives) and 387 biological relatives of controls. The sample sizes for the adoptive relatives of probands and controls were 173 and 194.

To avoid confusion, a brief recapitulation of the differences in strategies between the Rosenthal and the Kety approaches is in order. For Rosenthal the proband is a hospitalized and psychiatrically registered schizophrenic parent of an adoptee, and then the children of such parents become the focus of attention. For Kety the adoptee who has become a schizophrenic, hospitalized and psychiatrically registered, is the proband, and then the biological and adoptive families of such adoptees become the focus of attention. Parents, having been "screened" by societal forces for marriage and childbearing, are likely to have a lower liability for schizophrenia than adoptees who become schizophrenic.

Starting with papers published in 1975, Kety et al. have had the earlier

Table 7.4. *Schizophrenic adoptees ("Kety strategy"): schizophrenia in their biological and adoptive relatives*

Group	N	% definite (B) or doubtful (D) schizophrenia[a]	95% confidence intervals
Biological parents of schizophrenic adoptees	66	12.1	5.5–22.5
Biological parents of control adoptees	65	6.2	1.7–15.0
Adoptive parents of schizophrenic adoptees	63	1.6	0–8.5
Adoptive parents of control adoptees	68	4.4	0.9–12.4
Biological half sibs of probands	104	19.2	12.1–28.0
All adoptive sibs plus full and half sibs of control adoptees	143	6.3	3.0–11.9

[a]Based on records or interviews.

information from national registers on relatives supplemented by fieldwork interviews. Table 7.4 presents the findings reported for the Copenhagen sample using both register and interview data. These authors (1968) once used the term "extended spectrum," which included character disorders, psychopathy (including imprisonment and delinquency), and suicide, but now use the term soft spectrum, which seems to include only inadequate and schizoid personalities (Kety et al., 1978). They are quite open about the eventual definition of both hard and soft spectrum and treat their findings as preliminary ones. The results in Table 7.4 are in line with the genetic expectation that the biological relatives of the schizophrenics with whom they have had little or no contact have an excess of schizophrenia whereas the adoptive relatives who reared them or were reared with them, but with whom they have no genes in common, have very low, general population rates. The differences observed between biological relatives of schizophrenic adoptees and of control adoptees are statistically significant and quite reliable. The rate of B or D in the adoptive parents of schizophrenic adoptees is the lowest (1.6%) of any of the rates reported in Tables 7.2, 7.3, and 7.4. The rate in biological half sibs of 19.2% is unexpectedly high given that they are second-degree relatives sharing an average of only 25% of their genes with the probands (see Figure 4.7); we would expect them to have a rate half of that in first-degree relatives such as the parents or the offspring of schizophrenics. We shall return to these half-sib data.

Not tabled, but reported by Kety et al., is the fact that the rates of schizoid or inadequate personality in the biological relatives of schizophrenics and of controls did not differ (7.5%). Using families as their units of analysis, they found that 42% of the biological families of schizophrenic adoptees versus 9% for the control adoptees' families contained a definite (B) schizophrenic (the figures rising to 52% and 15%, still very significant, when D cases were included). The significant difference disappeared (though the trend remained) when their total spectrum was used, the rates escalating to 70% and 47% (15% of the *adoptive* families of schizophrenic adoptees contained a "total-spectrum" case).

Kety et al. were rightfully mindful of the prevalence of their concepts in the general population and have provided important basic data. There is strong reason to believe that the children of clear psychotics and mental retardates were prevented from entering the adoptee pool by the policies of the Danish authorities of the time (Mednick, 1977). If this resulted in a marked reduction of the subsequent prevalence of schizophrenic adoptees, the Danish adoption strategies discussed so far would have had their task of finding needles in haystacks made even more difficult. The 74 schizophrenic adoptees found in the national sample of 14,500 lead to a prevalence of 0.51% at the 1975 follow-up when their mean age was about 40. For the Copenhagen contingent the prevalence was 0.60%. A sample of *non-adoptees* was then drawn from the Copenhagen area who were matched to the adoptees for age, sex, and social class of *rearing* family (controls usually lived on the same street). The prevalence of definite schizophrenia (B) using the same criteria of record review without the benefit of information from a field interview was 0.57%. Kety et al. conclude from these findings that no significant screening out of relevant adoptees occurred. However, an alternative explanation should be considered. Kety et al. (1978, p. 30) provide prevalence data for the adoptive relatives and all biological control relatives for the Copenhagen study with a value of 1.3% for B from hospital records.[1] The twofold difference between a value of 0.60% and one of 1.3% leads us to suggest that screening out of potential schizophrenic adoptees had in fact taken place, with its attendant complications for understanding the meaning of the results. We can reconcile this interpretation with the near-perfect match in prevalence of B in the nonadopted controls by noting that their rate of 0.57% may well have resulted from the excellence of the matching procedures, which yielded a relatively advantaged social class of non-adoptees with an expected lowered prevalence of schizophrenia (cf. Chapter 2). It is informative to have the newest results of this project, which report

---

[1] The prevalences were 1.8% from adding interview information for B, and 4.0% for B + D.

that the prevalence of definite schizophrenia (B) was the same in the biological relatives of the nonadopted schizophrenics found among the matched Copenhagen sample as in the biological relatives of the proband adoptees (4.9% vs. 4.7%). This might be taken as some support for our conjectures because the affected relatives of nonadopted schizophrenics were mostly chronics whereas those of the adoptee probands were mostly border-line schizophrenics (B3) or doubtful cases (D) (Kety et al., 1978, p. 31).

Nevertheless, the interim findings for the national sample continue to fuel genetic interpretations. Using blindfolded diagnoses from abstracts of hospital charts, only the biological relatives of proband adoptees had a highly significant concentration of schizophrenic spectrum disorders, 5.9%, compared to biological relatives of controls (1.0%) and the adoptive relatives of probands (1.3%) and of controls (1.3%). As might have been expected, the rate was highest in the biological relatives of probands with chronic schizophrenia (N = 37); 17 (7.8%) were B or D and, consistent with arguments against splitting, 10 were latent schizophrenics (B3) or doubtful schizophrenics (D). Although none of the 61 biological relatives of acute probands (B2) had been diagnosed as schizophrenic from chart review, 4 (6.6%) were called D after field interviews by a Danish clinician who was not informed about their family history.

Another major puzzle piece has been supplied by Kety and colleagues' careful analyses of the biological half sibs of the schizophrenic proband adoptees as a function of parental sex and of parental mental status. This also provides the opportunity, promised earlier in Chapter 5, to unpack the few studies in the literature on half sibs of schizophrenics. Differences in the rate of schizophrenia, if any, between paternal half sibs of schizophrenic adoptees and maternal half sibs can contribute to the problems of assessing the contributions of alleged prenatal and perinatal events (obstetrical complications) to the development of schizophrenia. We have already shown that lowered birthweight in MZ twin pairs is not associated with which twin becomes schizophrenic (Table 6.6), and we have pointed out that in the Rosenthal strategy (Table 7.2) the offspring were born and adopted many years before the mothers' hospitalizations. In the Kety data, 14/63 (22.2%) of the paternal half sibs were definite or uncertain schizophrenics compared to 6/41 (14.6%) of maternal half sibs. Because the former did not share the same womb and birth canal whereas the latter did, these results go in the opposite direction from that predicted by a contribution from these kinds of obstetrical factors.

In Table 7.5 we set out for comparison the results of the three most recent studies of half sibs of schizophrenics. Not known (except for Kety) is the extent to which the half sibs were actually raised with the schizophrenic

Table 7.5. *Schizophrenia in the half siblings of schizophrenics*

Study	No. of half sibs	Prevalence (percentage)		
		Schizophrenia, definite	Schizophrenia, definite and uncertain	Schizophrenia, schizoid personality, or spectrum
Kallmann (1938)	100[a]	5.0	6.0	14.0
Bleuler (1978)	188[b]	3.7	5.3	8.0
Kety et al. (1975)	104	9.6	19.2	29.0

	Common parent affected	Common parent unaffected
Kallmann (1938)	19% of 21[b]	1.7% of 57.5[b]
Bleuler (1978)	—	3.7% of 188[b]
Kety et al. (1975)	34% of 15[c]	3.6% of 89[c]

[a]Over age 20.
[b]Data are age corrected (certain schizophrenia).
[c]Data are not age corrected (certain schizophrenia).

parent. The bottom of the table shows an important subdivision of half-sib rates as a function of the mental status (schizophrenic or not) of the biological parent the half sibs shared in common; small sample sizes demand caution in interpreting the percentages.

The pooled age-corrected risk for definite schizophrenia in three older studies in the literature is 3.2%, the same as that reported by Bleuler for his large Swiss sample; that risk may be compared with one of about 8.5% for full sibs. The difference in Table 7.5 between Kety's 19.2% or 29.0% and the other studies highlights the different diagnostic orientations and criteria of the investigators. Kety's rates would actually be somewhat higher if they could be age corrected. If we concentrate on the results with the cases called definite schizophrenia in all the studies, the results look much more homogeneous. The rates in the top half of the table are confounded because, in many of the families, a parent is also schizophrenic. Thus a half sib might be a first-degree relative of a schizophrenic parent, in addition to being the second-degree relative of their schizophrenic half sib. The half sib's overall risk should be quite high in such instances. The degree of inflation of the half-sib rates through such a mechanism is shown in the bottom of the table. Bleuler's rates do not change because the common parent shared by half sibs was, with one exception, not schizophrenic. When the common parent is unaffected, we would expect the risk to approach the general population risk of 1%; it is 1.7% for Kallmann, 3.7% for Bleuler, and 3.6% for Kety. It would closely approach the risk in full sibs, 10%, only if there were some very strong tendency for the *second spouse of a normal parent* of a schizophrenic to resemble the first spouse's genotype. When the shared parent is schizophrenic, both the Danish and German studies agree in finding a much higher risk to half sibs (19% for Kallmann and 34% for Kety, rising to 24% and 53% when uncertain schizophrenics are added in). One might have predicted a rate not far from the average of 17% (see Table 5.1) observed for the full sibs of schizophrenics when one parent is also affected. The 53% rate for B or D from the Kety data is of the order one would find with a disease like Huntington chorea if it were to be studied with the half-sib design.

What might account for the appreciably higher rates of schizophrenia-related disorder in the Danish work on half sibs as highlighted here? We are not sure, but we would suggest that they are in part accounted for by a high prevalence of personality-disordered and other psychiatrically conspicuous persons in the biological families of Copenhagen adoptees at the time, an appreciable heritability or genetic component of many such disorders, and a wide concept of borderline schizophrenia and uncertain schizophrenia on the part of the judges. We know, for example, that the same strategy employed by Schulsinger (1972) to study the families of adoptees who were psychopathic personalities (European usage) turned up a large number of biological relatives in a psychopathic spectrum but not in the schizophrenic spectrum. What we are seeing, on this view, would be the largely independent genetic influences of both schizophrenic and other heritable disorders, combined in some families of the Danish adoptees in ways that are not typical of schizophrenics found through other strategies. The suggestion is supported by the high degree of assortative mating for "spectrum disorders" already noted, for example, 45% of female co-parents in the Rosenthal studies. A high heritability for personality disorders and affective disorders as well as for schizophrenia would account for the comparatively *low* amounts of psychopathology among relatives of control adoptees as the latter were chosen because they were *not* in the psychiatric register. Our line of reasoning warrants close scrutiny for flaws.

These ideas are admittedly conjectural and in the service of the superego for genetic theorists. The high degrees of psychopathology seen in the half sibs could have a major environmental component and could reflect cultural transmission. That is, the half sibs might have stayed with a disturbed biological parent or been subjected to various kinds of institutional care. Although such happenings may not be sufficient to produce schizophrenia, they may have produced "inadequate personalities" of the kind that might have been diagnosed as definite or uncertain latent or borderline schizophrenia (B3 or D3). A disposition among interviewers and among judges using their summaries not to miss possible schizophrenia-related disorders may be among the reasons for high spectrum rates throughout the Danish studies, even though blindfolding was in effect for group membership. All the adoption strategies applied to schizophrenia are a marvelous tour de force and have produced the first really new data in decades; we hope we have not been hypercritical in our effort to scrutinize them.

Overview of adoption results

The adoption studies reviewed in this chapter support the broad genetic hypothesis because they show that sharing an environment with a schizophrenic does not account for the familial aggregation of cases. Furthermore, such factors as the presence of schizophrenia or related illnesses in the rearing family are *ruled out* as primary environmental causes of schizophrenia. One of the more plausible hypotheses before 1966 was that the genes did predispose one to schizophrenia, but that the transmitter of the "schizogenes" also transmitted a schizophrenogenic environment, making it hopeless to apportion relative weights to genes and environments in the transmission of schizophrenia. Both the necessity and the sufficiency of the specific kinds of schizophrenogenic environments provided by schizophrenic parents have been refuted by the adoption studies. Clearly, the studies do not rule out environmental factors, even intrafamilial ones such as "communication deviances" (Singer, Wynne, & Toohey, 1978), in the etiology of schizophrenia, but such factors are not specific to the parents of schizophrenics. The causal environmental factors may be like the fava bean's role in anemia in that they are quite common in some environments but only result in disorder when interacting with specially predisposed genotypes.

An admirable degree of self-criticism accompanies the recent reports on the adoption strategies (Kety et al., 1976; Wender et al., 1973, 1974). Only certain biological parents gave or were permitted to give their children for legal adoption; within-own-family placements were excluded; some of the adoptees were abnormal before placement and have led to appropriately "purified" groups from which they have been excluded; adopting parents represent a restricted range of rearing experiences biased toward health; a strong correlation was uncovered between the social class of biological parents and of adoptive parents; and children who were fostered rather than adopted did not enter the initial pool of adoptees (and would be interesting to follow up). Moreover, the mates of schizophrenics whose children are put out for adoption are probably not representative of the spouses of schizophrenics in general because they include a higher proportion of socially inadequate individuals who could not or would not jump into the breach. None of these problems erodes our principal conclusions about the consistency and strong confirmation of the importance of genetic factors, so far unspecifiable.

Although this book has focused so far on the genetical pieces in the schizophrenia puzzle, a few comments from us about the efforts to identify environmental puzzle pieces are in order. After reviewing the relevance of research on early infantile autism and on childhood schizophrenia, we shall look at a small sample of posited environmental puzzle pieces.

BIBLIOGRAPHY

Biron, P., Mongeau, J-G., & Bertrand, D. Familial aggregation of blood pressure in 558 adopted children. *Canadian Medical Association Journal*, 1976, *115*, 773–774.

Bleuler, M. *The schizophrenic disorders: Long-term patient and family studies* (Siegfried M. Clemens, trans.). New Haven: Yale University Press, 1978.

Bohman, M., & von Knorring, A-L. Psychiatric illness among adults adopted as infants. *Acta Psychiatrica Scandinavica*, 1979, *60*, 106–112.

Carter-Saltzman, L. Biological and sociocultural effects on handedness: Comparison between biological and adoptive families. *Science*, 1980, *209*, 1263–1265.

Heston, L. L. Psychiatric disorders in foster home reared children of schizophrenic mothers. *British Journal of Psychiatry*, 1966, *112*, 819–825.

Heston, L. L., & Denney, D. Interactions between early life experience and biological factors in schizophrenia. In D. Rosenthal & S. S. Kety (Eds.), *The transmission of schizophrenia.* Oxford: Pergamon Press, 1968, pp. 363–376.

Hutchings, B., & Mednick, S. A. Registered criminality in the adoptive and biological parents of registered male criminal adoptees. In R. R. Fieve, D. Rosenthal, & H. Brill (Eds.), *Genetic research in psychiatry.* Baltimore: Johns Hopkins University Press, 1975, pp. 105–116.

Kallmann, F. J. *The genetics of schizophrenia.* New York: Augustin, 1938.

Kety, S. S., Rosenthal, D., Wender, P. H., & Schulsinger, F. The types and prevalence of mental illness in the biological and adoptive families of adopted schizophrenics. In D. Rosenthal & S. S. Kety (Eds.), *The transmission of schizophrenia*. Oxford: Pergamon Press, 1968, pp. 345–362.

Kety, S. S., Rosenthal, D., Wender, P. H., & Schulsinger, F. Studies based on a total sample of adopted individuals and their relatives: Why they were necessary, what they demonstrated and failed to demonstrate. *Schizophrenia Bulletin*, 1976, *2*, 413–428.

Kety, S. S., Rosenthal, D., Wender, P. H., Schulsinger, F., & Jacobsen, B. Mental illness in the biological and adoptive families of adopted individuals who have become schizophrenic: A preliminary report based on psychiatric interviews. In R. R. Fieve, D. Rosenthal, & H. Brill (Eds.), *Genetic research in psychiatry*. Baltimore: Johns Hopkins University Press, 1975, pp. 147–165.

Kety, S. S., Rosenthal, D., Wender, P. H., Schulsinger, F., & Jacobsen, B. The biological and adoptive families of adopted individuals who become schizophrenic: Prevalence of mental illness and other characteristics. In L. C. Wynne, R. L. Cromwell, & S. Matthysse (Eds.), *The nature of schizophrenia: New approaches to research and treatment.* New York: Wiley, 1978, pp. 25–37.

Kirkman, H. N. Glucose-6-phosphate dehydrogenase. In H. Harris & K. Hirschhorn (Eds.), *Advances in human genetics.* New York: Plenum Press, 1971, pp. 1–60.

Laing, R. D. Is schizophrenia a disease? *International Journal of Social Psychiatry,* 1964, *10,* 184–193.

Lidz, T. *The origin and treatment of schizophrenic disorders.* New York: Basic Books, 1973.

Mednick, S. A. Some considerations in the interpretation of the Danish adoption studies. In S. Mednick & K. O. Christiansen (Eds.), *Biosocial bases of criminal behavior.* New York: Gardner Press, 1977, pp. 159–164.

Mednick, S. A. Berkson's fallacy and high-risk research. In L. C. Wynne, R. L. Cromwell, & S. Matthysse (Eds.), *The nature of schizophrenia: New approaches to research and treatment.* New York: Wiley, 1978, pp. 442–452.

Paikin, H., Jacobsen, B., Schulsinger, F., Godtfredsen, K., Rosenthal, D., Wender, P. H., & Kety, S. S. Characteristics of people who refused to participate in a social and psychopathological study. In S. A. Mednick, F. Schulsinger, J. Higgins, & B. Bell (Eds.), *Genetics, environment and psychopathology.* Amsterdam: North Holland, 1974, pp. 293–322.

Rosenthal, D. Two adoption studies of heredity in the schizophrenic disorders. In M. Bleuler & J. Angst (Eds.), *The origins of schizophrenia.* Berne: Huber, 1971, pp. 21–34.

Rosenthal, D. Discussion: The concept of subschizophrenic disorders. In R. R. Fieve, D. Rosenthal, & H. Brill (Eds.), *Genetic research in psychiatry.* Baltimore: Johns Hopkins University Press, 1975, pp. 199–208.

Rosenthal, D., Wender, P. H., Kety, S. S., Schulsinger, F., Welner, J., & Østergaard, L. Schizophrenics' offspring reared in adoptive homes. In D. Rosenthal & S. S. Kety (Eds.), *The transmission of schizophrenia.* Oxford: Pergamon Press, 1968, pp. 377–391.

Rosenthal, D., Wender, P. H., Kety, S. S., Schulsinger, F., Welner, J., & Rieder, R. Parent-child relationships and psychopathological disorder in the child. *Archives of General Psychiatry,* 1975, *32,* 466–476.

Schneider, K. *Klinische Psychopathologie* (9th ed.). Stuttgart: Thieme, 1971.

Schulsinger, F. Psychopathy: Heredity and environment. *International Journal of Mental Health,* 1972, *1,* 190–206.

Singer, M. T., Wynne, L. C., & Toohey, M. L. Communication disorders and the families of schizophrenics. In L. C. Wynne, R. L. Cromwell, & S. Matthysse (Eds.), *The nature of schizophrenia: New approaches to research and treatment.* New York: Wiley, 1978, pp. 499–511.

Wender, P. H., Rosenthal, D., & Kety, S. S. A psychiatric assessment of the adoptive parents of schizophrenics. In D. Rosenthal & S. S. Kety (Eds.), *The transmission of schizophrenia.* Oxford: Pergamon Press, 1968, pp. 235–250.

Wender, P. H., Rosenthal, D., Kety, S. S., Schulsinger, F., & Welner, J. Social class and psychopathology in adoptees: A natural experimental method for separating the roles of genetic and experiential factors. *Archives of General Psychiatry*, 1973, *28*, 318–325.

Wender, P. H., Rosenthal, D., Kety, S. S., Schulsinger, F., & Welner, J. Cross-fostering: A research strategy for clarifying the role of genetic and experiential factors in the etiology of schizophrenia. *Archives of General Psychiatry*, 1974, *30*, 121–128.

Wynne, L. C. Concluding comments. In L. C. Wynne, R. L. Cromwell, & S. Matthysse (Eds.), *The nature of schizophrenia: New approaches to research and treatment*. New York: Wiley, 1978, pp. 534–542.

8   Infantile autism and childhood schizophrenia: pieces or not?

If early infantile autism and childhood schizophrenia are simply early-appearing variants of the kinds of schizophrenia we have discussed so far, the findings and advances for the disorders are interchangeable and heuristically complementary. If they are not, or if autism is not related and childhood schizophrenia is, confusion is fostered by the continued indiscriminate use of the information. Controversies about the relative contributions of genetic factors, prenatal and perinatal hazards, parental personalities, and child-rearing experiences to the development of both early infantile autism and childhood schizophrenia are too often based on dogmatic assertions rather than scientific evidence. The purpose of this chapter is to examine the evidence implicating the childhood psychoses as early variants of adult schizophrenia and the evidence implicating genetic factors in their etiology, even if these genetic factors are not the same as those in adult schizophrenia.

The phenomenology of the phenotype

Differential diagnoses of childhood psychoses are much more difficult to make than in adult schizophrenia because we must depend almost exclusively on watching as opposed to a verbal interchange that permits sampling of cognitions, perceptions, and feelings. Childhood psychoses have been described as early expressions of schizophrenia; as a syndrome of extreme withdrawal, noncommunicative language, and obsessive desire for sameness; as a failure of ego development; and as pandevelopmental retardation, to mention a few (see DeMyer, Hingtgen, & Jackson, 1981). Only recently have there been attempts to make the diagnostic criteria for these conditions more objective and reliable for research use, let alone in clinical practice. These efforts still lack the rigor, described in Chapter 1, of structured interviews for diagnosing adult schizophrenia. We believe a meaningful distinction can be made on both behavioral and genetic grounds between

149

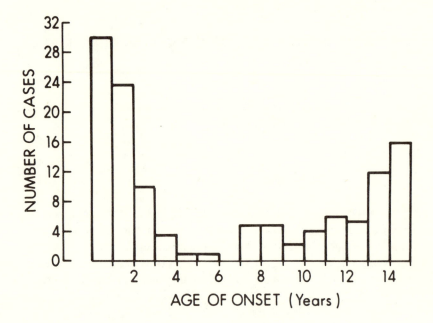

Figure 8.1. Age of onset distribution for pooled English and Japanese cases of childhood psychoses. (After Rutter, 1974.)

psychoses that begin in infancy and those that begin near puberty. Initial evidence favoring a qualitative difference between the classes of childhood psychoses arises from the discontinuity observed in the distribution of ages of onset seen in Figure 8.1. Michael Rutter constructed this figure from the pooled results of cases observed by others in England and Japan. It is clear that most cases are first detected within 2½ years after birth *or* in late childhood and early adolescence. Few psychoses begin in the gap between ages 3 and 11. Another feature that distinguished infantile autism from schizophrenia as we know it is the course of illness; only the latter runs an episodic course with remissions and relapses.

Some of the salient characteristics of early- and late-onset childhood psychoses as well as of brain damage syndromes of childhood on the one hand and of adult schizophrenia on the other are set out in Table 8.1. A + indicates the symptom or sign is fairly common, a − indicates rarity, and +/− suggests an intermediate value. Regrettably, more refined evaluations are not possible at this state of the art of child psychopathology. Most of the information is self-explanatory but a few signs require comment. By "extreme aloneness" we mean something far more pervasive than Eugen

Table 8.1. *Phenotypic indicators of organic syndromes, childhood psychoses, and adult schizophrenia*

Characteristic	Psychotic or severely retarded children with known neurological damage	Childhood psychosis		Adult schizophrenia
		Early onset	Late onset	
Extreme aloneness	+	+	−	−
Mental retardation	+	+	−	−
Males more often affected	+	+	+	+/−
Stereotyped ritualistic behaviors	+	+	+/−	+/−
Pronoun reversal	−	+	−	−
Echolalia	+/−	+	−	−
"Odd" since birth or early infancy	+/−	+	−	−
Delayed speech, extreme	+/−	+	−	−
Distinct motor anomalies (e.g., toe walking)	+	+	−	−
Perceptual disturbances	+	+	−	−
Abnormal EEG/seizures	+	+	−	−
Unremitting course	+	+	−	−
Increase in birth & pregnancy complications	+	+	−	−
Disordered stream of thought	−	−	+	+
Hallucinations	−	−	+	+
Blunted or incongruous affect	−	−	+	+
Phenothiazines ameliorate psychosis	?	−	+	+

Bleuler's definition of "autism" in adult schizophrenics, which, even when present, is difficult to observe. The presence of the symptom in adults often does not preclude completion of schooling, working, a few friends, and even marriage. In contrast, extreme aloneness as a symptom in childhood psychoses refers to an almost total absence of interpersonal relationships with anyone – parents, siblings, or strangers. Stereotyped ritualistic mannerisms are sometimes seen in adult schizophrenics and, when present, seem to form part of a delusional system in which they function to ward off evil, ensure good luck, and so on. In childhood psychoses the rituals appear to be automatic, invariant in different situations, and to lack a cognitive component. Formal thought disorder may not be evident until a child reaches advanced, formal operational levels of cognitive development. Normally, this kind of Piagetian competence does not occur until near puberty. However, when early-onset psychotic children mature, their cognitive processes resemble more closely the cognitive deficits seen in retarded persons than they do those seen in adult schizophrenics. Hallucinations and delusions are rare or absent in early-onset cases followed up into adulthood. Antischizophrenic drugs such as the phenothiazines reduce the motor activity of psychotic children but do little to change the core psychotic symptoms. The overall impression from Table 8.1 is that early-onset childhood psychoses are nearer to the organic brain damage syndromes whereas the later-onset childhood psychoses, most of which are called childhood schizophrenia, show considerable overlap with the phenomenology of adult schizophrenia.

Problems of prevalences and causes

Regardless of how childhood psychoses are defined and diagnosed, almost everyone agrees that even as a whole they are extremely rare, occurring in about 1 in 2,600 children. Schizophrenia in adults, by contrast, is 30 times more frequent by the end of the risk period. Psychoses beginning in infancy are even rarer – a prevalence of 1 in 10,000 infants. It has also been reliably observed that 1 in 30 to 1 in 50 children, even in countries such as Sweden with well-developed social support systems, are mentally retarded. The rareness of childhood psychoses together with the commonness of a condition liable to be confused with it sets the stage for researchers' frustration. Table 8.2 summarizes the prevalence studies for the childhood psychoses and for early infantile autism when it has been separated from the whole.

The very low base rate of childhood psychoses makes it particularly difficult to develop valid diagnostic tools. If a clinician were to formulate research diagnostic criteria that allegedly separated psychoses from other severe childhood developmental deviations, they should, in principle, advance the field. However, no diagnostic system is perfect. We must always contend with the false positives (a child called psychotic who is really retarded) and the false negatives (a child called retarded who is really psychotic). Suppose that the fallible criteria were used to evaluate every child in a district with 10,000 children, and that most of them were normal except the expected number of mentally retarded, emotionally disturbed, hyperactive, and brain-injured children. In addition, as we have seen, there is 1 child among these 10,000 with an infantile-onset psychosis. After evaluating all the children, the clinician claims that there are two cases of "infantile autism." However, in our simulation of omniscience, we know there was only one genuine case so that the second case was a false positive. Only 1 error in 10,000 appears to be an enviably low error rate. However, another investigator, knowledgeable about the base rate problem, does not even bother to evaluate the 10,000 children with research diagnostic criteria and concludes that *none* of them has "infantile autism." The second investigator has achieved the very same error rate as the first but at much less effort and expense – each has been wrong 1 time in 10,000. Of course, such batting averages are not the only considerations. The social cost of a false negative is more serious here than that of a false positive because the latter child (probably mentally retarded and/or emotionally disturbed) may benefit from the same kinds of treatment provided for early infantile autism.

Advances in our knowledge about the etiology(ies) of the childhood psychoses will depend on the accurate characterization of a phenotype for genetic analyses. The rarer the disorder, the greater the likelihood of including false positives. Scrutiny of the published studies of "autistic children" suggests that a large proportion of the cases were probably not "Leo Kanner specimens" but were suffering from some other kind of developmental deviation such as an organic brain syndrome, perhaps associated with perinatal anoxia, or from CNS trauma of other sorts. One of the most arresting facts in the literature comes from the important work of the experienced child psychiatrist, Stella Chess, on the characteristics of children with congenital rubella (i.e., their mothers were infected with measles virus during pregnancy). Chess (1977) reports that among 243 children with congenital rubella 10 showed a complete syndrome of infantile autism and a further 8 had a partial syndrome; thus the prevalence of autism in this population exposed in utero to this virus was 741 per 10,000. Could most cases of autism simply be due to undetected intrauterine infections from this virus?

Conservative diagnostic standards are urged for these rare conditions. We

Table 8.2. *Prevalence of childhood psychoses*

| | Size of population (approx.) | Prevalence (per 10,000) | |
| | | Infantile autism | All childhood psychoses |
Investigator			
Rutter (1966)	9,000	—	4.4
Lotter (1966)	78,000	2.0	4.5
Brask (1967)	46,000	4.3	5.4
Treffert (1970)	900,000	0.8	2.5
Wing et al. (1976)	25,000	2.0	4.8

are not advocating the abandonment of DSM-III, nor do we believe the conditions are too rare to be important. The point of this discussion is that diagnostic inflation may erode the value of research into the causes of these conditions and their relations to adult schizophrenia.

Familial morbidity in childhood psychoses

If childhood psychoses are genetically continuous with and overlap schizophrenia, then there should be an elevated rate of schizophrenia in the parents and siblings of child probands. Only a handful of studies provide the kinds of evidence we need to evaluate this problem. The rates, not risks, of (adult) schizophrenia and/or childhood psychoses in the first-degree relatives of childhood psychotics, early and late onset separated, are given in Table 8.3. Most of the investigators do not give the age distributions of their samples, which prevents us from calculating lifetime morbid risks. It should be noted that the research was all done by child psychiatrists who are spread along a diagnostic and therapeutic spectrum ranging from biological to psychodynamic with varying commitments to eclecticism. The raw prevalences for parents in the table are probably not too much off from the MR because they are well into the risk period, unlike the sib rates, which must be taken as minimum ones. None of the research details the criteria by which the relatives were diagnosed. The widely varying rates in the original reports, from zero in Kanner to 21% of parents in Meyers and Goldfarb, and the idiosyncratic features of others (e.g., only 2 of 18 "schizophrenics" ever hospitalized) mean that diagnostic practices were anything but uniform. In order to provide some comparability with the data already presented in Table 5.1 for parents and sibs of schizophrenics, we counted only hospitalized cases in Table 8.3, footnoting the remainder. Too often the schizophrenia in sibs is not specified as child or adult onset. As a first approximation to useful information, we have lumped all psychotic conditions together.

Overall there appears to be a relationship between the age of onset in the proband children and an increased rate of adult schizophrenia in first-degree relatives, given the values in Table 5.1. Two studies provide usable data on the occurrence of schizophrenia in relatives when probands fell ill after age 5, a convenient dividing line (cf. Figure 8.1). Of the 268 parents, 9% have been hospitalized for schizophrenia, a rate considerably higher than the MR of 5.5% in Table 5.1 for parents of adult-onset schizophrenics. The 9% rate is close to the risks for other first-degree relatives. Because early onset can be an indicator of severity and an indirect indicator of genetic loading, we would expect the relatives of childhood-onset schizophrenics to have higher-than-usual risks (confirmed), and, if on a continuum with very early-onset autism, the relatives of these cases should have even higher risks. The latter expectation is uniformly disconfirmed, and most instances are close to zero rates!

Of the 290 sibs of late-onset cases in Table 8.3, about 7% are also affected. Further follow-up should see a rise in that uncorrected rate.

The family data do suggest that preadolescent schizophrenia, or as some call it, late-onset childhood psychosis, can represent rare, early onsets of the usual, adult type of schizophrenia. That is not to say that all late childhood or early adolescent psychoses are manifestations of an inherited predisposition to schizophrenia. Alternative rare explanations such as brain tumors or viral infection sequelae should be considered after simpler causes such as street-drug intoxications have been excluded. Today's adolescents are impelled to try a wide variety of brain disorganizers. Preexisting neuroses or personality deviations may be escalated into schizophreniform symptom pictures.

In addition to the regular sibships of "preadolescent schizophrenia" reported by Kallmann and Roth, these investigators also found 52 pairs of twins in which one or both members had a preadolescent schizophrenia. Counting only cases where the co-twin broke down before age 15, the raw, pairwise concordance rate for 17 MZ pairs was 71% whereas it was only 17% for the 35 DZ pairs (24 same-sex and 11 OSDZ). Adding five co-twins who broke down after age 15 boosts the MZ and DZ rates to 88% and 23%, respectively. Both of these rates are higher than Kallmann's observations in adult twins (see Table 6.2), leading Kallmann and Roth to conclude that

preadolescent schizophrenia is determined genetically to the same extent and apparently by the same gene-specific deficiency state, as is assumed in regard to the adult form of the disease. The difference between the preadolescent and adult types seems to lie, at least in part, in a number of secondary factors which lower the constitutional resistance or interfere with the containability of early cases.

Table 8.3. *Prevalence of selected psychotic conditions in first-degree relatives of infantile and childhood psychotics*

Investigator	Age of onset in probands (yrs.)	Parents hospitalized for schizophrenia		Sibs	
		Total no.	% affected	Total no.	% psychotic
Early onset					
Kanner (1954)	<2	200	0	131	2.3
Creak and Ini (1960)	[a]	204	1.7[b]	234	0.7
Meyers and Goldfarb (1962)	≤5	84	2.4[c]	48	8.3
Lotter (1967)	<4½	60	0[d]	62	0[e]
Rutter and Lockyer (1967)	<5	126	0	85	0[f]
Kolvin et al. (1971)	<3	92	1.1	68	0
Fish (1977)	<2	70	5.7	44	4.5
Bender (cited in Fish, 1977)	<2	100	7.0	[g]	—
August et al. (1981)	<3	—	—	71	2.8

Late onset

Kallmann and Roth (1956)	7–11	204	8.9[h]	234	7.7
Kolvin et al. (1971)	>5	64	9.4	56	1.8
Bender (cited in Fish, 1977)	>2	100	12	[g]	—

[a]Ages not reported but most known to be early onset.

[b]Other psychiatric disorders include one case each: dementia following head injury, anxious depression, anorexia nervosa (schizophrenia?).

[c]Eighteen cases of schizophrenia in 84 parents (21.4%) were reported, but only two cases were hospitalized.

[d]Five parents reportedly had been hospitalized for psychiatric care and include one case each: recurrent depression, reactive depression, amphetamine psychosis, possible paranoid psychopath, no diagnosis available.

[e]In addition there were reported one case of "depressive psychosis" with IQ 56, one case "very autisticlike" with IQ 65, and one case with severe personality disorder, possible retardation, but friendly.

[f]Plus one questionable case of "autism"; at age 9 was described as "somewhat unusual" but "appeared quite normal and certainly could not be termed psychotic."

[g]Bender's sibling data were not subdivided by age of onset in proband. Among the 87 sibs of early- plus late-onset probands, 13.8% were diagnosed schizophrenic.

[h]Ten additional cases of "uncertain schizophrenia" were also reported.

A problem arises from the fact that Kallmann and Roth's statewide (New York) longitudinal survey for preadolescent schizophrenics produced 52 pairs of twins but only 50 singletons, very unlike the general population ratio of about 1 pair of twins for every 100 singletons. They offer no explanations for the composition of their samples. It has been argued that twins might be more vulnerable to developing schizophrenia, but that is certainly not the case in adult schizophrenia. Twins *are* more at risk for brain injury and severe mental retardation. About 2% of the general population surviving infancy are twins, but more than 3% of institutionalized retardates are twins – a 50% excess. Severe brain damage (a possible "secondary factor" lowering "constitutional resistance") may have contributed to the very early onset in Kallmann and Roth's cases of preadolescent schizophrenics, which were rare – constituting only 0.6% of all first admissions and only 1.9% of all schizophrenics in state hospitals in New York State. Additionally or alternatively, some of the twins called schizophrenics may have been misdiagnosed cases of organic brain syndromes.

Both family and twin data suggest that late-onset childhood psychoses are, at least in some cases, genetically related to adult schizophrenia and represent instances where adult schizophrenia begins at an unusually early age. However, this conclusion should be viewed as a challenge to future researchers, not as an established fact.

Combining five studies in Table 8.3 that report data for cases where the probands' disorders began *before age 5* (Kanner; Meyers & Goldfarb; Lotter; Rutter & Lockyer; Kolvin et al.), we find a 0.5% rate of hospitalized schizophrenia in parents and a 1.8% rate of schizophrenia or schizophrenic-like childhood psychoses in sibs. These values are *not* significantly different from the rate of schizophrenia in the general population. Such a result suggests that *early*-onset childhood psychoses including infantile autism are *not* genetically the same as adult schizophrenia.

Barbara Fish's data, on the other hand, are at variance with these conclusions. The 5.7% rate of schizophrenia in parents of her early-onset (< 2 years) childhood psychotics does suggest a continuity between early-onset cases and adult schizophrenia. In addition, Fish reports previously unpublished data of Lauretta Bender's showing a 7% rate of schizophrenia in parents of childhood psychotics whose onset was less than 2 years. What might account for their results?

Part of the disagreement might arise from different diagnostic criteria for schizophrenia. The two sets of data (Bender's and Fish's) that claim a link between infantile psychoses and adult schizophrenia are American (from New York State), whereas most of those showing no such link are European. It is generally agreed that the diagnostic criteria for schizophrenia are more conservative in Europe than in many parts of the United States. There are also problems of possible diagnostic contaminations and selective sampling. Both Bender and Fish refer to childhood schizophrenia "as a psychobiologic entity determined by an *inherited predisposition*, an early physiologic or organic crisis, and a failure in adequate defense mechanisms" (italics added) (Bender & Faretra, 1972). Starting with such a definition, there may be a tendency to limit the diagnosis of childhood schizophrenia to cases where there is a positive family history of schizophreniclike psychopathology. Additionally, such a definition raises the expectation of finding schizophrenia in family members of childhood psychotics and may result in overdiagnosing schizophrenia in their relatives. To minimize such problems, modern genetic family studies of adult schizophrenia have used probands unselected with regard to family history (e.g., taking consecutive admissions to a hospital) and have had probands' relatives diagnosed by blindfolded clinicians (unaware of the proband's diagnosis).

Fish points out another difference between the American and European studies: The European samples appear to contain a fairly large percentage of children with signs of organic brain damage whereas, she claims, the American studies exclude such cases. Children with psychoses associated with organic brain damage would not be expected to have an excess of schizophrenic relatives, and the European studies find virtually none. Although the European investigators may include many cases of psychoses with organic brain damage, we see no reason why they should systematically exclude cases, if any, that are genetically related to schizophrenia. The fact that the rate of schizophrenia in parents and sibs of the European probands is the same as the population base rates suggests that cases related to adult schizophrenia are at least very rare among an already rare syndrome.

Our tentative conclusion from family studies is that the vast majority of early-onset childhood psychoses are not genetically related to adult schizophrenia. Final conclusions require more research using up-to-date methodology (cf. Fish, 1977).

Genetic considerations

Claiming that early-onset childhood psychoses are genetically different from adult schizophrenia is not, of course, to deny that other genetic factors could be important. If genetic factors are important, however, they are not inherited in a simple Mendelian fashion. The family data are very different from Mendelian expectations, consanguinity rates are not elevated, and biochemical abnormalities suggesting an inborn error of metabolism have not been found. There are reports of excess serotonin (a neurotransmitter) in the blood of some autistic children, but the biochemical abnormality does not appear to be specific for autism. Many mentally retarded children and some normals also appear to have high levels of blood serotonin. Chromosomal abnormalities also seem unlikely etiological agents because psychotic children do not show multiple congenital malformations that most children with chromosomal abnormalities show. Chromosomal studies of psychotic children have not found any consistent abnormalities in number or morphology, although there are too few studies that use the refined staining and banding techniques now possible.

Two other genetic possibilities deserve consideration – rare mutations and polygenic inheritance. Although it is not our preferred choice of a theory for autism, a dominant mutation has been invoked to account for conditions such as some forms of human dwarfism. Even though the dwarfs do not reproduce very often, the incidence of the disorder continues at about 1 in 10,000 newborns; 7 out of every 8 new cases are attributed to "fresh" mutations in the germ cells of normal parents. The frequency of new mutations varies from gene to gene; a generally accepted average rate of 1 in 100,000 is not too far from the frequency of infantile psychoses in the general population. If new mutations were indeed the cause, we would expect parents and sibs to be unaffected. Identical twins would show a 100% concordance rate, fraternals would have a zero concordance rate, but 50% of the offspring of affected individuals would be affected. Males and females would be affected with equal frequency. We have seen that parents of children with early-onset childhood psychoses are virtually free of any psychosis, and the rate of psychoses among sibs is very low. Kanner reports 3 affected among 131 sibs, though he did not see the cases himself and no descriptions of the affected sibs are given. Meyers and Goldfarb observed 4 affected sibs among only 48. This unusually high rate probably reflects the investigators' very broad definition of schizophrenia: Apparently, none of the four was hospitalized and their purported psychoses do not appear to be infantile varieties. Fish found 1 case of autism and 1 case of childhood schizophrenia among 44 sibs. Three other investigators found no cases among a total of 215. If we count all reported cases of autism and other psychoses among the sibs of autistic children we find a total of 11 affected among 509 for a maximum rate of 2.2%. However, none of these cases is fully documented. There are no published case histories of these individuals nor were their diagnoses confirmed by blindfolded, independent clinicians who were unaware of the proband's diagnosis. As a consequence, we must consider that, at a minimum, the rate of autism among sibs is zero. Nevertheless, a recent preliminary report (Minton et al., 1980) also claims to find a higher-than-expected rate of autism among sibs of autistics. The truth likely lies somewhere between our maximum 2.2% and minimum 0% estimates. We hope future investigators will publish case histories of all probands and secondary cases and make an effort to have "blind" assessments of affected individuals.

At the risk of belaboring the diagnostic issue, we should point out that for any set of parents randomly selected, the chances of having a child with some severe psychological abnormality are *not* trivial and are probably in the order of 2% to 5%; some would say even 10% or higher if all forms of significant learning disabilities are included. Parents with an autistic child are, regrettably, not immune to these population base rates and about 2% to 10% of their other children will have serious behavioral or scholastic problems. Knowledge that the parents have one psychotic child could easily influence the diagnosis of the second abnormal child, especially if the second abnormal child is diagnosed in infancy when there are few objective criteria to guide such a decision. Such biases may account for some of the suspected cases of autistic mentally retarded sibs footnoted in Table 8.3. We should not be too surprised when authors (e.g., August, Stewart, & Tsai, 1981; Minton et al., 1980) report behavioral and cognitive abnormalities in sibs of autistics unless the frequency of these abnormalities significantly exceeds base rate expectations or those in appropriately matched control groups. We must also remember that ascertainment biases may lead to research samples that do not accurately represent nature. For the sake of illustration, a family with two affected children has twice the chance of being "discovered" and included in a sample of families of autistics than does a family with only one affected. Such ascertainment biases will lead to overrepresentation of multiply-affected families. As a consequence, artificial differences may be created between study groups of autistics and their families compared to controls unless the methods of obtaining the controls are identical to the methods of obtaining the experimental group (on ascertainment bias, see Bodmer & Cavalli-Sforza, 1976, p. 724).

Because virtually all individuals with early-onset childhood psychoses never reproduce, there are no data on offspring of these individuals. Such data would be invaluable, however, in evaluating a hypothesis of a rare mutation. Lacking such data, we must turn our attention to twin studies.

Twin studies of autism

Over the years many case studies of single pairs of twins with autism have been reported. However, pooling such single case studies does not provide a satisfactory set of twin data (see Chapter 6). Furthermore, in many of the reported case histories, zygosity diagnoses were not confirmed and many of the cases were questionably deserving of what Kanner might have diagnosed as infantile autism. The only systematic study of early-onset psychoses (before age 5) attempted to find all autistic twins in Great Britain. Susan Folstein and Michael Rutter found 11 MZ and 10 SSDZ pairs of twins. Four of the MZ and none of the DZ pairs were concordant. At face value these results suggest that there is a genetic predisposition to developing infantile autism. However, such an interpretation must be made with caution.

Before any firm conclusions about genetics can be drawn from twin data it is necessary to rule out the possibility that the twinning process itself might contribute to the development of the trait under study. That is, the trait should occur no more often in twins than it does in singletons. (We have already noted, for example, that there is an overrepresentation of twins among institutionalized retardates.) The twinning process is associated with a higher risk for pregnancy and birth complications that may result in brain damage or other congenital malformations. Furthermore, MZ twins have more congenital malformations than DZ twins, and MZ twins are more often concordant for birth defects than are DZ twins. It is also known that pregnancy and birth complications occur more frequently in individuals who develop infantile autism. Thus the higher concordance rate for autism among MZ twins could be due to genetic effects and/or to nongenetic but biological hazards associated with the twinning process. If the latter is true, there should be an overrepresentation of twins, especially MZ twins, among autistic children just as there is an overrepresentation of twins among institutionalized retardates.

To test such a hypothesis we obviously need precise estimates of the rates of autism in twins and singletons. Unfortunately, the estimates of the population base rates for autism range from about .8 to 4.5 per 10,000 (Table 8.2). The frequency among twins in the British study was about 2.5 per 10,000. We can conclude that although the rate in this twin sample does not exceed the population base rates to any large extent, the population base rates cover too broad a range to permit any conclusions about a relatively small increase, say in the range of a 20% to 50% excess. If, for example, the population base rate were precisely known to be 1 per 10,000, a 50% excess among twins would produce a rate of 1.5 per 10,000. Such a difference would not be detectable using the current imprecise range of population estimates from .8 to 4.5 per 10,000. The twin study results are not incompatible with a genetic hypothesis, but a simple dominant mutation theory would specify males and females being equally affected. Because such is clearly not the case, any dominant gene theory would have to be extended to include other factors, genetic or environmental, that differentially modified the penetrance of the gene in the different sexes. The twin data are also consistent with a prenatal brain damage hypothesis; a great many of the autistic twins in the

British survey do show neurological abnormalities such as seizures and other EEG abnormalities and many of them have histories that suggest possible prenatal difficulties.

Finally, we turn our attention to polygenic inheritance as a possible contributor to early-onset childhood psychoses. If a polygenic disorder leads to a condition that is incompatible with reproduction, as appears to be the case with infantile psychoses, we would expect parents of affected children to be free of the disorder although there may be something distinctive about them because they possess a subthreshold "dose" of the deleterious genes. Sibs (including DZ twins), however, should have an increased risk for the disorder and the risk to MZ co-twins should be even higher. The twin data are compatible with a polygenic theory that specifies different thresholds for males and females. The paucity of adequately documented cases of infantile psychoses in more than 500 sibs of early-onset childhood psychotics cannot support a polygenic theory and also argues against the many psychogenic theories that focus on general parental personalities, attitudes, or child-rearing practices. Counting the maximum 11 (2.2%) cases among sibs could suggest a familial clustering compatible with multifactorial (genetical and/or environmental) models. Histories of the parents themselves are apparently free of childhood psychoses and, in our view, there appears nothing particularly distinctive about them to indicate that they are carriers of psychosis-producing genes. The early and often-cited claims that most parents of infantile psychotics are emotional refrigerators or have other forms of deviant personalities have not been confirmed in more recent researches. When parents of psychotic children do exhibit an unusual trait, it may well be a reaction to having a very unusual child and not a cause of the child's psychopathology.

Discussion and conclusions

Both the genetic evidence and the phenomenology of childhood psychoses lead us to believe that a meaningful distinction can be made between psychoses that begin in the earlier years of life and psychoses that begin at or after puberty. The reader should not take our early-onset/late-onset dividing line of age 5 too rigidly. About 70% of Kolvin's late-onset childhood psychotics broke down after age 9. Adolescent maturation is a process that spans several years. The actual initiation of the process occurs at some unknown time before the beginning of the adolescent growth spurt, which may begin as early as age 7½ in girls but more typically begins between ages 9½ and 14½ in girls, and 10½ and 16 in boys. It would be most valuable to obtain measures of skeletal and endocrinological maturity in future studies of late-onset childhood psychoses. If our hunches are correct, these children should either be more biologically mature than their chronological age would indicate or they should have histories suggesting brain trauma.

We find *no* strong evidence to implicate genetics in the development of the *early*-onset variety, though the possibility of a rare dominant mutation or of polygenic inheritance cannot be ruled out. The same data (i.e., no or very few sibs affected) fail to support psychogenic causations. It is true that parents do not treat all their children alike, but we cannot accept the psychogenic view as credible until we see evidence explaining how normal parents, through subtle means, produce severe psychoses in one child whereas their others are normal. Given adequate sampling, social class is *not* related to childhood autism (Wing, 1980).

It seems far more parsimonious to postulate biological but not genetic, probably congenital, etiological factors, given: (1) the similarities in symptomatology shared by infancy-onset psychotics and children with known CNS trauma; (2) the ample evidence suggesting CNS pathology, which includes an increase in pregnancy and birth complications; (3) increased frequency of perceptual abnormalities; and (4) the association of autisticlike behavior with CNS viral infection, retrolental fibroplasia, metabolic disturbance, and degenerative diseases. Many of these contributors could be familial and biological without being genetic. The recent demonstration of enlarged left-temporal ventricular horns in 15 of 17 autisticlike children is the most direct evidence to date implicating organic etiology in general, and "language-hemisphere" dysfunction in particular. We hope further efforts to link anatomical and behavioral abnormalities will routinely employ noninvasive computerized tomography (CT brain scan) to study all psychotic children. The failure to find biochemical abnormalities specific for psychotic children is compatible with a dominant mutation or an organic etiology; a dominant gene, trauma, or toxins causing structural changes in the prenatal brain would leave no biochemical fingerprints. Viral infections during prenatal life, occurring before the development of immunological systems, could also cause permanent changes in the brain that would not be detected postnatally by serological techniques.

Data relevant to the genetics of *late*-onset childhood psychoses come from only two studies: One was carefully done but has a small (by most geneticists' standards) sample size; the other is larger but has some puzzling features. Tentative conclusions implicate genetic factors as important to the development of *late*-onset childhood psychoses, and these factors appear to overlap with genetic factors that add to the liability for adult schizophrenia. If these conclusions are correct, they require a reevaluation of the minimum age of onset for adult-type schizophrenia, which is often pegged at 15 years.

Cases beginning before age 15 are rare, but they may provide invaluable clues to maturational changes or environmental events that actualize a predisposition to schizophrenia. Thus, unlike information about the early-onset cases, late-onset childhood schizophreniclike psychoses can provide pieces for solving our schizophrenic puzzle.

BIBLIOGRAPHY

Achenbach, T. M., & Edelbrock, C. S. The classification of child psychopathology: A review and analysis of empirical efforts. *Psychological Bulletin*, 1978, *85*, 1275–1301.

August, G. J., Stewart, M. A., & Tsai, L. The incidence of cognitive disabilities in the siblings of autistic children. *British Journal of Psychiatry*, 1981, *138*, 416–422.

Bender, L. Schizophrenic spectrum disorders in the families of schizophrenic children. In R. R. Fieve, D. Rosenthal, & H. Brill (Eds.), *Genetic research in psychiatry*. Baltimore: Johns Hopkins University Press, 1975, pp. 125–134.

Bender, L., & Faretra, G. The relationship between childhood schizophrenia and adult schizophrenia. In A. R. Kaplan (Ed.), *Genetic factors in schizophrenia*. Springfield, Ill.: Charles C Thomas, 1972, pp. 28–64.

Bleuler, E. Dementia praecox or the group of schizophrenias (Joseph Zinkin, trans.). New York: International Universities Press, 1950. (Originally published 1911.)

Bodmer, W. F., & Cavalli-Sforza, L. L. *Genetics, evolution, and man*. San Francisco: W. H. Freeman, 1976.

Brask, B. H. The need for hospital beds for psychotic children: An analysis based on a prevalence investigation in the county of Aarhus. *Ugeskrift for Laeger*, 1967, *129*, 1559–1570.

Campbell, M. Pharmacotherapy in early infantile autism. *Biological Psychiatry*, 1975, *10*, 399–423.

Chess, S. Follow-up report on autism in congenital rubella. *Journal of Autism and Childhood Schizophrenia*, 1977, *7*, 69–81.

Corbett, J., Harris, R., Taylor, E., & Trimble, M. Progressive disintegrative psychoses of childhood. *Journal of Child Psychology and Psychiatry*, 1977, *18*, 211–219.

Creak, M., & Ini, S. Families of psychotic children. *Child Psychology and Psychiatry*, 1960, *1*, 156–175.

DeMyer, M. K., Hingtgen, J. N., & Jackson, R. K. Infantile autism reviewed: A decade of research. *Schizophrenia Bulletin*, 1981, *7*, 388–451.

Deykin, E. Y., & MacMahon, B. The incidence of seizures among children with autistic symptoms. *American Journal of Psychiatry*, 1979, *136*, 1310–1312. (a)

Deykin, E. Y., & MacMahon, B. Viral exposure and autism. *American Journal of Epidemiology*, 1979, *109*, 628–638. (b)

Finegan, J., & Quarrington, B. Pre-, peri-, and neonatal factors and infantile autism. *Journal of Child Psychology and Psychiatry*, 1979, *20*, 119–128.

Fish, B. Biologic antecedents of psychosis in children. In D. X. Freedman (Ed.), *Biology of the major psychoses.* New York: Raven Press, 1975, pp. 49–83.

Fish, B. Neurobiologic antecedents of schizophrenia in children. *Archives of General Psychiatry,* 1977, *34,* 1297–1318.

Fish, B., Campbell, M., Shapiro, T., & Floyd, A., Jr. Comparison of trifluperidol, trifluoperazine, and chlorpromazine in preschool schizophrenic children: The value of less sedative antipsychotic agents. *Current Therapeutic Research,* 1969, *11,* 589–595.

Folstein, S., & Rutter, M. Infantile autism: A genetic study of 21 twin pairs. *Journal of Child Psychology and Psychiatry,* 1977, *18,* 297–321.

Guthrie, R. D., & Wyatt, R. J. Biochemistry and schizophrenia. III. A review of childhood psychosis. *Schizophrenia Bulletin,* 1975, *12,* 18–32.

Hanson, D. R., & Gottesman, I. I. The genetics, if any, of infantile autism and childhood schizophrenia. *Journal of Autism and Childhood Schizophrenia,* 1976, *6,* 209–234.

Hauser, S., Delong, G., & Rosman, N. Pneumographic findings in the infantile autism syndrome, a correlation with temporal lobe disease. *Brain,* 1975, *98,* 667–688.

Kallmann, F. J., & Roth, B. Genetic aspects of preadolescent schizophrenia. *American Journal of Psychiatry,* 1956, *112,* 599–606.

Kanner, L. To what extent is early infantile autism determined by constitutional inadequacies? *Proceedings of the Association for Research in Nervous and Mental Disease,* 1954, *33,* 378–385.

Kolvin, I., Ounsted, C., Richardson, L., & Garside, R., III. The family and social background in childhood psychoses. *British Journal of Psychiatry,* 1971, *118,* 396–402.

Lotter, V. Epidemiology of autistic conditions in young children. I. Prevalence. *Social Psychiatry,* 1966, *1,* 124–137.

Lotter, V. Epidemiology of autistic conditions in young children. II. Some characteristics of parents and children. *Social Psychiatry,* 1967, *1,* 163–173.

Meyers, D., & Goldfarb, W. Psychiatric appraisals of parents and siblings of schizophrenic children. *American Journal of Psychiatry,* 1962, *118,* 902–908.

Minton, J., Shell, J., Campion, J. F., Green, W. H., Perry, R., Samit, C., & Campbell, M. *A study of siblings of autistic children.* Paper presented at the meeting of the American Academy of Child Psychiatry, Chicago, October 1980.

Rimland, B. The differentiation of childhood psychoses: An analysis of checklists for 2,218 psychotic children. *Journal of Autism and Childhood Schizophrenia,* 1971, *1,* 161–174.

Ritvo, E. R. Biochemical studies of children with the syndromes of autism, childhood schizophrenia, and related developmental disabilities: A review. *Journal of Child Psychology and Psychiatry,* 1977, *18,* 373–379.

Rutter, M. Behavioural and cognitive characteristics of a series of psychotic children. In J. Wing (Ed.), *Early childhood autism.* Oxford: Pergamon Press, 1966, pp. 51–81.

Rutter, M. The development of infantile autism. *Psychological Medicine,* 1974, *4,* 147–163.

Rutter, M. Infantile autism and other child psychoses. In M. Rutter & L. Hersov (Eds.), *Child psychiatry: Modern approaches.* Oxford: Blackwell, 1977, pp. 717–747.

Rutter, M., & Lockyer, L. A five to fifteen year follow-up study of infantile psychosis. I. Description of the sample. *British Journal of Psychiatry*, 1967, *113*, 1169–1182.

Treffert, D. A. Epidemiology of infantile autism. *Archives of General Psychiatry*, 1970, *22*, 431–438.

Wing, L. Childhood autism and social class: A question of selection? *British Journal of Psychiatry*, 1980, *137*, 410–417.

Wing, L., Yeates, S. R., Brierley, L. M., & Gould, J. The prevalence of early childhood autism: Comparison of administrative and epidemiological studies. *Psychological Medicine*, 1976, *6*, 89–100.

9   Environmental puzzle pieces: multifactorial contributors

Within the broad diathesis–stressor framework for understanding schizo-phrenia that we are trying to develop in this book, we have assumed a certain kind of interchangeability (called fungibility by the legal profession) of the genetical and environmental contributors to the liability of developing schizophrenia (see Figure 4.3). The relative importance of environmental factors would then be a dynamic, varying function of where in the combined liability distribution a person was found at any particular time. We shall expand on this concept in Chapter 11. It accords well with the epigenetic view put forward by Margaret Singer, a psychodynamic clinical psychologist, and Lyman Wynne, a psychodynamic (transactional) psychiatrist, who study schizophrenia within the diathesis–stressor framework:

We assume that the individual's biologic capacities for focusing attention and for perceiving, thinking, and communicating gradually are shaped and modified by interchange with the environment during development. This viewpoint is *epigenetic:* The interchanges or transactions at each developmental phase build upon the outcome of earlier transactions. This means that constitutional and experiential influences recombine in each developmental phase to create new biologic and behavioral potentialities which then help determine the next phase. (Singer & Wynne, 1965, p. 208)

The inherent difficulties of trying to uncover important environmental contributors to the etiology, release, exacerbation, or amelioration of schizo-phrenia must be acknowledged at the outset. We have already mentioned the slim but tantalizing pickings from the study of MZ twins discordant for schizophrenia as pointers to specific stressors. Data gathered retrospectively from or about current schizophrenics dealing with their childhoods, their obstetrical histories, and so on are bound to be lacking in accuracy and completeness. Creative recoveries of early, premorbid hard data from archives by such researchers as Norman Watt, George Albee, Sarnoff Mednick, and Lee Robins (cf. Robins, 1979 for references to other "follow-back" research) were efforts to overcome the shortcomings of earlier data.

169

Data gathered prospectively may never be linked to schizophrenia because such a long time elapses between acquisition and the materialization of overt cases; good luck is also needed to pick the best predictor variables, ones that will not pass out of fashion as new research rejects received wisdom. Despite these kinds of barriers, a great deal of effort has been expended to implicate various intrafamilial (structural and emotional), interpersonal, sociocultural, and somatic (nongenetic) factors in our understanding of schizophrenia. We can touch on only a few of these factors, and then only in passing.

Bruce Dohrenwend, a social psychologist–epidemiologist, has lamented the fact that support for the importance of environmental factors in the etiology of schizophrenia is "argument by subtraction," that is, unaccounted-for variance after genetic variance has been subtracted. He goes on to say:

If socio-environmentally-induced stress is an important factor in the etiology of various types of psychiatric disorder in general populations, then life events such as marriage, birth of a first child, loss of a job, and death of a loved one are strategic as more proximal phenomena through which such stress is transmitted to individuals. Such events are eminently researchable. (1975, p. 387)

We can only agree with that view and hope that research will not only identify relevant events but also specify whether they are, in fact, differentially (vis-à-vis mental disorders in general) important for schizophrenia.

It is clear from the fact that only some 50% of the identical co-twins of schizophrenics are also affected even after lengthy observation times that genetic factors are not sufficient causes. It is clear from the reported increase in stressful life events for schizophrenics versus controls in the 6 months prior to admission (to be discussed) that stress is somehow relevant. And it is clear from the adverse impact on relapse rates of schizophrenics at home that a negative emotional atmosphere influences the course of the disorder (also to be discussed). The multifactorial view about the contributors to etiology and phenomenology implicit in the classical epidemiological emphasis on agent, host, and environmental background complicates our efforts to understand schizophrenia, but it is a necessary complication for a complex disorder.

Life events

In epidemiology relative risk is defined as the ratio of the rate of the disease among those exposed to an "agent" to the rate in those not exposed. Thus the death rate among nonsmoking British male physicians from carcinoma of the lung is .07 per 1,000. Among those smoking a pack a day (about 20 cigarettes) the death rate from this cancer is 20 times greater, or 1.39 per 1,000. From what has been presented in Chapters 5 and 6 about the lifetime risks of schizophrenia in the offspring and identical co-twins of schizo-phrenics, we can calculate that the relative risk (a kind of odds ratio) of offspring from sharing 50% of their genes with a schizophrenic is 13 and the relative risk from sharing 100% of their genes with a schizophrenic is about 50. This leads to the consideration that genotype is far more important in the causation of schizophrenia than smoking a pack a day is to causing death from lung cancer. On the other hand, the majority of smokers do not die of lung cancer, and the majority of offspring of schizophrenics are not affected. Paykel (1978) reports that 54% of normals matched to a sample of 50 first-admission schizophrenics in New Haven, Connecticut experienced at least one stressful event in the preceding 6 months. An event was defined as one of some 60 specific changes or crises (marriage, minor physical illness, family arguments, etc.). Seventy-eight percent of the schizophrenics reported such events. Limiting the field to undesirable events only, 42% of schizophrenics versus 14% of controls had one or more yielding a relative risk of 4.5. After the time period was constricted to the preceding month, the highest relative risk obtained from the life-event approach was 10.0 for suicide attempters. Exceedingly few schizophrenics concurred in any one event; the two most common events were court appearances (nine) and minor physical illnesses (eight). It is difficult to get enthusiastic about such findings as clues to the prevention or to the causes of schizophrenia.

In the research of George Brown and James Birley in London, crises and life changes were significantly associated with onset or relapse in the 3 weeks preceding admission for acute schizophrenia. Forty-six percent of patients versus only 14% of controls experienced such events as losing a job, moving house, and various domestic crises over which they had no control. Information was available to show that during the preceding 9 weeks both groups were equal, about 13% experiencing such events; it appeared that the onset of schizophrenia was accompanied by a sharp increase (from 13% to 46%) in the frequency of significant events. The relative risk for the 3-week period was 6.4. See Paykel (1978) and references therein for details on the calculation of relative risks.

Christine Vaughn and Julian Leff carried the program of social psychiatry research in London further by simultaneously examining the effect on relapse rate of medication versus stopping medication, low expressed (negative) emotion (EE) versus high, and (for the high-EE [negative] emotion group) intensity of contact with relatives at home over a 9-month period. The Social Psychiatry Unit had earlier shown that in the 9 months following discharge the relapse rate of patients from high-EE homes was 58% versus 16% from low-EE homes. The findings from the extension of this research are shown in Figure 9.1 for 128 schizophrenic patients. Subgroup 6 had the worst relapse rate; 92% of them succumbed in the worst of all worlds – high EE, intense contacts (more than 35 hours per week), and failure to maintain their phenothiazine medication. EE was rated on a scale that sampled critical comments, hostility, and emotional overinvolvement, and the cutting score was 6 such interactions. The lowest relapse rates were found in the low-EE homes with no effect in that setting of stopping medication. It seems medication was especially effective in protecting the high-EE patients, who spent fewer than 35 hours a week in contact with their parents or spouses (Group 3 in Figure 9.1). The medications plus the reduction in intensity of contact may have had an additive protective effect and should be kept in mind in the management of therapeutic efforts. "On medications" was defined as taking them for 8 months of the 9-month period.

The histories of our schizophrenic twins illustrated a diversity of precipitants. One twin was actually being trained to "expand his consciousness" after he joined an organized insight-seeking movement; this turned out to be as disastrous as looking for a gas leak with a match. Childbirth was a clear precipitant; there were recurring effects in one twin. In another pair, only the childless one was a schizophrenic. In yet another pair, one twin became psychotic after her second child but her MZ sister, despite four pregnancies (including one abortion on psychiatric grounds), was only neurotic. Obviously, whether childbirth triggers schizophrenia in a predisposed woman depends on factors other than genotype. Within pairs concordant for schizophrenia the same stressor may be more disrupting for one than the other as a function of how they experience it, which, in turn, depends on the kinds of epigenesis valued by Singer and Wynne.

In a seldom-cited study by Schofield and Balian (1959) comparing the personal histories of schizophrenic patients and a matched group of normals who were patients in the same hospital for nonpsychiatric reasons and who had no history of mental illness, a large amount of conventional wisdom was put to rest (or embarrassment). The normals were given a comprehensive clinical interview covering the usual psychiatric areas of concern. The most noteworthy finding was the high degree of overlap between the life history events experienced by both the normals and the schizophrenics. For example, the predominant relationship between the parents of both groups was one of affection (76% of both groups); interparental relationships of ambivalence, indifference, or hostility were slightly more common among the parents of *normals*. Overprotection and domination by mothers did characterize the schizophrenics (24% vs. 1%), but fully 65% of schizophrenics' mothers' relationships with them were characterized as healthy affection. Poor home conditions such as poverty, invalidism, and divorce were significantly more often found in histories of *normals*. Neither alcoholism nor early death of a parent distinguished between the two groups. Although 85% of the normals had average or better school achievements, only half had excellent deport-

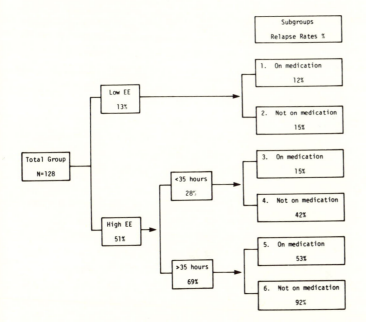

Figure 9.1. Nine-month relapse rates of 128 schizophrenic patients (71 in the low-EE group and 57 in the high-EE group) as a function of medication maintenance and exposure to negative emotional atmosphere. (After Vaughn & Leff, 1976.)

ment records; for the schizophrenics, 24% had difficulties in achievement but 82% had *excellent* deportment. Frequency of dating was not different in the two groups, and 1/3 of each were or had been married. Heterosexual adjustment was actually poorer among the normals (37% vs. 22%). When it came to contrasts in social adjustment and skills, the schizophrenics were disadvantaged with 61% rated as showing social withdrawal (vs. 10% in normals) and only 2% as adept in social intelligence (vs. 23% in normals). Such comparisons, however, may simply reflect the beginnings of the disease process. For such global constructs as a "life plan," 74% of schizophrenics were rated as vague or confused but so were 32% of the normals. A summary of this study confirms the impression of a high degree of overlap between normals and schizophrenics in the area of life events. Of the 35 separate contrasts, 37% showed no reliable differences; for 14% of the contrasts, the normals were, contrary to expectations, the disadvantaged group.

We need to look more closely at the area of communication deviances in the transmission of schizophrenia. Note that the term transmission leaves open the question of the role of genes and environment in the familiality of schizophrenia. If, for example, the parents in the Danish studies who adopted the children who became schizophrenics all treated them in a specific way, it would undermine our faith in the genetic half of our diathesis–stressor causal model. None of the adoptive parents in the Danish studies have been examined in ways that would permit the detection of their own modes of communicating. That would have required a longitudinal prospective study that began in 1924 together with a reliable and valid measure of "schizophrenicity." However, a pilot study conducted in Maryland by Wender, Rosenthal, and Kety on the characteristics of the adoptive parents of schizophrenics obtained independent ratings of parental psychopathology and parental communication deviances (from tape-recorded Rorschach records). Margaret Singer, a gifted clinical psychologist, first made a global assessment of parental Rorschach communication and was able to predict perfectly the status of three groups of offspring: 7 schizophrenic offspring reared by their biological parents, 9 different schizophrenic offspring reared by their adoptive parents, and 10 nonschizophrenic offspring reared by their adoptive parents. Systematic scoring of parental couples for communication deviances (Singer, Wynne, & Toohey, 1978) revealed no difference between the biological parents of schizophrenics and the adoptive parents of (different) schizophrenics; however, both of these groups were more deviant than adoptive parents of normals (.122, .121, and .049 were the mean frequencies, respectively, per couple).

Wender et al. had earlier reported that parental *diagnoses* did not distinguish between the adoptive parent groups, although ratings of the interviews showed the adoptive parents of schizophrenics to be more disturbed than the adoptive parents of normals. The results of the Singer and the Wender analyses were seen as complementary (Singer et al., 1978, p. 510) and as consistent with the hypothesis that both genetic and experiential factors can interact to produce an overt case of schizophrenia. Such a view is the essence of the diathesis–stressor framework. The likelihood that, reversing the direction of the assumed causal arrow, disturbed offspring cause disturbances in their caretakers whether adoptive *or* biological cannot be discounted. Certain kinds of communication deviances as contributory factors in some cases of schizophrenia, as triggers or as straws that break the camel's back, complement the research on expressed emotion we have described. This area has been extensively scrutinized by Hirsch and Leff (1975) and Leff (1978); Wynne's comments are also of interest (1978, pp. 534–542).

Obstetrical complications as predisposing factors

The kinds of life events and within-family milieus we have discussed sometimes serve either as precipitants of schizophrenia or as predisposing contributors, but not in a uniform way across individuals. This is another way of calling attention to an interaction effect between stressors and diatheses or predispositions. Of many other classes of environmental factors, obstetrical factors have been repeatedly implicated as possibly predisposing in some cases of schizophrenia. We have already examined one such factor, namely, lowered birthweight in identical twins, and found it lacking in explanatory power, but this is only 1 factor among some 60 that obstetricians might choose to examine.

"Obstetrical complications" (OCs) is a term used to cover pregnancy complications, birth complications, and neonatal complications (up to 4 weeks postpartum). It is important to distinguish among studies that focus on OCs in births to schizophrenic mothers (or wives of schizophrenics), OCs determined retrospectively in the lives of current schizophrenics themselves, and OCs determined in infants who will be followed prospectively to see what develops that may be relevant to schizophrenia. The available evidence is far from conclusive and is often contradictory with positive findings not replicable for one reason or another. Two sets of findings are frequently cited by those who claim a special importance for OCs in the etiology of schizophrenia: the Pollin et al. study at the NIMH on discordant schizophrenic MZ pairs (see Chapter 6), and the two different studies by Mednick and colleagues in Denmark on children born to schizophrenic mothers. Findings in the Danish work can only be preliminary because the "true" schizophrenics in the original high-risk study are only now showing up (Schulsinger, 1976) and the offspring in the second high-risk study, which began at birth, are still too young. A most thorough and thought-provoking review of this area of research is provided by Thomas McNeil and Lennart Kaij (1978), who have themselves made contributions to resolving the problems in their southern Swedish samples. They show that our focus on birthweight was too specific because a broad view of OCs in the MZ twin studies we used permits the conclusion that the twin with the most OCs is affected or affected more severely (72% of the time).

According to McNeil and Kaij, the kinds of perinatal-risk characteristics used in most retrospective studies pale in the face of prospectively designed studies. Few subjects, high risk or not, are born without showing something that might have seemed highly relevant had it been found retrospectively in a schizophrenic. Every one of us has, after all, experienced the trauma of birth. The proband in one of our fraternal female pairs weighed only 3.5 pounds at birth, was a breech delivery, had bilateral ptosis (droopy eyelids suggestive of brain or neck injury), and a "twisted right leg." Her sister weighed 6.75 pounds and was a normal presentation. The proband was rejected by her parents whereas her co-twin, different on every count – attractive, successful, well married, a mother – was the picture of mental health at follow-up. The proband was a consensus schizophrenic, although one of her chart diagnoses was paranoid state due to a birth injury. She was in all senses the ugly duckling. Perhaps nothing could prevent the vicious circles in her life, which finally led to schizophrenia. However, without the inferred genetic predisposition to schizophrenia, we would have predicted some other kind of psychiatric disability.

Twins *are* more liable to OCs than singletons, and MZ deliveries are more at risk than DZ. Moreover, males are at a greater risk than females. Thus, if OCs had a *specific* etiological role in schizophrenia and were not just moderator variables or contributors to a network of causes added to a genetic predisposition, we would have certain expectations: *Prevalences* of schizophrenia should be higher in MZ males than in MZ females, higher in MZs than in DZs, higher in males than in females, and so on. No such predictions have been confirmed for schizophrenia, although they have been for mental retardation.

In a longitudinal study of the children of schizophrenics, other psychiatric cases, and two normal control groups we conducted at the University of Minnesota (Hanson, Gottesman, & Heston, 1976), neither perinatal history nor the presence of single neurological abnormalities distinguished the schizophrenics' offspring. By age 7 neither physical growth nor psychological test findings showed conspicuous abnormalities. In some of the Swedish work of McNeil and Kaij no significant differences in total number of OCs were found between experimental (offspring of schizophrenics) and control infants. When they did occur, they were unrelated to the severity of the mothers' illnesses. Although experimentals and controls did not differ in birthweight, there was a larger proportion of babies small for gestational age in the high-risk sample.

Until recently there was no reliable or prospective information on the number of OCs in schizophrenics themselves. Information on the offspring of schizophrenic patients has many limitations and the findings are inconsistent. When complications or neonatal deaths are reported in excess in a particular sample, they could implicate the genotype of the child, intrauterine environmental factors, medication toxicity, or unreported attempts at self-abortion. The crux of the matter is that until high-risk infants, carefully examined at birth, are followed up well into adulthood, we shall not know whether those who did have OCs, even when combined with childhood behavior problems or deviant psychophysiology, will become the ones who develop schizophrenia. We shall address the issue of combining single, unpredictive factors into unique configurations in the next section.

If we look for a moment at epilepsy and mental retardation, we see that even there it is not easy to implicate OCs and other biological factors such as virus infections and anoxia as causal. When the condition to be forecast has its onset some 30 to 50 years after an event that allegedly predisposes to it, the problems seem insurmountable. If one accepts the usefulness of Pasamanick and Knobloch's (1960) concept of a continuum of reproductive casualty, schizophrenia must surely be at its least specific end.

By using careful, collected-at-birth obstetrical records for adults who became process schizophrenics, for schizophreniclike psychotics, and for their normal matched controls, McNeil and Kaij found only the process schizophrenics to have reliably more OCs than their controls, mainly due to neonatal complications. We concur with the many reservations expressed by McNeil and Kaij about the quality of research in this area, and with their conclusion that OCs seem to be independent stressful factors that may interact with the genetic influences and are risk-increasing factors to be taken seriously in the search to understand the etiology and phenomenology of schizophrenia. It is the task of further research to specify which ones, how seriously, and in what proportion of cases (NIMH, 1981).

Environmental factors in combination

Powerful environmental causes or contributors to schizophrenia are difficult to identify. If environmental factors are interaction effects only, clues provided from the studies reviewed so far, including the MZ twins discordant for schizophrenia, will continue to frustrate our search. In other words, a factor may cause schizophrenia only in the relatively few individuals who are genetically predisposed and may have no noticeable effect as an independent cause of schizophrenia in the population as a whole. The test of this idea, as mentioned earlier, would be to determine the risk for schizophrenia among persons exposed to the suspect "vector" but who are not selected because they are related to a schizophrenic. It is important to discover precipitating factors even if they are not etiological in their own right. Factors suggested by twin studies may select forces that are twin-specific, for example, relative dominance within a pair, and not be useful in the study of singleton schizophrenics.

Because inferiority in birthweight, submissiveness, and poor school achievement have been implicated singly as associated with the sicker of two MZ twins, it seems reasonable that such factors have a cumulative effect on the risk for developing schizophrenia, even if they are not completely independent. Taken one at a time, we might expect the disadvantaged twin to have some kind of adjustment problem; but when all occur simultaneously such a twin should be at great risk for psychiatric disorder compared to twins as a whole, and some should even be psychotic. The spared twin in the pair should be healthier than twins in general. Setting aside genetic considerations for a moment, triply disadvantaged twins should become delinquent, neurotic, or schizophrenic as a function of such factors as the quality of parental communication or identification with the psychologically sicker parent.

In addition to Tienari's study in Finland on schizophrenia in twins, he studied an entire cohort of male identical twins born in a certain region of Finland from 1920 to 1929 and assessed them according to a number of intrapair differences, including school achievement, dominance–submissiveness (relative to each other), and birthweight. After a personal examination of the 160 men from 80 pairs, he classified them as normal, deviant personality, neurotic or psychopathic, or psychotic. Twenty-two pairs of MZ twins were found in which the same twin was disadvantaged on all three factors. Table 9.1 shows the psychiatric adjustment classification of the members of the 22 pairs as well as that for the remaining twins in the cohort. Table 9.2, derived from 9.1, shows the sample divided into abnormal and normal groups in two different ways. From the distribution of the entire sample of 160 twin individuals we can calculate that in the subsample of 22 individuals 10 would be normal and 12 abnormal. The upper part of Table 9.2 shows precisely that distribution among the 22 "inferior," triply disadvantaged twins. In other words, the cumulative effect of these particular environmental contributors has had no particular role in causing psychiatric abnormality.

If deviant personalities are combined with the normals and contrasted with the more overt kinds of psychopathology, the bottom of Table 9.2 shows a tendency for the disadvantaged twin to be "sick" more often than expected (seven vs. four). However, although the environmentally advantaged twins in such pairs would be expected to have a lower than average risk of psychopathology, they have their full share (four vs. four).

For this Finnish cohort of male twins the combination of stressors such as low birthweight, plus intrapair submissiveness, plus low school achievement does not determine psychiatric abnormality over the twin population as a whole. We believe such a demonstration weakens naïve enthusiasm about easily discovering environmental factors or constellations of such factors that will predict schizophrenia independently of a genetic predisposition. We seek and would welcome the identification of the kinds of environments that, at the sociological or interpersonal level (see Leff's and Vaughn's earlier-cited work), or at the physiological level (e.g., learning stress management by biofeedback or "brain nutrition"), facilitate or prevent the most malignant manifestations of schizophrenia in those individuals predisposed to it.

Summary and conclusions

When geneticists try to estimate formally the contribution of genetic factors to the liability to developing schizophrenia (see Chapter 4), the value of that

Table 9.1. *Intrapair differences and psychiatric abnormality: effect of cumulative differences in birthweight, dominance, and school achievement*

Psychiatric classification (Tienari)	Pairs in which same twin is inferior in all variables			Twins from other pairs (4)	All twins (5)
	(1) Inferior twin	(2) Expected[a]	(3) Superior twin		
Normal	10	(10)	11	52	73
Deviant personality	5	(8)	7	46	58
Neurotic or psychopathic	4	(2)	3	12	19
Psychotic	3	(2)	1	6	10
Total persons	22	(22)	22	116	160

[a]Calculated (to nearest whole number) from Column (5).

Table. 9.2. *Cumulative intrapair differences and psychiatric abnormality*

Investigator's psychiatric classification	Twins differing consistently from partner in birth-weight, dominance and school achievement (22 pairs)		
	Inferior twin	Expected[a]	Superior twin
Normal	10	10	11
Not normal	12	12	11
Alternative division			
Normal or deviant	15	18	18
Neurotic, psychopathic, or psychotic	7	4	4

[a]Derived from all 80 pairs in group.

statistic, called the heritability and symbolized h^2, is quite high – in the neighborhood of 70% (Rao et al., in press). The magnitude of h^2 is much less informative about the importance of environmental factors for most schizo-phrenics than might be assumed (or feared). One of the reasons high heritability does an apparent injustice to the real power of environmental factors is that heritability is a concept from *population genetics* according to which $(1 - h^2)$, or 30%, indicates the strength of environmental differences over the population as a whole. In this system the what's-left-over from genetic liability becomes the "environmentability."

Although environmental factors may contribute only about 30% to the individual differences in the liability to schizophrenia in the whole popula-tion, they will be critical factors when they occur to someone who is in the "neighborhood" of the threshold in the distribution of combined liability (see Figure 4.6). Thus even individuals with a high risk for schizophrenia on genetic grounds, say the MZ co-twins of schizophrenics, could in theory avoid a breakdown by avoiding the environmental factors that added liability "units" and pushed their twin over the threshold. It is true that various lines of evidence reviewed in this chapter and the adoption work converge to discredit shared family environment as important. However, that still leaves as important for the individual those aspects of the environment/ecology not shared or those not experienced in the same way by others. Much of the work we mentioned earlier by the social psychiatrists connected with the Institute of Psychiatry in London (Brown, Birley, Wing, Leff, etc.) speaks to the role of such presumptive *idiosyncratic* stressors and objective life events of many kinds in precipitating onsets and relapses in some schizophrenics. Individuals who happen to be at the extreme tail of a (separate) distribution of genetic liability will easily become cases and will rarely have such objectively defined stressful life events prior to their breakdowns; for those individuals almost any environment they experience appears to be sufficiently stressful. For the much larger number of individuals who are not so extremely predisposed on genetic grounds, however, the relatively gross events catalogued by the Dohrenwends and others mentioned in this chapter working in the field of social psychiatry make common sense and will presumably play a much larger role in their schizophrenia puzzles. Perhaps we have belabored the point, but the majority of the population do not develop schizophrenia (or major affective disorders) even when they are exposed to severe and multiple stressors. Only those in the zone of combined liability near the threshold of overt schizophrenia will have their illnesses triggered by augmentation of liability from environmental sources. This line of reasoning from the diathesis–stressor framework makes it clear that although the genes may be necessary but not sufficient for causing schizophrenia, the environmental contributors may also be necessary but not sufficient, and not yet specifiable other than on a case-by-case basis.

BIBLIOGRAPHY

Arey, S., & Warheit, G. J. Psychological costs of living with psychologically disturbed family members. In L. N. Robins, P. J. Clayton, & J. K. Wing (Eds.), *The social consequences of psychiatric illness*. New York: Brunner/Mazel, 1980, pp. 158–175.

Barrett, J. E., Rose, R. M., & Klerman, G. L. *Stress and mental disorders*. New York: Raven Press, 1979.

Bloom, B. L., Asher, S. J., & White, S. W. Marital disruption as a stressor: A review and analysis. *Psychological Bulletin*, 1978, *85*, 867–894.

Brown, G. W., Birley, J. L. T., & Wing, J. K. Influence of family life on the course of schizophrenic disorders: A replication. *British Journal of Psychiatry*, 1972, *121*, 241–258.

Dohrenwend, B. P. Sociocultural and sociopsychological factors in the genesis of mental disorders. *Journal of Health and Social Behavior*, 1975, *16*, 365–392.

Dohrenwend, B. P., & Dohrenwend, B. S. Psychiatric disorders and susceptibility to stress. In L. N. Robins, P. J. Clayton, & J. K. Wing (Eds.), *The social consequences of psychiatric illness*. New York: Brunner/Mazel, 1980, pp. 183–197.

Goldberg, E. J., & Comstock, G. W. Epidemiology of life events: Frequency in general populations. *American Journal of Epidemiology*, 1980, *111*, 736–752.

Hanson, D., Gottesman, I. I., & Heston, L. L. Some possible childhood indicators of adult schizophrenia inferred from children of schizophrenics. *British Journal of Psychiatry*, 1976, *129*, 142–154.

Hirsch, S. R., & Leff, J. P. *Abnormalities in parents of schizophrenics* (Maudsley Monograph No. 22). London: Oxford University Press, 1975.

Inghe, G. Mental and physical illness among paupers in Stockholm. *Acta Psychiatrica Scandinavica*, 1958, Suppl. 121, 112–168.

Jacob, T. Family interaction in disturbed and normal families: A methodological and substantive review. *Psychological Bulletin*, 1975, *82*, 33–65.

Kind, H. The psychogenesis of schizophrenia: A review of the literature. *British Journal of Psychiatry*, 1966, *112*, 333–349.

Lane, E. A., & Albee, G. W. On childhood intellectual decline of adult schizophrenics: A reassessment of an earlier study. *Journal of Abnormal Psychology*, 1968, *73*, 174–177.

Leff, J. Social and psychological cause of the acute attack. In J. K. Wing (Ed.), *Schizophrenia: Towards a new synthesis*. London: Academic Press, 1978, pp. 139–165.

McNeil, T., & Kaij, L. Obstetric factors in the development of schizophrenia: Complications in the births of preschizophrenics and in reproduction by schizophrenic parents. In L. C. Wynne, R. L. Cromwell, & S. Matthysse (Eds.), *The nature of schizophrenia: New approaches to research and treatment*. New York: Wiley, 1978, pp. 401–429.

Mednick, S. A., Schulsinger, F., Higgins, J., & Bell, B. (Eds.). *Genetics, environment, and psychopathology*. Amsterdam: North-Holland, 1974.

Moore, M. R., Meredith, P. A., & Goldberg, A. A retrospective analysis of blood-lead in mentally retarded children. *Lancet*, April 2, 1977, pp. 717–719.

National Institute of Mental Health. Risk factor research in the major mental disorders. DHHS Publication No. (ADM)81–1068. Superintendent of Documents, U.S. Government Printing Office, Washington, D.C. 20402, 1981.

Pasamanick, B., & Knobloch, H. Brain damage and reproductive casualty. *American Journal of Orthopsychiatry*, 1960, *30*, 298–305.

Paykel, E. S. Contribution of life events to causation of psychiatric illness. *Psychological Medicine*, 1978, *8*, 245–253.

Pollin, W., & Stabenau, J. R. Biological, psychological and historical differences in a series of monozygotic twins discordant for schizophrenia. In D. Rosenthal & S. S. Kety (Eds.), *The transmission of schizophrenia*. Oxford: Pergamon Press, 1968, pp.317–332.

Rabkin, J. G. Stressful life events and schizophrenia: A review of the research literature. *Psychological Bulletin*, 1980, *87*, 408–425.

Rao, D. C., Morton, N. E., Gottesman, I. I., & Lew, R. Path analysis of qualitative data on pairs of relatives: Application to schizophrenia. *Human Heredity*, in press.

Robins, L. N. Longitudinal methods in the study of normal and pathological development. In K. P. Kisker, J. E. Meyer, C. Müller, & E. Strömgren (Eds.), *Psychiatrie der Gegenwart*. Vol. 1. *Grundlagen und Methoden der Psychiatrie* (2nd ed.). Heidelberg: Springer-Verlag, 1979, pp. 627–684.

Schofield, W., & Balian, L. A comparative study of the personal histories of schizophrenic and nonpsychiatric patients. *Journal of Abnormal and Social Psychology*, 1959, *59*, 216–225.

Schulsinger, H. A ten-year follow-up of children of schizophrenic mothers: Clinical assessment. *Acta Psychiatrica Scandinavica*, 1976, *53*, 371–386.

Serban, G. Stress in schizophrenics and normals. *British Journal of Psychiatry*, 1975, *126*, 397–407.

Singer, M. T., & Wynne, L. C. Thought disorder and family relations of schizophrenics. IV. Results and implications. *Archives of General Psychiatry*, 1965, *12*, 201–212.

Singer, M. T., Wynne, L. C., & Toohey, M. L. Communication disorders and the families of schizophrenics. In L. C. Wynne, R. L. Cromwell, & S. Matthysse (Eds.), *The nature of schizophrenia: New approaches to research and treatment*. New York: Wiley, 1978, pp. 499–511.

Sturgeon, D, Kuipers, L., Berkowitz, R., Turpin, G., & Leff, J. Psychophysiological responses of schizophrenia patients to high and low expressed emotion relatives. *British Journal of Psychiatry*, 1981, *138*, 40–45.

Tienari, P. On intrapair differences in male twins with special reference to dominance-submissiveness. *Acta Psychiatrica Scandinavica*, 1966, Suppl. 188, 1–166.

Vaughn, C., & Leff, J. P. The influence of family and social factors on the course of psychiatric illness. *British Journal of Psychiatry*, 1976, *129*, 125–137.

Watt, N. Patterns of childhood social development in adult schizophrenics. *Archives of General Psychiatry*, 1978, *35*, 160–170.

Wender, P. H., Rosenthal, D., & Kety, S. S. A psychiatric assessment of the adoptive parents of schizophrenics. In D. Rosenthal & S. S. Kety (Eds.), *The transmission of schizophrenia*. Oxford: Pergamon Press, 1968, pp. 235–250.

Woerner, M. G., Pollack, M., & Klein, D. F. Pregnancy and birth complications in psychiatric patients: A comparison of schizophrenic and personality disorder patients with their siblings. *Acta Psychiatrica Scandinavica*, 1973, *49*, 712–721.

Wynne, L. C. Concluding comments. In L. C. Wynne, R. L. Cromwell, & S. Matthysse (Eds.), *The nature of schizophrenia: New approaches to research and treatment*. New York: Wiley, 1978, pp. 534–542.

10   The social biology of schizophrenia

Social biology, not to be equated with sociobiology (Wilson, 1975), can be defined as knowledge about the observable biological and sociocultural factors that affect the composition of human populations and, in principle, their evolution. With respect to schizophrenia, we will be interested in facts about sexuality, marriage, fertility (actually, fitness as defined by the number of offspring), divorce, obstetrical complications, and patterns of morbidity and mortality. Questions about eugenics and genetic counseling will be touched on in passing. Such sociobiological issues as speculative, post hoc evolutionary "explanations" for the origin and perpetuation of schizophrenia are difficult issues as well for social biology. However, the highlighting of the difficulties will be interesting in its own right.

Only a sampling of the observations relevant to the social biology of schizophrenia can be attempted in this book. The time is not yet ripe for a final synthesis of these observations with theories about the etiology of schizophrenia and the likely models for its transmission. Nevertheless, the basic facts will help to dispel some of the myths that have accumulated about schizophrenia and that must be reckoned with in the eventual solving of the schizophrenia puzzle.

Sexuality of schizophrenics

Very little systematically collected information about the sex life of schizophrenics, either premorbidly or postmorbidly, is available. The data we will review about marriage and fertility will permit some inferences. Clinical impressions abound but are so idiosyncratically anecdotal as to be useless for generalizing. We are indebted to Manfred Bleuler (1978) for having taken the trouble to explore this sensitive topic with his 208 probands (100 men, 108 women) and their relatives in his longitudinal research. Even though recent Swiss urban sexual mores are different in many ways from those of the rest of

Europe and the United States, the information he collected can serve as a backdrop to the following section. He was able to group his probands into four categories based on their "erotic life" prior to the onset of their schizophrenia.

Nonerotic: no love relationship and no sexual relations – 24 men, 40 women

Erotically discreet: "natural love relationships" and no or clandestine sexual relations – 43 men, 14 women

Erotically active: maintained several intimate relationships, sometimes producing illegitimate children – 16 men, 42 women

Sexually perverted: 1 each voyeur, homosexual, and incest with brother

Information on the remaining 26 was insufficient to categorize. Bleuler was impressed by both the large proportion of nonerotics and the rarity of perverts. As might be expected, a large proportion of the nonerotics never married and most but not all could be called schizoid premorbidly. (In the entire proband sample only 1/4 were premorbidly "schizoid-pathological," and a further 1/3 "schizoid within the norm.") Sixty-eight of the probands had married before their schizophrenia could be detected clinically: 11 of 28 marriages of men were happy and successful before the onset of schizophrenia, as were only 13 of 40 marriages of women. The remainder were rated as more or less "poor." It is important to note that of the total of 184 children born to the probands, 78% were born *before* the probands were first hospitalized. In this sample of children only 15 were born out of wedlock, 12 before the onset of psychosis, suggesting more restraint than the normal population.

Bleuler, based on his experience with the local population, concluded that the prepsychotic sexuality of schizophrenics, except for the frequency of sexually restrained males, did not depart from his expectations. Alcoholics, he believed, were much worse off in this area than schizophrenics. Bleuler's findings about the civil statuses of his probands (and of a much larger sample of admissions), and as compared to controlled census information, anticipate and confirm the data from other countries we will report later. The wealth of data will repay efforts at secondary analyses. Very briefly, he found the following.

	Males (%)		Females (%)	
	Probands	Census	Probands	Census
Single	52	21	48	20
Married	27	73	18	63
Divorced	16	3	19	5
Widowed	4	3	15	12

Barbara Stevens's (1969, 1970) London study of the marriage and fertility patterns of 813 schizophrenic women and 482 women with affective disorders casts further light on the sexuality of these kinds of patients. The schizophrenics had an average of 1.04 children per patient of whom 19% were illegitimate (161 children out of 843). In the comparable population of normal London women in the 1960s, the illegitimacy rate was 13%. The histories available for the schizophrenic women suggested that no more than 3% could be described as promiscuous; information of this kind for the general population was not available. Even fewer were known to be homosexual ($N = 13$); 15% never showed an interest in the opposite sex. The apparent excess of illegitimacy was probably due to the diminished chances for marriage of the schizophrenics before admission to hospital. A more fine-grained analysis of the data reveals the interesting observation that most out-of-wedlock births were the result of a serious affair rather than of a promiscuous relationship. Fully half of the single schizophrenic women had been seriously involved with a man and of them 1 in 5 had a child before admission and 1 in 8 had a child after admission. Such pockets of variation show how complicated the area of sexuality can be. Another instance of this variation was the finding that 5 out of the total sample of women each had had 4 or 5 illegitimate children. A review of the personality characteristics of the schizophrenics confirms the common-sense expectation that the schizoid patients had the lowest illegitimacy rate whereas those with marked psychopathic (sociopathic) tendencies had the highest.

Marriage, fertility, and divorce

Let us now examine other data relevant to the social biology of schizophrenia. Larson and Nyman (1973) carefully compiled the completed fertility of male schizophrenics in Sweden; females were excluded so as to minimize false positive diagnoses, for example, involutional melancholics called schizophrenic. They used the entire birth cohort of males only born from 1881 to 1900 and followed them up to 1966, when they were well through the risk periods of both schizophrenia and parenthood. The longitudinal approach yielded a complete sample of schizophrenics in which 32% did not have their first symptoms of overt schizophrenia until after age 40.

The rural catchment area in southeastern Sweden contained 153 schizophrenic probands, of whom 110 or 72% *never* fathered a child. The remaining 43 men produced 131 children. Larson and Nyman present their data by Kraepelinian subtypes, which are useful as an indication of severity. Table 10.1 shows the average number of children for each category, including married *and* unmarried, that is, the *net fitness* of schizophrenics. It is clearly below replacement value (0.9 children overall) except for the paranoid and schizoaffective subgroups. As shown many times in the literature, marital fertility of 3.0 children probably did not differ from the comparable general population. Severity of schizophrenia had a clear impact on these men's chances of marriage and reproduction. Fully 85% of the nuclear cases (hebephrenic and catatonic) were unmarried and childless, and 54% of the paranoid schizophrenics were unmarried and 61% of them childless. This careful study also examined the fertility of the probands' siblings so as to collect evidence about alleged fitness advantages suggested by the balanced polymorphism theory of Huxley et al. (1964).

Of the nuclear-case sibs, 81% were parents compared to 74% of the paranoids' sibs and there was no difference in their mean marital fertility (3.1 vs. 3.0). In the sample of sibs, the morbid risk for schizophrenia of the two groups of probands was 19.1% and 7.6%, respectively.

The reduced fertility of schizophrenics as a whole is evidence of strong negative natural selection pressures. Such negative selection is clearly evident, but it is somewhat diminished in populations practicing effective means of birth control. That is, a fixed mean fitness in schizophrenics will look relatively less disadvantaged as the typical family size in the general population decreases, and differential disadvantages can even disappear.

Let us look at a few more studies related to the reproduction of schizophrenics. Ødegaard analyzed the fertility in marriage, the marriage rate, and the reproductive rate relative to the general Norwegian population for the first admissions to all mental hospitals in the period 1936–1955. Data for schizophrenic men and women can be compared with those for manic-depressives. The data do not include children born after a first admission, a point we shall address shortly. It can be seen in Table 10.2 that marital fertility is somewhat reduced for schizophrenics, and both the marriage rate and the relative rate of reproduction are greatly reduced, especially for males. There is no evidence that biological factors, that is, sterility per se, are involved here. Most evidence (Ødegaard, 1946; Stevens, 1969; Vogel, 1979) points toward the importance of premorbid personality traits reducing the opportunities for, and interest in, marriage and childbearing.

When schizophrenics are followed over time after they are first admitted to a mental hospital, it is clear that their subsequent increases in marriage rate or in reproductivity are rather small. Erlenmeyer-Kimling, Rainer, and Kallmann (1966) in a New York State cohort of schizophrenics admitted from 1934 to 1936 found that the initial ever-married rate of 49% for female patients was only 52.5% 7 years later, and only 54% 27 years later. Their number of children per schizophrenic, over these same intervals, went from

Table 10.1. *Number of children produced by male Swedish schizophrenics*[a]

Subtype	N	Average age of onset	N children	Average children per schizophrenic
Hebephrenic	28	26.1	11	0.4
Catatonic	20	27.4	5	0.3
Simple	8	28.5	1	0.1
Mixed	20	36.6	14	0.7
Schizoaffective	11	39.0	14	1.3
Paranoid	66	42.0	86	1.3
Total	153	35.6	131	0.9 (SD 1.7)

[a]Derived from Larson and Nyman (1973).

0.8 to 0.9 to 1.0. We have already mentioned comparable findings from Swiss schizophrenics.

Even the schizophrenics who manage to get married have a very high risk of marital disruption with its dire consequences for childbearing and child rearing. In a new approach to this phenomenon, Slater, Hare, and Price (1971), using patients admitted in London in the 1950s and 1960s, showed that married schizophrenics spent the lowest proportion of the *risk period for parenthood* (20–44) in the married state of all diagnostic groups – 42% of the general population time (18 years) for males and 60% for females. For the same time period in New York State, Erlenmeyer-Kimling et al. (1969) found that 40% (females) to 60% (males) of ever-married diagnosed schizophrenics were divorced or permanently separated. What evidence there is suggests that, as in the case of marriage versus singlehood, premorbid personality problems influence the selection of married schizophrenics for divorce. We may wish to conclude that durable marriages among schizophrenics have selected the "healthiest" schizophrenics through two difficult "screens."

The information we have outlined about the marital and fertility patterns of schizophrenics bears directly on the social and the biological components of the concept of social biology. The impact on the former is self-evident; the impact on the latter is indexed only by the total reproductivity of schizophrenics. A useful overview of relevant data is provided by Erlenmeyer-Kimling, Wunsch-Hitzig, and Deutsch (1980) and can also be gleaned from the data in Table 10.3 from Slater et al.'s (1971) study of London inpatients and outpatients. It is clear that even with the improvements in the treatment of schizophrenia, neither male nor female schizophrenics are replacing themselves in the population. The data from large samples of manic-

Table 10.2. *Darwinian fitness in Norwegian psychiatric patients as percentage of general population*[a]

	Schizophrenics		Affective psychoses	
	Male	Female	Male	Female
Marriage rate	38	53	91	93
Marital fertility	93	92	85	82
Relative reproduction[b]	36	48	77	76

[a]Derived from Ødegaard (1972) for period 1936–1955.
[b]Fertility × marriage rate.

depressives and neurotics serve as important comparisons and as challenges to simplistic explanations.

No eugenic alarms, in our opinion, need be sounded based on the data we have presented. There is, however, a great need for humane understanding of the problems of living and coping created for the *individual* schizophrenic who has a baby, whether by design or by inattention to contraception. We shall return to the related topic of genetic counseling for schizophrenia later in this chapter. Tracking changes in the patterns of fertility is important but can be confounded by variations in diagnostic standards over time (see Chapter 1), national (including race, rural-urban, and religion) differences, and secular trends (cf. Bleuler, 1978, pp. 357–372; Erlenmeyer-Kimling et al., 1980; Stevens, 1969).

If, for whatever reasons, the nonschizophrenic sibs of schizophrenics, some of whom are presumed to be "gene carriers," do have increased relative fitness, it would help to explain the perpetuation of the disease despite the strong negative selection described so far. However, no studies exist to support such a contention. In fact, social selection (Yokoyama & Templeton, 1980) appears to be operating to *lower* the reproductivity of sibs relative to the general population, even if it is higher than that of their sick sibs (cf. Bleuler, 1978; Buck et al., 1975; Lindelius, 1970, p. 357). The tentative findings (Erlenmeyer-Kimling & Paradowski, 1966) in support of greater relative fitness in unaffected sisters have since been corrected to show no difference (Erlenmeyer-Kimling, 1978).

Patterns of mortality and morbidity

There are two reasons why it is logical to be concerned with the patterns of mortality (death) and morbidity (disease statuses and resistance) for schizo-

Table 10.3. *Marital and fertility data, London patients, 1952–1966[a]*

Marriage and fertility groupings	Females			Males		
	Schiz.	Manic-dep.	Neurosis[b]	Schiz.	Manic-dep.	Neurosis[b]
Number of patients	1,086	2,692	5,596	1,003	1,606	3,902
Number of children[c]	907	3,715	6,397	452	2,218	4,168
Children per patient	0.9	1.4	1.1	0.5	1.4	1.1
Children per marriage	1.7	1.9	1.6	1.5	1.9	1.6
Children per fertile marriage	2.2	2.4	2.1	2.2	2.4	2.2
Proportion of patients ever married (%)	54.0	79.1	73.6	32.7	79.1	69.6
Proportion of marriage childless (%)	24.9	20.1	23.4	27.7	21.5	25.1
Proportion of patients with children (%)	38.9	61.1	54.0	21.8	58.2	49.4

[a]Derived from Slater, Hare, and Price (1971).
[b]Excludes obsessionals.
[c]Includes illegitimate children.

phrenics. On the one hand, the information will contribute to our knowledge about the structure and composition of human populations, and on the other, it will contribute to possible explanations for the perpetuation of schizo-phrenia, if one or another physiological advantage can be demonstrated. In order to be relevant to evolutionary kinds of speculation, such physiological advantages as increased resistance to disease or decreased mortality relative to the general population would have to appear early enough in the lives of schizophrenics to augment their reproductive potential. In the classical example often invoked as an analog for positing a balanced polymorphism for schizophrenia, the carriers for one gene for sickle-cell anemia (a recessive disease) are less affected by malaria, a potentially fatal disease, and therefore can transmit the sickle-cell gene to the next generation where it may combine with another and appear as the disease itself. Individuals with both of the disease-producing genes develop anemia and die early; individuals with neither of the disease-producing genes die early as a result of malaria. Those with one of the genes for sickle-cell anemia not only avoid anemia but also avoid the dire consequences of malaria, and thereby have a selective advantage over either of the two homozygotes in a malarial environment. Unfortunately, however, such a clear, classical, balanced polymorphism is not an analog for schizophrenia.

Vital statistics maintained on psychiatric patients for the nineteenth and twentieth centuries show that psychiatric patients have excess mortality, and schizophrenics are no exception. Excess mortality can be defined as the death rate of psychiatric patients divided by the corresponding rate for the general population, standardized for age. The picture of mortality differs somewhat from study to study depending on whether the data are restricted to deaths occurring within a mental hospital over time or whether a study design allows for the follow-up of individuals ever admitted and diagnosed as schizophrenic. It is clear that at least during the first half of the twentieth century and perhaps for another decade or two after that, schizophrenics had excess mortality to the extent of a 200% to 500% increase. In Sweden, for example (Larsson & Sjögren, 1954), a male schizophrenic once admitted to hospital would have only 68% of the life expectancy remaining for a member of the general population. The corresponding percentage for female schizo-phrenics was 54%. Explanations for the excess mortality tended to center mainly on tuberculosis. It was clearly in excess in psychiatric patients and ac-counted for approximately 1/3 of all deaths in schizophrenics. This gave rise to many speculations about genetic relationships between schizophrenia and tuberculosis, which are seldom heard nowadays. With improvement in health care in Western industrialized societies, tuberculosis has tended to disappear as a major cause of death in schizophrenics. Even up to the middle of the 1950s, however, tuberculosis led to an excess of mortality from 7 to 13 times the population rate in all patients suffering from functional psychoses. The excess mortality rate has since dropped to only about 2. The rational explanation for the association between deaths from tuberculosis and the diagnosis of schizophrenia seems to have been given by Alström in 1942. He believed that it was due to the large weight loss, which lowered the resistance to tuberculosis and increased the susceptibility to infection. It is probable that the antischizophrenic drugs (introduced in 1954) have virtually eliminated weight loss; they even appear to cause an increase in weight. The leading cause of death among psychiatric patients nowadays is bronchopneumonia; this is in large part associated with the increasing age of psychiatric patients of all types, including those with organic and senile psychoses.

Saugstad and Ødegaard (1979) have provided important new data about mortality in Norwegian psychiatric hospitals for the past 25 years, using the national case register of mental disorder. These data give the cause of death for some 10,000 deaths in Norwegian mental hospitals from 1950 to 1974. The data are also compared with the period between World Wars I and II. It is clear that the causes of death among those with functional psychoses must be separated from those with organic psychoses, including senile dementia. In recent times, pneumonia has been joined by cardiovascular diseases and suicide as the leading causes of death. The Norwegian investigators paid special attention to cardiovascular diseases and cancer. It was clear that cancer does not account for excess mortality among schizophrenics. It was also clear that cardiovascular disease did cause excess mortality (from 50% in females to 80% in males, and was increasing). It may be a paradox of treating schizophrenia with phenothiazine medication that the price paid for the relief of stress and psychotic symptoms is an increase in cardiovascular deaths mediated by diminished physical activity and increased body weight. It was difficult for the investigators to assess the impact of increased smoking on the causes of death, and no mention was made of the role of diet or hypertension as contributory risk factors.

Suicide appears with alarming frequency as a cause of excess mortality in schizophrenia. As other causes of death have receded in importance, suicide has climbed to where it will rank first or second as a cause in some recent studies. This is so whether we are talking about deaths that occur in hospital or those that occur in schizophrenics followed for a long time after their initial admissions. In the large Norwegian series of deaths, violent death recently ranked first as the cause of excess mortality among those with functional psychoses; the major cause of violent death was suicide. Excess mortality from violent death among the male Norwegian schizophrenics rose from 120% to 360% between 1950 and 1974. It was only exceeded by the affective psychoses in males, where the excess increased from 280% to 630% for the same period. The fact that these suicides occurred in hospital despite the precautions taken suggests how desperate these people are to escape from their too often unrelieved torment.

Among Bleuler's (1978) probands followed for some 22 years, about ⅓ were dead at follow-up. After deaths associated with the treatment for the acute phase of schizophrenia, suicide was the most common cause, accounting for 13% of all deaths. In the general population of Switzerland, suicide accounted for from 1% to 3% of deaths. The 40-year follow-up of psychiatric patients conducted by Tsuang, Woolson, and Fleming (1980) in Iowa showed that some 10% of all deaths among schizophrenics were associated with suicide, a figure that did not differ from the suicide rate in those with affective psychoses. Given the usual ratio between suicide attempts and completed suicide, the frequency of suicide attempts among schizophrenics is likely to be 20% to 30%.

Lindelius and Kay (1973) in Sweden, as well as others, have noted that the method of committing suicide is very often a frighteningly violent one. The suicides committed by schizophrenics are not limited to the early phase of the illness but extend throughout the course. Suicides were committed both while the patients were in periods of remission as well as when they were acutely psychotic with additional symptoms of agitated depression. Bleuler (1978) was prompted to say:

I know and fear the danger of suicide late in the course of schizophrenias. The older view [that it occurred most frequently at the beginning of psychosis] corresponded to the concept that in the course of time the inner life of schizophrenics "was extinguished, dulled, or burned out," and that in time they would lose their "internal dynamics" and their capacity to suffer. But the fact that years and decades after onset of illness suicides continued to occur points to the fallacy of that outdated assumption. (p. 306)

It is relevant to our discussion here to note that the sibs of schizophrenics also have a very high frequency of death by suicide even when they are not known to be schizophrenic themselves. This, of course, raises the question as to whether these suicides should be counted as "schizophrenic equivalents."

Morbidity

From the evidence we have reviewed, it is clear that the continued prevalence of schizophrenia cannot be accounted for by any decreased mortality among schizophrenics themselves. This has led some investigators to speculate about increased resistance to infection, either bacterial or viral, and to other diseases. Resistance to diseases that used to be killers in infancy, when mortality is highest, might provide promising leads to a physiological advantage for those who follow this line of thought. Suggestions are beginning to appear in the literature (Roberts & Kinnell, 1981; Torrey & Peterson, 1976; Tyrrell et al., 1979) that virus infections of some kind might be a partial cause of schizophrenia or at least a contributor to etiological heterogeneity. Demonstrations of specific resistances or susceptibilities between schizophrenics and the general population and between schizophrenics and other kinds of psychiatric disorders could be useful as clues to pathogenesis (mechanisms of the disease process itself) as well as to a search for genetic markers (to be discussed in Chapter 12).

According to Baldwin (1979), who conducted a broad overview of the relationships between schizophrenia and physical diseases, at least 20 diseases have been claimed to occur in excess in schizophrenics, and a further 6 have been claimed to occur less often than expected. Although unsubstantiated clinical observations and plain speculative suggestions accounted for a large proportion of the literature citations, there were a few exceptions. In principle the demonstration of an association between schizophrenia and the rarer physical diseases would require the following of 10,000 schizophrenics for 20 years in order to provide definite proof. Baldwin's review led him to the following conclusions:

Most of the suggested antagonisms and supposed deficiencies of diseases in schizophrenia, including cancers, epilepsies, allergies, diabetes, and myasthenia gravis, have arisen from interpretations of clinical "non-experience" based on more or less impressionistic overestimations of whatever is to be expected by chance. There is not as yet sufficient sound epidemiological evidence for any of them, and the only negative association for which the evidence is now fairly strong is that with rheumatoid arthritis. (p. 617)

Reports of reduced occurrences of asthma, hay fever, and other allergic phenomena are difficult to test directly given the obligation to protect schizophrenics from harmful experimentation. The sometimes-suggested diminished response to histamines is inconclusive because the protective effects of antischizophrenia medication have not been eliminated (Matthysse & Lipinski, 1975). A direct study of the immunological and allergic responsiveness of chronic schizophrenics was conducted sometime in the 1960s by Hussar, Cradle, and Beiser (1971). Although it is the kind of study not likely to be approved nowadays by committees set up to protect human subjects, it is worth reporting for the clear results obtained. Twenty-one chronic schizophrenics and 21 normal controls sharing the same hospital environment and food were injected with diphtheria toxoid (0.5 cc) on day 1 and on day 31. The investigators measured serum antibodies and the development of allergic skin reactions to the toxoid. They found no difference between the schizophrenics and the normal controls in their ability to form antibodies after exposure to the diphtheria toxoid. Furthermore, there was no difference between the two groups in sensitization to the toxoid. This direct test and refutation of one of the many hypotheses about schizophrenics being protected from serious physical disease is quite compatible with the general conclusions from the Baldwin survey. The enthusiasm for studying human leukocyte antigens (HLA) stems in part from the possibility of an auto-immune or antigenic component in the etiology of schizophrenia (Roberts & Kinnell, 1981; Torrey & Peterson, 1976). It is far too early to write the final story on this kind of research, but the allocation of research resources should take into account the literature reviewed here. Certainly the negative association with (i.e., protection from) rheumatoid arthritis should be pursued for further leads to the pathogenesis of schizophrenia or as a clue to genetic association with the HLA complex (McGuffin, 1979).

Explanations for the continued prevalence of schizophrenia in the face of the evidence about excess mortality, excess morbidity, and decreased fitness in schizophrenics and their relatives are found wanting. By and large schizophrenics have no advantages and are usually disadvantaged with respect to normal populations or individuals with other psychiatric disorders.

Infant mortality and obstetrical factors for children of schizophrenics

Another aspect of the social biology of schizophrenia that has attracted considerable attention concerns infant mortality and the quality of reproduction of schizophrenics. The information is important in its own right; it also provides further clues about possible physiological advantages and biological factors that could be contributors to etiology, either in interaction with the genotype or on their own. Furthermore, selective factors operating early that would lead to excess fetal or neonatal deaths would distort the facts available for accurate genetic modeling. Useful guides to the literature in this area may be found in McNeil and Kaij (1978), Hanson, Gottesman, and Heston (1976), Fish (1977), and Watt et al. (in press).

By and large, initial results in this area showing poor quality of reproduction by schizophrenics had not been replicated but continue to be cited. A number of studies showing high rates of neonatal death, congenital malformations, and increased perinatal deaths used general population values as their contrast information. When similar studies were done later using appropriately matched controls, the differences tended to disappear or to become statistically nonsignificant.

Three groups of investigators have had access to the host of pregnancy and delivery variables carefully collected from subgroups of the nationwide Collaborative Study of Cerebral Palsy, Mental Retardation, and Other Neurological and Sensory Disorders of Infancy and Childhood, conducted by the Perinatal Research Branch of the National Institute of Neurological Diseases and Stroke (NINDS) at 12 hospitals (Niswander & Gordon, 1972). Although the project was not intended to cast light on problems of schizophrenia, it could be used for such a purpose because a number of the mothers and/or fathers involved as parents of the consecutive babies delivered turned out to have schizophrenia. The Minneapolis, Boston, and New York City samples, although differing somewhat in sample composition and diagnostic criteria for schizophrenia, found no statistically significant increased incidence of fetal and neonatal deaths when comparing schizophrenic offspring to those of closely matched control groups. No statistically significant differences in birthweights were observed between the children of schizophrenics and their appropriate controls. A few studies have reported tendencies for the high-risk children to have lower birthweights.

Among the conclusions from McNeil and Kaij's masterful overview of this area are the following: The majority of studies show no differences in birthweights for the children born to schizophrenics compared to controls, and there are no differences in the rates of pregnancy complications, birth complications, neonatal complications, and total obstetrical complications in various aspects of reproduction in schizophrenics compared to controls. Such findings, it should be noted, do not tell us whether obstetrical complications do or do not contribute to the development of schizophrenia in those children of schizophrenics who do become schizophrenic later in life. Looking at a large number of careful studies of neuromotor functioning in the children of schizophrenic parents shows that various kinds of abnormalities are seen early in the lives of these children (Erlenmeyer-Kimling et al., in press). The conclusion that obstetrical complications are one more risk-increasing factor in the etiology of schizophrenia that deserves our attention cannot be refuted by any of the findings we have reviewed. It is, however, very difficult to establish an event as a cause of a condition that may have its onset 30 or 40 years after the event. Granting the importance of such risk-increasing factors, we have yet to determine, using high-risk, prospective strategies, which factors are specific, how serious they are, and in what proportion of cases they are relevant. Table 10.4 illustrates some of the variables available to the NINDS investigators that have been analyzed.

Table 10.4. *Representative obstetrical, growth, and neurological variables available in NINDS protocols*

Pregnancy and delivery	Physical growth	Neurological
Number of pregnancies	Birthweight	Complete neurological examinations were performed at birth, 4 months, 1 year, and 7 years
Fetal deaths	Gestational age	
Neonatal deaths	Neonatal length	*Neonatal examination:*
Gestational age	Neonatal head circum.	Abnormal tonic neck reflex (R)
Birthweight	1-year weight	Tremors
% males	1-year height	No step R
Apgar (1, 2, 5 minutes)	4-year weight	Ankle clonus
Number of mothers with:	4-year height	Incurvation of trunk
No complications reported	7-year weight	No placing R
Vaginal bleeding (by trimester)	7-year height	No patellar jerk
Severe physical illness		No auditory R
Hyperemesis		Abnormal Moro
Iron deficiency anemia		Abnormal traction R
Hypothyroid		Abnormal pupil R
Pre-eclampsia		Abnormal withdrawal R
Diastolic hypertension		No rooting R
Excess weight gain		No palmar grasp
Abruptio placentae		Abnormal prone position
False labor		Abnormal eye movements
Premature rupture of membranes		Motor lethargy
Compound presentation		
Caesarian section		
Full breech delivery		
Induced labor		
Placental size		
Placental infarcts		
Placental thrombi		
Placental true cysts		

Although it is reasonable to subscribe to the concept that pre- or perinatal traumas lead to a "continuum of reproductive casualty" (Pasamanick & Lilienfeld, 1955) in all infants, we doubt that such a continuum includes true schizophrenia. It must be recalled that the large number of father–child pairs of schizophrenics rules out transmission through in-utero effects, and the fact that children of schizophrenic mothers are at no greater risk than children of schizophrenic fathers further argues against the notion that obstetrical factors have a special and specific place in the etiology of schizophrenia. It is important to note that the absence of reliable increases in obstetrical complications, including low birthweight, combined with observations of deviant neuromotor function early in life implicates the genotype interacting with ubiquitous events as a cause of the neuromotor dysfunction. Further evidence to support the nonspecificity of obstetrical complications comes from the observation that the risk of schizophrenia to children born before the onset of schizophrenia in their parents is not higher or lower than the risk to children born after the onset in their parents. It is also well to remind ourselves (see Chapter 7) that the risk to the maternal half sibs in the Danish adoption studies was not different from the risk to the paternal half sibs. Findings in the studies of discordant twins (Chapter 6) also support this line of reasoning. We shall return to the strategy and the results of prospective studies of the children born to schizophrenics in the final chapter. Unlike the mature field of organic psychiatry for adults (Lishman, 1978), pediatric organic psychiatry has yet to be developed.

Some of the findings in this chapter suggest that in our attempts to solve the schizophrenia puzzle, we must be alert for pieces that may not even be pieces!

Genetic counseling

A chapter on the social biology of schizophrenia is an appropriate place for a brief discussion of genetic counseling. The subject must be approached with humility and great caution because the decisions about reproduction, marriage, and divorce are very personal ones made by individuals who are particularly vulnerable to both incompetent and competent advice. It is well to be reminded at the outset that genetic counseling for schizophrenia or for any other psychiatric condition as well as for other common medical disorders is an art and not a science, and that the road to hell is paved with good intentions.

So far as we can tell, very little genetic counseling about schizophrenia actually goes on despite the number of writings about the topic. The individuals seeing schizophrenics seldom offer genetic counseling. Patients themselves and their relatives are rarely informed enough about the disorder even to know what questions to ask. The information that patients and their relatives do have is often misinformation that may lead to unnecessary guilt and self-limitation in the areas of marriage and reproduction. Even though the evidence reviewed so far in this book exonerates parents from having caused their child's schizophrenia by their methods of rearing, the knowledge that the parents may have contributed genes that somehow or other eventually led to their child's schizophrenia may have replaced one devil with another. A point to stress for families of those 90% of schizophrenics who have apparently normal parents is that there was no way to predict such an outcome for a particular family.

In the typical genetic counseling situation for rare medical disorders, information is given to families who have already had an affected child or are at risk of having a child with some hereditary disorder known to "run in their family." Given the information in Chapter 1 about the age of onset distribution for schizophrenia, it would be rare to find parents of a schizophrenic who had any concerns about their own further reproduction. What is usual when counseling is sought in this area is that the parents of schizophrenics are concerned about their schizophrenic offspring's plans for marriage and reproduction. These parents will also be concerned about the risk of their other unaffected children becoming ill and about the prospects for all of their grandchildren.

Both professionals and relatives who find their way to a genetic counselor often have much stronger beliefs in the genetic component of schizophrenia than are warranted, and they fear the worst. The counselor, therefore, is in a position to bring good news and relief from anguish. Under ideal conditions genetically relevant information should only be dispensed when it is requested voluntarily so as to avoid the invasion of privacy. However, the realities of everyday life seem to require, in our opinion, that informed professionals should take the initiative in offering rational genetic counseling. We would suggest that the offer be put in the form of a leading question. If the lead is not picked up by the relative or the patient, more harm than good is likely to ensue if the matter is pursued.

The low utilization of genetic counseling stems in part from its past confusion with the eugenics movement. That particular ideological fusion of human genetics with politics was an explosive and disastrous mixture that we are still trying to live down. The genocidal practices of Nazi Germany in the 1930s and 1940s in the misguided hope of sanitizing the human gene pool must never be forgotten. However, genetic counseling must be disassociated from the eugenics movement. The goal of genetic counseling is to relieve the suffering of individuals and at the same time to protect their rights. The problems of society cannot be solved by the authoritarian imposition of naïve eugenic principles. Even in the 1980s many states have laws forbidding marriage of the "insane" (as well as of retardates, epileptics, and alcoholics) and permitting sterilization for problems manifested in behavior. Fortunately, neither class of laws is enforced.

Genetic counseling for schizophrenia involves much more than casual fact finding and casual rate giving; it is much nearer to the practice of a psychotherapist than to that of a "genetic bookie." The range of ethical and social questions that arise in a counseling session is quite wide, and is only growing wider. The counselor must avoid the temptation to play God or to foist his own values and fears about mental illness onto his clients (Kessler, 1979; Reilly, 1977).

The most frequent situation we have encountered is the one where the spouse of a newly diagnosed schizophrenic wants to know the risk of schizophrenia developing in their already-born children. If the couple does not have children, the request for advice may be covering a more important question the spouse is reluctant to raise. The implicit question is whether he or she should now start divorce proceedings and then work through the inevitable guilt feelings. One of the responsibilities of the counselor is to determine the motivation and the timing for the questions that do arise so as to answer the real questions. Sometimes adoption agencies will inquire as to the suitability of a particular child with an allegedly schizophrenic parent being put up for adoption to a particular family. There is often no way to confirm the validity of the diagnosis of the biological parents. The kinds of decisions to be made require very careful detective work and face-to-face meetings with the parties involved to increase the accuracy of judgments; the use of the telephone as a source of relevant information is to be avoided. In both the biological and the adoption situations, the art of counseling requires information about the personalities and the strengths and weaknesses of the individuals involved.

The actual estimation of the empirical or recurrence risk for schizophrenia is just *one* of the elements in the genetic counseling situation. The term risk takes on a narrower meaning here than the term morbid risk as we have used it so far. The concern now is with a *future* development of schizophrenia rather than with some calculations about entire classes of grandparents or aunts and uncles. The relatives of a child with a schizophrenic parent are primarily concerned with ways to minimize the actualizing of the risk for schizophrenia. It should be crystal-clear by now that both environmental and genetical factors are crucial in the development of the disorder. Regrettably, we cannot specify either the genetical or the environmental factors. The information about the empirical risks given in Chapters 5, 6, 7, and 8 together with the considerations about environmental contributors in Chapter 9 should all be consulted. The common-sense advice – to provide the best possible environment for the mental and physical growth of the child – deserves repetition. Relatives should be warned not to "overdiagnose" the ordinary vicissitudes of behavior, especially during adolescence. There is increasing reason (cf. Breakey et al., 1974; Bowers, 1977) to warn against the exposure to hallucinogenic drugs such as LSD and amphetamines because they may trigger a predisposition that would otherwise stay unexpressed. Certain prescription drugs are suspected of affecting neurotransmitters, including the dopamine pathways of the brain, and caution is urged in their use with individuals who may be genetically vulnerable to schizophrenia (cf. Crow, Johnstone, & Owen, 1979; Snyder, 1980). The proliferation of cults, encounter groups, and sensitivity-training groups, whether connected to religious organizations or not, prompts us to warn against exposure of individuals-at-risk to unsupervised, intensely emotional, "mind-expanding" experiences that often use techniques akin to brainwashing. Our warning cannot as yet be supported by controlled research designs.

A further practical suggestion is to obtain comprehensive health insurance for individuals at risk before their "insurability" comes up for question. In those families where one parent has already become schizophrenic, we strongly recommend family planning and the avoidance of further children. This can be justified on pragmatic clinical grounds wherein emotional and financial burdens as environmental stressors are to be avoided, rather than on any kind of genetic grounds. It is the ethical responsibility of the counselor to refer these families to other sources if he or she is unable (for personal reasons) to include family planning within the range of advice. Freedom to choose is paramount in the genetic counseling situation, and choosing should be based on the most accurate information.

Once the counselor is satisfied that he or she has accurate diagnostic information about the individuals in the pedigree, including second- and third-degree relatives, an actuarial risk can be calculated for the future development of schizophrenia in the sibs or children of schizophrenics. Calculation involves a computer program that makes the assumption that the disorder is determined multifactorially and uses the fact that the lifetime risk in the population is 1% and that the observed risk in sibs, one of our more accurate benchmarks, is close to 10%. The risks that can be calculated within this framework go beyond the information in Chapters 5 to 7 in that they do not require knowledge about the "true mode of transmission" or about the proportion of liability that is actually genetic versus environmentally connected. Furthermore, other affected relatives and other *unaffected* relatives are simultaneously taken into account. We cannot go into the details of derivation, but the interested reader should consult Smith (1971), Bonaiti-Pellié and Smith (1974), and Lalouel (1978). The methods will apply to any familial disease with an underlying liability. Unlike counseling for conditions that mendelize into neat 25% or 50% segregation ratios, counseling for a common, genetically conditioned disorder involves a different empirical risk for every family. This is bound to be confusing both for professionals and laymen, and it is no wonder if the recipients of "rate" information choose to interpret it in an all-or-none fashion; that is, the dreaded event will or will not happen in their families. The risks provided in Table 10.5 were derived with Smith's computer program, RISKMF. The objectively determined risk values, we emphasize again, are only points of departure for the wider counseling process. The figures apply only to individuals reared within their natural families and cannot be used in the adoption situation without clinical extrapolation based on the information in Chapter 7.

The precision implied by carrying the calculations to one decimal point is misleading. The risks are only approximations and must be taken with a number of grains of salt. Values in the table are lifetime risks because the "condition" is not congenital. Adjustments will certainly have to be made for the variable age of onset of schizophrenia, as discussed in Chapter 2 in the section on Age, Sex, and Risks. It will help to use the table if Figure 4.4 is kept in mind. A careful study of the tabled values reveals how unaffected first-degree relatives reduce the risk in the various pedigrees depicted. The table may be extended by noting that each additional unaffected sib will reduce the risk by the same amount as one unaffected sib. For example, with no parents affected and two sibs affected, the risk is 14.5%. By adding one unaffected sib to this family, the risk is reduced to 13.3%, whereas adding yet another unaffected sib reduces the risk to 12.0%, and so on.

Additional information about unaffected second- and third-degree relatives did not turn out to affect the recurrence risks using the Smith program. The risks are importantly changed by knowing whether affected individuals occurred on only one side or on both sides of the pedigree; this is shown in the bottom half, middle columns, of the table when only one parent is affected. In other words, when the second-degree relative who is affected is on the same side of the family as the affected parent, the risk is only 10.6%; when the affected second-degree relative is on the side of the family *opposite* to that of the affected parent, the risk goes up to 19.0%. The basic reason is that each side of the family contributes independent (genetic) information for calculating the risks to their descendants. Notice, for example, that with no parents affected and two sibs affected, the risk to another sib is 14.5%, whereas with no sibs in the family and both parents affected, the risk to a child (a "one-sib" family) is 41.1%. Thus we have two first-degree relatives affected in each

Table 10.5. *Projected recurrence risks for schizophrenia with varying family histories*

Pedigree	Number of schizophrenic parents			
	None	One		Both
		Same side	opposite side	
No sibs	0.9	8.5		41.1
1 sib *unaffected*	0.9	7.6		36.5
1 sib *affected*	6.7	18.7		45.9
1 sib A + 1 sib U	6.2	16.6		41.9
1 sib A + 2 sibs U	5.5	14.8		38.9
2 sibs A	14.5	27.8		50.6
2 sibs A + 1 sib U	13.3	25.0		46.4
2 sibs A + 2 sibs U	12.0	22.4		43.4
1 2° relative A	2.7	10.6	19.0	45.3
1 sib A + 1 2° A	10.3	21.5	28.3	50.5
1 sib A + 1 2° A + 1 sib U	9.4	19.0	25.4	46.0
2 sibs A + 1 2° A	18.6	30.8	35.7	54.9
2 sibs A + 2 2° A + 1 sib U	19.9	30.0	38.0	54.1
1 3° relative A	1.7	9.6	13.3	42.8
1 sib A + 1 3° A	8.6	20.2	23.8	48.3
1 sib A + 1 3° A + 1 sib U	7.9	17.8	21.2	44.0
1 sib A + 1 2° A + 1 3° A	11.9	23.1	32.3	52.9
2 sibs A + 1 2° A + 1 3° A + 1 sib U	18.5	28.9	35.5	52.3

Note: Risks estimated assuming a lifetime risk of 1% in the general population and a lifetime risk of 10% in sibs of schizophrenics (correlation in liability of .40) in RISKMF computer program (Smith, 1971).

case, but with quite different consequences for the recurrence risks generated for schizophrenia. The vast range of risks tabled, from a little bit under the population risk of 1% all the way up to 54.9%, shows some of the complexities involved in genetic counseling. It is certainly sobering, for example, to compare the risks of developing schizophrenia when one parent is affected (the central column of the table) with the very much simpler view of the problem given in the earlier chapters. One last caution should be added: The tabled values have very wide confidence limits (cf. Smith, 1971, p. 583).

With the facts and conjectures gathered under the rubric "social biology" behind us, we can now tackle the difficult task of describing and understanding some of the genetic models proposed for the transmission and development of schizophrenia.

BIBLIOGRAPHY

Allen, R. M., & Young, S. J. Phencyclidine-induced psychosis. *American Journal of Psychiatry*, 1978, *135*, 1081–1084.

Alström, C. H. Mortality in mental hospitals with especial regard to tuberculosis. *Acta Psychiatrica Scandinavica*, 1942, Suppl. 24.

Baldwin, J. A. Schizophrenia and physical disease. *Psychological Medicine*, 1979, *9*, 611–618.

Beauchamp, T. L., & Childress, J. F. *Principles of biomedical ethics.* New York: Oxford University Press, 1979.

Bleuler, M. *The schizophrenic disorders: Long-term patient and family studies* (Siegfried M. Clemens, trans.). New Haven: Yale University Press, 1978.

Bonaiti-Pellié, C., & Smith, C. Risk tables for genetic counseling in some common congenital malformations. *Journal of Medical Genetics*, 1974, *11*, 374–377.

Bowers, M. B., Jr. Psychoses precipitated by psychotomimetic drugs. *Archives of General Psychiatry*, 1977, *34*, 832–835.

Breakey, W. R., Goodell, H., Lorenz, P. C., & McHugh, P. Hallucinogenic drugs as precipitants of schizophrenia. *Psychological Medicine*, 1974, *4*, 255–261.

Buck, C., Hobbs, G. E., Simpson, H., & Winokur, J. M. Fertility of the sibs of schizophrenic patients. *British Journal of Psychiatry*, 1975, *127*, 235–239.

Caplan, A. L. (Ed.). *The sociobiology debate: Readings on ethical and scientific issues.* New York: Harper & Row, 1978.

Crow, T. J., Johnstone, E. C., & Owen, F. Research on schizophrenia. In K. Granville-Grossman (Ed.), *Recent advances in clinical psychiatry.* London: Churchill Livingstone, 1979, pp. 1–36.

Erlenmeyer-Kimling, L. Fertility of psychotics: Demography. In R. Cancro (Ed.), *Annual review of the schizophrenic syndrome* (Vol. 5). New York: Brunner/Mazel, 1978, pp. 298–333.

Erlenmeyer-Kimling, L., Marcuse, Y., Cornblatt, B., Friedman, D., Rainer, J. D., & Rutschmann, J. The New York high-risk project. In N. F. Watt, E. J. Anthony, L. C. Wynne, & J. Rolf (Eds.), *Schizophrenia: Children at risk.* Cambridge University Press, in press.

Erlenmeyer-Kimling, L., Nicol, S., Rainer, J. D., & Deming, W. E. Changes in fertility rates of schizophrenic patients in New York State. *American Journal of Psychiatry*, 1969, *125*, 916–927.

Erlenmeyer-Kimling, L., & Paradowski, W. Selection and schizophrenia. *American Naturalist,* 1966, *100*, 651–665.

Erlenmeyer-Kimling, L., Rainer, J. D., & Kallmann, F. J. Current reproductive trends in schizophrenia. In P. H. Hoch & J. Zubin (Eds.), *Psychopathology of schizophrenia.* New York: Grune & Stratton, 1966, pp. 252–276.

Erlenmeyer-Kimling, L., Wunsch-Hitzig, R. A., & Deutsch, E. Family formation by schizophrenics. In L. N. Robins, P. J. Clayton, & J. K. Wing (Eds.), *The social consequences of psychiatric illness.* New York: Brunner/Mazel, 1980, pp. 114–134.

Fish, B. Neurobiologic antecedents of schizophrenia in children. *Archives of General Psychiatry*, 1977, *34*, 1297–1318.

Gottesman, I. I., & Erlenmeyer-Kimling, L. (Eds.). Differential reproduction in individuals with physical and mental disorders. *Social Biology*, Supplement, 1971.

Hanson, D., Gottesman, I. I., & Heston, L. L. Some possible childhood indicators of adult schizophrenia inferred from children of schizophrenics. *British Journal of Psychiatry*, 1976, *129*, 142–154.

Hussar, A. E., Cradle, J. L., & Beiser, S. M. A study of the immunologic and allergic responsiveness of chronic schizophrenics. *British Journal of Psychiatry*, 1971, *118*, 91–92.

Huxley, J. A., Mayr, E., Osmond, H., & Hoffer, A. Schizophrenia as a genetic morphism. *Nature*, 1964, *204*, 220–221.

Kessler, S. (Ed.). *Genetic counseling: Psychological dimensions.* New York: Academic Press, 1979.

Lalouel, J. Recurrence risks as an outcome of segregation analysis. In N. E. Morton & C. S. Chung (Eds.), *Genetic epidemiology.* New York: Academic Press, 1978, pp. 255–284.

Larson, C. A., & Nyman, G. E. Differential fertility in schizophrenia. *Acta Psychiatrica Scandinavica,* 1973, *49*, 272–280.

Larsson, T., & Sjögren, T. A methodological psychiatric and statistical study of a large Swedish rural population. *Acta Psychiatrica Scandinavica*, 1954, Suppl. 89.

Lindelius, R. (Ed.). A study of schizophrenia: A clinical, prognostic, and family investigation. *Acta Psychiatrica Scandinavica*, 1970, Suppl. 216.

Lindelius, R., & Kay, D. W. R. Some changes in the pattern of mortality in schizophrenia in Sweden. *Acta Psychiatrica Scandinavica*, 1973, *49*, 315–323.

Lishman, W. A. *Organic psychiatry: The psychological consequences of cerebral disorder.* London: Blackwell Scientific, 1978.

Matthysse, S., & Lipinski, J. Biochemical aspects of schizophrenia. *Annual Review of Medicine,* 1975, *26*, 551–565.

McFalls, J. A. *Psychopathology and subfecundity*. New York: Academic Press, 1979.

McGuffin, P. Is schizophrenia an HLA-associated disease? *Psychological Medicine*, 1979, *9*, 721–728.

Niswander, K., & Gordon, M. *The women and their pregnancies*. Philadelphia: W. B. Saunders, 1972.

Ødegaard, Ø. Marriage and mental disease: A study in social psychopathology. *Journal of Mental Science*, 1946, *92*, 35–59.

Ødegaard, Ø. Marriage rate and fertility in psychotic patients before hospital admission and after discharge. *International Journal of Social Psychiatry*, 1960, *6*, 25–33.

Ødegaard, Ø. The multifactorial theory of inheritance in predisposition to schizophrenia. In A. R. Kaplan (Ed.), *Genetic factors in "schizophrenia."* Springfield, Ill.: Charles C Thomas, 1972, pp. 256–275.

Omenn, G. S., & Motulsky, A. G. Intrauterine diagnosis and genetic counseling: Implications for psychiatry in the future. In D. A. Hamburg & H. K. H. Brodie (Eds.), *American handbook of psychiatry* (Vol. 6). New York: Basic Books, 1975, pp. 643–664.

Pasamanick, B., & Lilienfeld, A. M. Association of maternal and fetal factors with development of mental deficiency. I. Abnormalities in the prenatal and paranatal periods. *Journal of the American Medical Association*, 1955, *159*, 155–160.

Reich, W. T. (Ed.). *Encyclopedia of bioethics*. New York: Free Press, 1978.

Reilly, P. *Genetics, law, and social policy*. Cambridge: Harvard University Press, 1977.

Roberts, D. F., & Kinnell, H. G. Immunogenetics and schizophrenia. *Psychological Medicine*, 1981, *11*, 441–447.

Saugstad, L. F., & Ødegaard, Ø. Mortality in psychiatric hospitals in Norway 1950–74. *Acta Psychiatrica Scandinavica*, 1979, *59*, 431–447.

Slater, E., Hare, E. H., & Price, J. Marriage and fertility of psychotic patients compared with national data. In I. I. Gottesman & L. Erlenmeyer-Kimling (Eds.), Fertility and reproduction in physically and mentally disordered individuals. *Social Biology* Supplement, 1971.

Smith, C. Recurrence risks for multifactorial inheritance. *American Journal of Human Genetics*, 1971, *23*, 578–588.

Snyder, S. H. *Biological aspects of mental disorders*. New York: Oxford University Press, 1980.

Stevens, B. C. *Marriage and fertility of women suffering from schizophrenia or affective disorders*. London: Oxford University Press, 1969.

Stevens, B. C. Illegitimate fertility of psychotic women. *Journal of Biosocial Science*, 1970, *2*, 17–30.

Torrey, E. F., & Peterson, M. R. The viral hypothesis of schizophrenia. *Schizophrenia Bulletin*, 1976, *2*, 136–146.

Tsuang, M. T., Woolson, R. F., & Fleming, J. A. Causes of death in schizophrenia and manic-depression. *British Journal of Psychiatry*, 1980, *136*, 239–242.

Tyrrell, D. A. J., Crow, T. J., Parry, R. P., Johnstone, E., & Ferrier, I. N. Possible virus in schizophrenia and some neurologic disorders. *Lancet*, April 21, 1979, pp. 839–844.

Vogel, H. P. Fertility and sibship size in a psychiatric patient population: A comparison with national census data. *Acta Psychiatrica Scandinavica,* 1979, *60,* 483–503.

Watt, N., Anthony, E. J., Wynne, L., & Rolf, J. (Eds.). *Schizophrenia: Children at risk.* Cambridge University Press, in press.

Wilson, E. O. *Sociobiology: The new synthesis.* Cambridge: Harvard University Press, 1975.

Yokoyama, S., & Templeton, A. The effect of social selection on the population dynamics of Huntington's disease. *Annals of Human Genetics*, 1980, *43*, 413–417.

11   Genetic models and theorizing

Human beings are unwieldy subjects for genetic analysis compared to fruit flies and mice, and schizophrenia is a difficult, complex phenotype for any kind of analysis. It is no wonder, then, that we are only now getting a start on solving the schizophrenia puzzle by sorting and organizing the more important genetical and environmental pieces. At present, the number of missing puzzle pieces is too great to solve the puzzle. Some of the missing pieces will come from the fields of neurochemistry, neuropharmacology, recombinant DNA, and from such rapidly developing fields as computerized axial tomography and positron emission tomography (cf. Passonneau et al., 1980). Patience is mandatory. Even with Huntington disease, a relatively simple mendelizing autosomal dominant disorder with complete penetrance, we cannot specify the exact nature of the genetic disorder at the molecular level of a gene product. The gene is inferred and not yet excisable from DNA by restriction enzymes. We cannot account for the variable age of onset, covering almost the entire life span, and we cannot detect which of the offspring of affected individuals are destined to develop the disease, although 50% of them do so. Even when the mode of transmission for other genetic disorders has been clearly identified as that of recessive inheritance, which we know to be associated with an enzyme deficiency, we cannot identify the enzyme in some 70% of all the known recessive disorders (McKusick, 1978, p. xvi). Although the pattern of inheritance of color blindness, one of the oldest known genetic disorders, was known in the early 1700s, it was not assigned to the X chromosome until 1911, and in the 1980s we are still dependent on a behavioral test to identify cases and know little about the disorder's biological basis.

Once the existence of an important genetic predisposition to schizophrenia has been established, using the information provided thus far in this book, it becomes important to provide a theory for the mode of its transmission. We do not yet know how this disorder is transmitted genetically, for reasons just given. In some sense, specification of the genetic model or models for the mode(s) of transmission may be premature. To the extent that theorizing will have heuristic value, we will present an overview of some of the more promising approaches to model construction in efforts to account for the data so far presented in this book. In the first instance, theories can provide a scheme for systematically collecting puzzle pieces and comparing them for inconsistencies and imperfections. Heuristic models encourage the formation of testable hypotheses that should lead to the falsification of some notions and the strengthening of others. Needed but missing puzzle pieces may also be identified as the model develops thus leading to the initiation of specific research enterprises in both clinical and basic science areas. As we have indicated, different genetic models have different implications for the kinds of studies that should command the scarce research resources available; they have implications for the kinds of molecular pathology to be expected, such as enzyme deficiencies for recessives, mutations in structural proteins for dominants, and who-knows-what for polygenic disorders. In a well-nourished population with variation in height under very strong genetic control, we have no knowledge about the biochemical differences between tall and short adults (pygmies excepted); most of the remarkable successes in increasing the food value of plants and animals by genetic selection programs are not reducible to biochemical differences. Advances in theorizing that attempt to account for developmental and physiological aspects of schizophrenia should provide suggestions for rational treatment, for the detection of cases premorbidly, and for suggestions leading to the eventual prevention of schizophrenia.

Let us remind ourselves what is meant by saying that a disorder or a disease is a genetic one, or that it results from the epigenetic interaction of some genetic predisposition (diathesis) with environmental contributors (stressors). We have interpreted the information provided thus far to mean that a large and rather specific genetic "something" interacts with nonspecific, rather commonplace, environmental factors.

There is no reluctance to call galactosemia a genetic disease. All babies born with this homozygous recessive disorder (a prototypical inborn error of metabolism) become affected when exposed to milk, which is a universal agent in their diets. Thus when the genetic predisposition is relatively rare and the relevant environmental factor is common, it is easy to recognize an inherited genetic disease. We do not have the mental habit that would permit us to say that milk causes galactosemia. At the other end of the continuous scale of the relative importance of genetical and environmental factors in the causation of disease, we can pick a contrasting illustration. Exposure to measles virus is usually sufficient to cause measles in those not inoculated against it. Thus when the genetic predisposition is relatively common or universal and the relevant environmental factor is infrequent or acute, a disorder is readily recognized as an environmental one. The hemolytic anemia that follows the eating of fava or broad beans is called favism and is a textbook example of a disease that is both a genetical and an environmental one. It results from a genotype-by-environment interaction wherein only those persons with the particular enzyme variant develop the disease, and then only after eating the beans. For this X-linked recessive trait, which is quite common in people from Mediterranean regions, both the gene and the bean are necessary for the associated disease to appear. In this instance, neither causal factor alone is sufficient, and the disease is *both* a genetical and an environmental one.

Schizophrenia falls between the two clear extremes of galactosemia and measles and has aspects that are suggestive of the interaction observed in favism. It is the relative prevalence of the genetic predisposition to developing schizophrenia compared with the relative prevalence of alleged environmental causes that leads us to prefer calling it a genetic disorder. We would not cluster schizophrenia at that genetic end of the continuum with galactosemia, PKU, and Huntington disease, nor would we cluster it at the other end of the continuum with measles, cholera, and the plague. It belongs somewhere in between with diabetes, cardiovascular disease, and the familial-congenital malformations. For the three latter conditions, the unspecified but relatively specific genetic predisposition must share the spotlight with (often unspecified) discrete factors in the environment that cause some and not others with the genotype to develop the disorder. Adding to the complexity of these middle-of-the-continuum conditions is the strong likelihood that the effects of identified environmental factors may be interaction effects only. By that we mean to say that the effects of environmental risk factors may be interaction effects only that operate on the relatively few genetically predisposed individuals to produce schizophrenia but that will have no adverse effects on the population as a whole (Serban, 1975). Extreme values of the risk factors, of course, could produce some psychopathology in almost everyone, but not psychopathology deserving the diagnosis of schizophrenia.

Causal networks in the gene-to-behavior pathway

The molar-molecular, macro-micro, and holistic-reductionist kinds of organizing dimensions are paralleled in the field of genetics by population genetics–molecular genetics. The ends of the continuum are associated with different kinds of data-collecting techniques. As we have suggested, information collected throughout the range of the dimension will be required for the solving of the schizophrenia puzzle. The vast majority of data we have reviewed so far are associated with the population genetics end. That is, to the extent that the data are relevant to a genetic puzzle, they provide information about the molar, macro, and holistic phenomena that requires integration into a gene-to-behavior pathway. Like clinical research in other areas of biology, the majority of research in psychiatric genetics represents prescientific first steps on the long road to the complete understanding of psychopathology. Many of the steps will require retracing and restarting in more valid directions as more information is generated in the field of psychiatric genetics.

Because schizophrenia does not appear to be the result of a single abnormal gene product, we are forced to give priority to various multifactorial models for explaining its etiology. The term "multifactorial" covers both the situation where the genetic contribution could be a single major locus plus multiple environmental and/or genetic factors, as well as multiple genetic factors and multiple environmental factors. The latter model is termed a polygenic model, the former a mixed model. The idea that schizophrenia can be caused by a single, sufficient genetic factor can be rejected (O'Rourke et al., in press). J. H. Edwards (1969, p. 59) has described the predicament in working with multifactorially determined traits:

> Clearly where we can catch and study the enzyme, or work on the ends of a unique route, we are working at a single-factor level; where we observe the ends of a route which is not unique, we may or may not be able to make interpretations at the single-factor level. Where we are dealing with the results of several of many metabolites, as in total growth (as in height or weight) or the consequences of incoordinated embryonic growth (as in malformations) or with some part of the metabolic net influenced by numerous pathways, we can plausibly assume that the number of factors is very large; the sheer complexity of the situation limits us to some simple summarizing index, although we must appreciate that a single number can tell us little about the structure of anything very complex.

A wider appreciation of the difficulties we face in trying to construct genetic models for the phenomena of schizophrenia can be gotten by studying Figures 11.1 and 11.2. Figure 11.1 (Neel & Schull, 1954) presents part of the causal network or chain of consequences or "pedigree of causes" (Grüneberg, 1952) set into motion by the relative deficiency of insulin or by failure to use it efficiently, which occurs in diabetes. The figure says nothing about the causes of the fundamental defects that lead to the failure of certain cells in the pancreas to produce the needed hormone in sufficient amounts or that make other cells resistant to using it (Jarett, 1979). It is clear, however, that single-gene explanations are inadequate (cf. Notkins, 1979; Suarez, Reich, & Trost, 1976; Suarez, Hodge, & Reich, 1979). The readily observable symptoms of diabetes are not directly related to the insulin deficiency; some of the symptoms are the results of efforts to compensate for some of the physiological consequences of the insulin deficiency. The mode of transmission for diabetes is unknown. We are fond of diabetes, which has been called a geneticist's nightmare, as an analog to the problems we face in schizophrenia research.

Facing the diagram of the partial causal network for diabetes is a partial causal network for schizophrenia that is a product of P. E. Meehl's speculative daring (personal communication, 1966; 1972). Despite the number of connecting causal arrows, it represents for Meehl a network of minimal complexity. The exact definitions of the terms used in the figure are not critical at this point. (Meehl's ideas are given in depth in Meehl, 1973.) The model sketched is a multifactorial model wherein Meehl prefers a single major locus, called a "dominant schizogene," in addition to numerous "polygenic potentiators" that are shown in the figure as "pp." Such a model has been formally called a mixed model by geneticists (Cloninger et al., in press; Morton & MacLean, 1974). Meehl's list of polygenic potentiators (pp) includes the following: primary social introversion (high); anxiety parameter (high); aggression parameter (high, low); sex drive (low, high?); hedonic potential (low); energy level (low); polymorph-perverse eroticism (high); mesomorphic toughness (low); arousal parameter (low, high?); inhibitory parameter (low, high?); dominance (low); perceptual-cognitive parameters (field dependence, sharpener–leveler, augmenter–reducer, logical clarity, etc.); and Murray's "gratuities" (scarce) – brains, beauty, grace, special talents.

Unlike the elements in the diabetes picture, none of the elements in the schizophrenia network is presently reducible to physiological terms. Meehl's construction does for psychopathology what Neel and Schull's figure does for pathophysiology. Meehl describes the gene-to-behavior pathway in these terms:

Schizophrenia is a complicated collection of learned social responses, object-cathexes, self-concepts, ego-weaknesses, psychodynamisms, etc. These are dispositions of first or second order. They are *not* provided by our genes. They are acquired by social learning, especially learning involving interpersonal aversiveness. Assume the mutated gene (a structure) causes an aberrant neurohumor that directly alters signal selectivity at the synapse (Meehl, 1962). Then the gene is a *structure*; the gene-controlled synthesis of an abnormal substance (or failure to make a certain substance) is an *event*; the altered synaptic condition is a *state*; and the results of that state's existing at the billions of CNS synapses is an altered parameter of CNS function, i.e., a *disposition*. But this disposition is a disposition of at least third (perhaps fourth or fifth) order with respect to those molar dispositions that are the subject-matter of clinical psychiatry and psychoanalysis. Hence, an individual's being characterized by a certain genotype is a disposition of still higher order, because (presumably) the synaptic disposition itself is not an absolutely *necessary* consequence of the first link of the gene's action, since it could be avoided if we knew how to supplement the brain's inadequate supply of magic substance X, or how to provide a related molecule

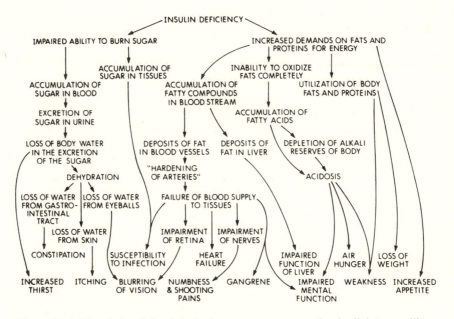

Figure 11.1. The chain of physiological consequences occurring in diabetes mellitus as a result of insulin deficiency. (Reprinted from Neel & Schull, *Human Heredity*, by permission of the University of Chicago Press. ©1954 by the University of Chicago.)

that would bring the parameters of CNS function back to the "normal" base. (1972, pp. 15–17)

One need not agree with Meehl's posited version of a dominant gene theory or with his speculative neurophysiology in order to agree with the heuristic value of his causal chain. Because his "schizogene" is not posited as a sufficient cause of schizophrenia, it cannot be refuted. Such complications to genetic models as incomplete penetrance and variable expressivity are not incorporated in either of the two figures.

By introducing the two figures at this point without further elaboration, we hope to communicate the general idea of a causal network, even when it is partial, preliminary, oversimplified, and sketchy. Edward's comments complement those of Meehl; the two together are enough to stop us from expecting easy solutions to our puzzle.

Diversity and unity in schizophrenia

In this book we have talked about and around the questions of heterogeneity. It is far from clear to what extent schizophrenia is etiologically genetically

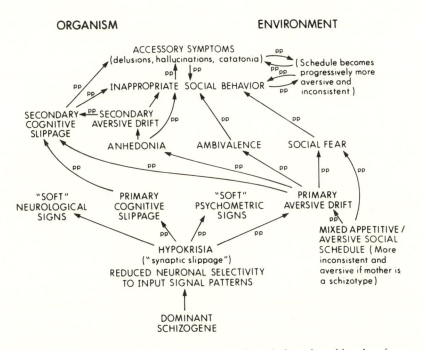

Figure 11.2. Speculative causal chains of psychopathology in schizophrenia as a consequence of synaptic slippage. (Courtesy of P. E. Meehl, 1966.)

heterogeneous or homogeneous. Furthermore, there is still an active debate as to which of the obvious clinical, phenotypic heterogeneities associated with schizophrenia reflect variations on one underlying theme versus overlapping variations of different themes. When Kraepelin (see Chapter 3) grouped hebephrenia, catatonia, and dementia paranoides together under one entity, it was recognized as a creative stroke of genius. Kraepelin read through the noise of the varying clinical pictures and recognized one basic theme. Eugen Bleuler's subtitle of his 1911 monograph – *The Group of Schizophrenias* – has been misinterpreted to suggest a wish on Bleuler's part to undo the lumping of Kraepelin. The use of the plural *schizophrenias* was intended as a challenge to a too-ready acceptance of the idea of etiological unity. Bleuler hoped his admission of uncertainty would serve to motivate research that would test the hypothesis. As we have seen in Chapter 5, his son, Manfred Bleuler (1978, p. 438), finds little evidence to suggest that the original lumping was in error.

We can pose two opposing hypotheses. One is that the components of the so-called spectrum of schizophrenic disorders comprise a genetic unity in the sense (see Figures 4.5 and 4.6) that they represent differing (lesser) amounts of liability in the schizophrenia liability distribution. Depending on how the components would be rank ordered for severity, each would require positing an additional threshold besides the one for schizophrenia itself. Other ways to preserve the concept of unity would involve positing the spectrum disorders as pleiotropic manifestations of one genotype or as variable expressions of one gene (see Figures 11.1 and 11.2). We would anticipate that as one moved along the spectrum from the deteriorated chronic cases through the well-preserved, late-onset paranoid schizophrenics, the good-prognosis schizoaffectives, and the borderline schizophrenics to the compensated and functioning schizotypal personalities, etiological heterogeneity would increase. That is to say (see Chapter 7), there are many ways of arriving at the end state called schizotypal personality and only some subset of those would be genetically related to schizophrenia.

The lumpers would prefer this hypothesis, and the splitters an opposite one. For them, the myriad of classifications and subtypes based on symptom homogeneity, or type of onset, course, or outcome, or type of premorbid personality or pre-Kraepelinian category would each have a different etiology (cf. Leonhard, 1979). Based on the evidence we have reviewed so far in this book, we join Manfred Bleuler in doubting that these varieties of splitting using clinical phenomenology will yield some sort of periodic table of elements.

For one possible way to understand heterogeneity, let us turn to the phenotype of mental retardation. We could also, incidentally, have used the phenotypes of deafness and blindness to make some of the same points. A very rough estimate of the causes of childhood blindness (G. R. Fraser & Friedman, 1967) suggests that 51% of instances are associated with environmental causes – prenatal (6%), perinatal (34%), and postnatal (11%); whereas 38% are associated with mendelizing genes – dominant (17%), recessive (16%), and sex-linked recessive (5%). It is further estimated that 15 different dominant genes contribute to the dominant category and that some 23 to 35 different recessive loci contribute to the recessive category. The remaining 11% of blindness phenotypes are associated with malformations with unknown or complex causes.

Childhood mental retardation has many environmental causes, including brain injury throughout the period of development, prenatal and postnatal viral infections, anoxia, and gross environmental deprivations. It also has many genetic causes, including chromosomal abnormalities, dominant gene loci, autosomal and X-linked recessive loci, and various polygenic combinations leading to low intellectual levels. Even if we restrict ourselves to the simple mendelizing conditions that have retardation as part of the clinical picture, we run the risk of being overwhelmed by genetic heterogeneity. At present (McKusick, 1978), some 2,800 definite plus probable Mendelian phenotypes have been identified for our species. The phenotypes comprise the very rare and the rare genetic diseases, the blood groups, and some congenital malformations known to mendelize. Some of the entries are based on the observation of single families. Excluded from the listing are chromosomal abnormalities and their effects, and the numerous diseases that have a polygenic component.

We have read through the descriptions of the almost 3,000 Mendelian phenotypes and have found that some 300 are associated with one or another degree of mental retardation or cognitive deficit. The vast majority (220) are associated with autosomal recessive conditions. It must be emphasized that the 300 phenotypes altogether account for only a very small proportion of the prevalence of cases diagnosable as mentally retarded because each individually is quite rare (PKU, for example, has a prevalence of 1 in 25,000). We can estimate that the total prevalence of mental retardation, defined as individuals with IQs under 70, is approximately 3.3% (Penrose, 1963; Robinson & Robinson, 1976). Down syndrome, by far the most common chromosomal abnormality associated with mental retardation, occurs with an incidence of 0.15% in newborns. A little extrapolation shows that the vast majority of cases diagnosed as mental retardation, using an IQ-test criterion, appear to be causally related to a multifactorial-polygenic system that underlies the genetic contribution to variation in normal intellectual ability.

To the extent that schizophrenia is like mental retardation, it would be foolish to use the diagnosis as a sufficient category in research into the etiology of schizophrenia. Like mental retardation, the combined phenotype as a source of probands with a subsequent look at the prevalence of disorder in their relatives would permit the conclusion that we were dealing with something familial. However, it would not permit the various signals to be discovered among the noises. We could not find out, for example, which of the various specific etiologies corresponded to the recessive inborn errors of metabolism and their different but specific dietary treatment requirements. It is not possible using presently available evidence to say how far the analogy between mental retardation and schizophrenia will hold.

Too much splitting may be a step backward. We are more hopeful about the use of endophenotypic (in contrast to exophenotypic/phenomenologic) information based on, for example, responders versus nonresponders to phenothiazines, normal versus abnormal brain scan, and even low versus normal platelet monoamine oxidase levels as potentially useful ways for approaching the issue of etiological heterogeneity. Some of the risk factors to be discovered may fall into Meehl's category of polygenic potentiators, but even that would be an important advance (cf. Sing & Skolnick, 1979, on risk factors in cardiovascular disease). Considering the complex pathway from genotype to psychiatric symptomatology and the difficulties in establishing heterogeneity even within such better-understood conditions as diabetes and cardiovascular disease, the odds are stacked against finding as much heterogeneity for schizophrenia as has been found for the mental retardations. For the near future, we may not know how far we are dealing with clinical diversity in genetic unity, and how far we are dealing with genetic diversity in clinical unity.

Overview of genetic transmission theories

The introductory material in Chapter 4 about modes of transmission, the concept of liability, and the concept of a threshold will serve as a prologue to the present discussion. Three major classes of theory have been invoked in order to account for the genetic mode of transmission in schizophrenia. The distinct-heterogeneity model generates the hypothesis that schizophrenia is composed of a large number of qualitatively separate diseases, some of them genetic in origin and others environmentally caused. It would accord with the facts about blindness and about the severe cases of mental retardation. On this model we would expect, for example, that catatonic schizophrenia would be controlled by a locus on one chromosome, poor-outcome schizophrenia by a locus on another chromosome, phenothiazine-responsive schizophrenia by another locus, and so on, and a schizophreniclike psychosis could be precipitated by amphetamine. On this heterogeneity model, the genetic varieties would each be expected to have pedigrees consistent with dominant or recessive inheritance. The second theory is the monogenic, or single-major-locus (SML) model; it generates the hypothesis that all schizophrenics possess the same abnormal gene at the same locus. The model would be like that in Huntington disease. The third class of theories can be called multifactorial-polygenic. These models generate the general hypothesis that schizophrenia is caused by the combination of a number of genes in combination with a number of environmental contributors. The simple versions of all three of these theories have been modified so much by their proponents that they overlap, borrow assumptions from each other, and do not run the risk of being refuted in any finalistic manner. All the theories make explicit or implicit use of the threshold concept because they deal with affected and unaffected individuals. It is generally agreed among theorizers that all schizophrenics are not exactly the same genetically and that some

1. DISTINCT HETEROGENEITY

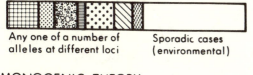

Any one of a number of   Sporadic cases
alleles at different loci   (environmental)

2. MONOGENIC THEORY

S gene necessary for all but symptomatic cases
of "Schizophrenia"

 Homozygotes (SS)

▢ Symptomatic schizophrenia (OO)

▨ Heterozygotes (SO)

3. MULTIFACTORIAL POLYGENIC THEORY

SOME HIGH RISK COMBINATIONS OF COMMON
GENES

AA Bb cc DD Ee ⎫   Σ6
Aa BB CC Dd EE ⎭ Very high risk   Σ8

AA BB Cc dd ee ⎫
Aa Bb Cc Dd Ee ⎬ High risk   Σ5
aa bb Cc DD EE ⎭

Capital letters indicate genes predisposing to
schizophrenia on illustrative model

Figure 11.3. Hypothetical genotypes at hypothetical schizophrenia-relevant loci of persons with schizophrenia according to three main theories.

causal contributors are more important than others. Sometimes the differences among proponents of different models are simply semantic or simply associated with intuitive preferences.

Figure 11.3 illustrates simple versions of each class of models. The number of genotypes illustrated and the proportion of phenotypes they account for should not be taken literally. The distinct-heterogeneity kind of model has worked well for blindness, deafness, and severe mental retardation. The schizophrenialike "symptomatic" psychoses described by Davison and Bagley (1969) such as those associated with temporal-lobe epilepsy, alcoholic hallucinosis, head injuries, and amphetamines would be some of those in the sporadic box.

The rectangle depicting the monogenic theory makes provision for the symptomatic schizophrenialike psychoses we have mentioned. The three possible genotypes at the "schizophrenia locus" are *SS, SO,* and *OO.* The model as applied to schizophrenia is *not* like that used for Huntington disease. Only a small proportion of the *SO* genotypes develop schizophrenia (all of the "*HO*" develop Huntington disease), thereby making room for the contribution of polygenic background factors and environmental contributors. The penetrance of the *S* gene is forced to be different (Matthysse & Kidd, 1976; Slater & Cowie, 1971) in each of the three genotypes, which is the same as saying that different proportions of each of the three genotypes are to the right of one threshold. No major effect of the hypothesized major gene has as yet been detected. The flexibility of the model after borrowing the liability and threshold concepts from multifactorial models prevents it from being refuted (but see O'Rourke et al., in press).

In order to illustrate the multifactorial-polygenic model, we have selected a relatively simple five-locus version (see Figure 4.3 for the two-locus, three-allele account) with only two possible alleles at each locus. It will be recalled from Figure 4.6 that, on this model, schizophrenia appears once an accumulation of genetical and environmental contributing factors exceeds a threshold value. Figure 11.3 only refers to the specific genetic liability axis from Figure 4.6. In our illustration here we assume that a capital-letter allele enhances the liability toward schizophrenia, whereas a lowercase allele decreases the liability. Our five-locus model provides us with 11 genotypic classes ($2n + 1$) in regard to the number of liability-increasing genes, that is, from 0 to a maximum of 10. The model actually generates 243 different genotypes ($3^n = 3^5$), but most are functionally equivalent to others. The 3 $\Sigma 5$ genotypes shown are a subset of 51 such five-liability-enhancing combinations. The genotypes illustrated as "high risk" ($\Sigma 5$) and "very high risk" ($\Sigma 6$ and $\Sigma 8$) are beyond the threshold because of additional liability factors and a shortage of assets. Some of even the "very high risk" genotypes would not be schizophrenics on this model. That most schizophrenic adults, approximately 80%, have no close relatives who are also schizophrenic is a fact expected on this model. Using standard methods of quantitative genetic analysis, the variation in the liability to developing schizophrenia appears to be under a high degree of genetic control, approximately 70% (Gottesman & Shields, 1967; Rao et al., 1981). This model typifies a diathesis–stressor theory in that the vulnerability to environmental stressors varies as a function of the degree of genetic loading. It is clear from the figure that individuals who are at increased risk for developing schizophrenia are genetically heterogeneous. Although this is a legitimate use of the term, it is not what the proponents of the first class of models have in mind. Not illustrated in the

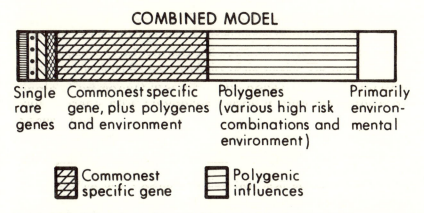

Figure 11.4. Schematic overview of the genetic constitutions of schizophrenics on a model combining the three theories of Figure 11.3.

figure is a low-risk genotype; for example, a $\Sigma 3$ individual could be *aa bb cC dd EE* with only three liability-enhancing alleles.

As we noted in Chapter 4, compatibility between some of the data about schizophrenia and the different models for the mode of transmission is a necessary but not a sufficient condition for the acceptance of a model. Various methods have been tried in order to demonstrate the superiority of one of the models in Figure 11.3 over another, but all have been found wanting. The data are sufficiently ambiguous to prevent, at this stage of our knowledge, a definitive solution. Another reason why a definitive solution is not yet at hand may be that all three major classes of theory are partially correct. One possible picture of how the genetics of schizophrenia may eventually turn out – a combined model that permits many flowers to bloom – is shown in Figure 11.4. It does not immediately lead to testable hypotheses but it does allow genetic theorizers to temporize. Again, the different proportions allocated to the different theoretical models should not be taken literally. We prefer to attribute multifactorial causes for the vast majority of cases of schizophrenia. In this respect we would be casting our lot with those who try to explain along these lines the etiology of the common "genetic diseases" such as some congenital malformations, the entire range of mental retardation, cardiovascular diseases, and diabetes.

Those cases of schizophrenia in the combined model assigned to the rectangle called "commonest specific gene, plus polygenes and environment" are intended to accommodate the kinds of theories preferred by Meehl, Heston (with schizoidia rather than schizophrenia as the phenotype of interest), and Slater. As we have noted, the flexible versions of the various models have considerable overlap with one another. In the Slater version of the SML model, the population lifetime risk is taken as 0.85%, which permits the calculation of the S gene frequency–3%. Within this model, the penetrance of the S gene is 100% in homozygotes (SS), but such genotypes account for only 10% of the schizophrenic phenotypes. All of the remainder, that is, 90%, would be SO heterozygotes; in these genotypes, the penetrance of the gene was calculated as only 13%. The normal homozygote (OO) cannot be affected with the genetic variety of schizophrenia. Once the SML model stipulates so low a penetrance as 13%, it opens the door to the influence of polygenic and environmental contributors, thereby making it a version of a multifactorial model.

Other geneticists who have played with the SML model have used different S-gene frequencies and different penetrance rates. Sometimes the results are incredible, although some of the versions provide compatible, if Promethean, fits to *some* of the data sets that are as good as any multifactorial-polygenic proposal. The major thrust of monogenic theories is to motivate a search for a simply inherited endophenotype that would be expected to occur in at least one parent of every schizophrenic. Such a task, as noted for Huntington disease, is not easy.

Although the following empirical observations are not exclusive deductions from a multifactorial-polygenic-threshold model, they seem to us more naturally compatible with such a model than with an SML model:

1. The non-Mendelian and increased risk of "schizophrenia-flavored" conditions other than schizophrenia proper in the relatives of schizophrenic subjects

2. The uneven and sharp drop in risk of schizophrenia as one moves from MZ twins to first- and second-degree relatives

3. The occurrence of pedigrees in which there are either unilateral or bilateral (maternal and paternal) or sporadic distributions of other affected relatives

4. The relationship between increasing risks of schizophrenia in relatives with increasing severity in the proband and with greater numbers of other affected relatives, and the risk-reducing effect of normal relatives

5. The absence of a proved SML disease as an analog to schizophrenia that is as common as schizophrenia and shows the observed pattern of risk in relatives; cystic fibrosis, one of the most common mendelizing disorders, has an incidence of approximately 1 in 2,500 newborns.

As Slater and Cowie (1971) put it, "Two genetical models are available, either of which provides an adequate framework for the observations, so that the worker is entitled to choose the model which suits his purposes best." Our preference for the multifactorial-polygenic framework leads us to look for specific and important contributing partial risk factors on both the diathesis and the stressor sides of the model.

Let us try to bolster our preference for a multifactorial-polygenic-threshold model with more information and another analogy, this time to the congenital malformation, cleft lip with or without cleft palate. Multifactorial-polygenic models can be divided into continuous and quasicontinuous or threshold ones. The most widely known polygenic models for IQ, height, and blood pressure posit a large number of underlying genes, all of whose effects are equal; with such traits, the phenotypic correlation between relatives is the same as the genetic correlation if the traits are completely heritable. The parent–child and sib–sib correlations for height or fingerprint-ridge count are very close to 0.50.

We will concentrate on the threshold versions of multifactorial theories as the most relevant background to our thinking about schizophrenia. This model has made analysis of such traits as schizophrenia, cleft lip, diabetes, and seizure susceptibility feasible, provided one accepts the working hypothesis that the *underlying* liability is continuously and normally distributed. Falconer (1965, 1967), Edwards (1969), and Smith (1970, 1971) have illustrated the methods involved that turn incidence data into correlations via the tetrachoric correlation coefficient, and we (Gottesman & Shields, 1967) were the first to study psychopathology with such methods. Data on the occurrence of cleft lip with or without cleft palate, CL(P), in the relatives of probands can be used to illustrate the threshold model (F. C. Fraser, 1980; Woolf, 1971). Because schizophrenia develops and is not congenitally observable like cleft lip, the analogy is wanting until it is appreciated that cleft lip also develops, but prenatally during embryogenesis. Such elegant data for a disorder with both a variable age of onset and the capacity for remission are not yet available.

The population incidence (q_g in Figure 4.5) of CL(P) can be taken as .001 (Woolf, 1971). The risk in sibs is .04, a low absolute value but still a 40-fold increase over the population risk; in second-degree relatives it is .0065 and in third-degree (first cousins), .0036. The sharp falling off of incidence as one moves to more remote relatives is one of the supports for polygenic theory; a simple dominant gene theory calls for the frequency of affected relatives to decrease by 1/2 in each step. An important parallel between CL(P) and schizophrenia is that the risk to parents is about 1/2 that in sibs although both are classes of first-degree relatives. In both disorders the reduced values probably represent the effects of social selection for who become parents; different values of q_g will be required to evaluate the significance to genetic theorizing of lower rates in parents when such selection is probable. Figure

4.5 shows the hypothetical distribution of the genetic liability to CL(P) or any other threshold character, for the general population as well as for the first-degree relatives of affected persons from the general population.

The horizontal (X) axis is for normal distribution deviate values of the posited multifactorially determined predisposition or liability to the threshold trait. At a point on the X axis (not drawn to scale) corresponding to a value of .001 (q_g) of the general population we can erect a vertical line (T) to represent the threshold value of liability beyond which all persons are affected; such a line would cut off 4.0% of the sibs (q_r) and only 0.36% of first cousins. The latter are not shown but they would have a mean liability between the general population value (G) and first-degree relatives (R). A sharp threshold between the liability of affected and unaffected persons is artificial; the threshold model implies an increasing likelihood of being affected as the polygenic predisposition increases.

The multifactorial-threshold model is supported by a demonstration of a relationship between the severity of the defect in the proband and the risk to the relatives, based on the assumption that the more genes, the more severe the condition, and the more genes, the more the relatives will have when the amount is halved, quartered, and so on. For CL(P), unilateral and bilateral affectation of the face form two levels of severity; in the sibs of unilateral cases the risk is 3.83%, in those of bilaterals, 6.71%; and the generalization holds for other degrees of relatives. Further support for the theory comes from the demonstration that the risk to probands' relatives, say sibs, increases with the number of other relatives affected (see Table 10.5); that is, families with two patients are more "high-risk" families than those with only one. In the case of CL(P), if no other relative is affected, the recurrence risk to a proband's sib is 2.24%; if an aunt or uncle is affected, the risk rises to 9.91%; finally, if a parent is affected, the risk to the sib of a proband rises to 15.55%. The malformation is too rare for there to have been extensive twin studies, but from the available evidence the risk to the identical twin of a proband is about 40%.

Using these data, estimates can be made of the heritability of the unobservable, underlying liability to CL(P). Heritability (h^2) is defined as the proportion of the total variability of the trait in the population that is due to transmissible genetic differences, in the absence of dominance and interaction between genes. The risks to MZ twins, sibs, and first cousins yield high h^2 estimates of 88%, 92%, and 100%, respectively, which are reasonably consistent values. Similar but not quite so high estimates emerge from the data we have summarized on the relatives of schizophrenics. The estimates are inflated by the inclusion of the transmission of shared, common environmental effects (cultural transmission), which can be resolved by the application of techniques known as path analysis (Li, 1975; Rao et al., in press; Rice, Cloninger, & Reich, 1980). The latter techniques reveal that, once assuming the multifactorial model, 70% of the variance in the combined liability to developing schizophrenia is genetically transmitted and 20% "culturally" transmitted.

We agree with Anderson (1972) that it is not too helpful to rely on evolutionary theory in deciding among genetic models; we simply do not know enough about how any human behavior evolved. However, the data we reviewed in Chapter 10 on the fertility or Darwinian fitness of schizophrenics are interesting and important in their own right. The question of how a disadvantageous genetic condition can be maintained at the observed prevalences in the population over time despite the greatly reduced fitness of both male and female schizophrenics can perhaps more readily be answered by polygenic than by monogenic theory. The former would obviate the need to find a selective advantage in gene carriers hypothesized by the balanced-polymorphism theory of Huxley et al. (1964). Response to natural selection against a polygenic trait associated with lowered marriage and fertility rates would be very slow. Genes in the system would only be eliminated from the gene pool when they were present in the rare individual at the tail end of the distribution, and those below the threshold would not be subject to negative selection. Schizophrenics could be thought of as part of the genetic load of our species, the price paid for conserving genetic diversity (cf. Dobzhansky, 1970; Lerner, 1958). Attempts at invoking evolutionary (pseudo-) explanations for either the origin or the perpetuation of schizophrenia may be futile and useless, muddling the line of genetic reasoning.

It would be incorrect to assume that because a trait such as the liability to schizophrenia is inherited polygenically the search for cause has ended and relevant specific genetic loci are undiscoverable in principle. The genes underlying continuous variation are not qualitatively different from those associated with discontinuous traits at the molecular level – both are subject to the same rules of inheritance because they are chromosomal and thus segregate, show dominance, epistasis, linkage, and genotype–environment interactions. From the beginning of this century geneticists have succeeded in identifying specific loci in polygenic systems and in locating them on specific chromosomes by linkage with major genes; however, these feats were accomplished with genetically tractable organisms such as wheat and fruit flies. It is heuristically important to us to learn that whenever polygenic variation has been studied under *laboratory conditions* (e.g., inbreeding, backcrossing, availability of chromosome markers), a few handleable genes have proved to mediate a large part of the genetic variance under study (Thoday, 1967). One locus in wheat accounted for 83% of the variance in ripening date, with three others jointly accounting for 14%. Only five loci for such "weighted genes" for bristle number in fruit flies accounted for 88% of the observed variation; but we must add the striking fact that separable components of the complex character permitted their study as more or less discontinuous variables. Sewall Wright (1934a,b) concluded that three or four major factors (genes) controlled the threshold character polydactyly (extra toes) in inbred lines of guinea pigs.

Encouraged by the demonstration that the genes in polygenic inheritance need not be and often are not roughly equal in their effects on the phenotype, and bolstered by our clinical observations on what appears to be "excess" similarity for facets of the schizophrenia picture between pairs of affected relatives on the simpler equal-effects assumption, we hazard the speculation that there are a few genes with large effects in the polygenic system underlying many schizophrenias. In other words, we view the etiology of schizophrenia as being due to a weighted kind of multifactorial-polygenic system with a threshold effect. Some of the heuristic implications of our speculations about "high-value" genes in the polygenic system underlying schizophrenia include a focusing on partitionable facets of the syndrome such as neurotransmitter receptor morphology, number, and subtype, paranoid features, genetic polymorphisms of proteins in brain and blood, variation in brain scans, and neurophysiology, on the chance that ordinary twin, adoption, and family studies will reveal one or more of the high-value genes segregating in a clear Mendelian pattern. There are already suggestions in the human genetics literature that a gene associated with a biochemically different insulin in juvenile diabetics may be identified as one of the polygenes causing insulin-dependent diabetes (Notkins, 1979), and that one facet of total cholesterol may segregate as a Mendelian trait (Elston et al., 1975; Morton et al., 1978; Sing & Skolnick, 1979) in the multifactorial system relevant to cardiovascular disease.

The contribution of specific genetic factors to the genetic liability to schizophrenia analogous to the specific contributors in the diabetes and cardiovascular disease examples forms only part of the picture with respect to the combined liability to developing schizophrenia. General genetic contributors that serve as modifiers or potentiators, together with general environmental contributors that serve the same functions, each define dimensions of liability (see Figure 4.6) that combine with the specific genetic liability as well as with genetical and environmental assets to determine the net liability and the position of an individual vis-à-vis the threshold at a particular time.

Diatheses, stressors, and the unfolding of schizophrenia

The static, cross-sectional depiction of schizophrenia implied by the threshold models in Figures 4.5 and 4.6 as well as by the causal networks we invoked in Figures 11.1 and 11.2 is unsatisfactory. While we wait for the advances in the neural sciences that will permit the identification of some relevant, final common pathway involved in the pathogenesis of schizophrenia with a consequent identification of endophenotypes worth measuring as indicators of the underlying liability, we can add to our models the necessary complication of ontogenesis or "development." By adding the dimension of time to our models of liability, we can represent a more dynamic and realistic view of a person's trajectory across the epigenetic landscape (Hanson & Gottesman, 1979; Waddington, 1966). The intention is to incorporate the concepts of changes in effective genotype by gene regulation (the switching on and off of genes by environmental inputs) (Brown, 1981), by possible critical periods (prenatal and postnatal), and by ecological inputs (assets and liabilities) to a dynamic system (cf. Chapter 4). Figure 11.5 is a rough attempt at a more realistic multifactorial model.

The time axis starts from the moment of egg fertilization, so that possible prenatal factors could show their influence on values of the combined liability scale. Ontogenetic constitutional changes as well as random events will influence the path of the trajectories leading to both downward and upward inflections in the curves. We would expect, given our conception of epigenesis, that augmentations or reductions in liability that occurred close together in time would have a cascade (a snowball) effect and would be more influential than the same forces spread out in time. The figure shows the trajectories marking the changes in the combined liability toward developing schizophrenia for three genotypes over, say, the first 50 years of life; one of the genotypes, G_2, is represented by a pair of identical twins.

G_1 indicates the trajectory of a person with a low (for schizophrenics generally) combined *genetic* liability to schizophrenia who develops a late-onset paranoid schizophrenia. He or she could be a $\Sigma 5$ (Figure 11.3) with moderate values on the other four axes of Figure 4.6. Over time, environmental contributors to liability, say first the death of a spouse and then the onset of deafness, cause upward deflections of the trajectory to the threshold (TT), culminating in a late-onset paraphrenia (Kay & Roth, 1961). The line at the bottom of the zone of the so-called schizophrenic spectrum disorders is intended to convey the idea of a need for a second threshold (T'T') in our model; Wright invoked a second threshold to account for the imperfectly formed fourth digit seen in crosses between a four-toed and a three-toed line of guinea pigs with liabilities to polydactyly. Improvements in the threshold

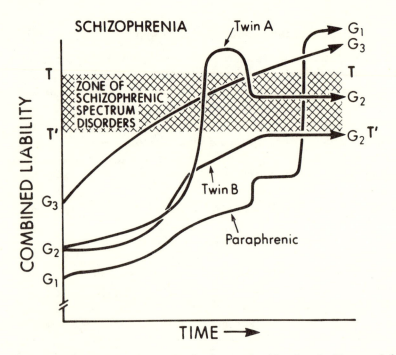

Figure 11.5. The epigenesis (development) of schizophrenia illustrated for three different genotypes interacting with stress (see text).

model by Reich, James, and Morris (1972) and Reich et al. (1979) to include multiple thresholds could, in principle, permit a choice between competing models.

G_2 could be the divergent trajectories of a pair of identical twins, say $\Sigma6$ (cf. Figure 11.3) with moderate other scores; only the A-twin encounters the sufficient factors over time, leading to schizophrenia with an acute onset for a person with his genotype. The B-twin at the time of observation is discordant for schizophrenia, but close to the posited threshold of schizophrenic spectrum disorders. Subthreshold values of combined liability make it clear why so many first-degree relatives can have normal personality-test scores and normal lives (Gottesman & Shields, 1972), and why two phenotypically normal parents are the rule for the vast majority of schizophrenics. The A-twin is shown to have an acute onset with an indistinguishable premorbid personality, followed by a remission from schizophrenia into a chronic schizotypal personality disorder.

G_3 is the posited trajectory of a person with a high genetic (specific liability of $\Sigma8$ and general liability, also high) loading needing very little in the way of environmental contributors to make him schizoid; he is shown as having a poor premorbid personality, an insidious onset, and a deteriorating course. A great many other life trajectories could have been drawn to illustrate the unfolding of schizophrenia. It is easy to see how the hospitalization data in pairs of twins and the fascinating life-span histories of the schizophrenic Genain monozygotic quadruplets (Rosenthal, 1963) augment our total perspective about the pathogenesis and the epigenesis of schizophrenia.

Conclusions

For the time being, the case for a necessary and important genetic basis for developing schizophrenia rests on the compatibility of the pattern of increased risks to various degrees of relatives with plausible genetic models. The continuing exclusion of any specific environmental factors as sufficient causes indirectly supports a genetical stance. It is clear that ordinary Mendelian models for the rare genetic diseases will not be suitable for explaining the mode of transmission for such a common disorder as schizophrenia. Furthermore, there are very few families in which we find recessive or dominant gene segregation ratios (25% or 50%). We suggested that some combination of the plausible models including distinct heterogeneity, the flexible single major locus (monogenic), and multifactorial-polygenic-threshold models does the most justice to the final puzzle. We have emphasized the difficulties of choosing between any two competing models on the basis of currently available data. We are all handicapped by our ignorance of what may be suitable indicators of the liability toward developing schizophrenia. No suitable *corpus delicti* for the neurochemical or the neurophysical geneticists has yet been discovered.

Methods developed by quantitative geneticists permit us to use qualitative clinical genetic information in order to arrive at an estimate of the heritability of the underlying, unobserved predisposition. We agree with Curnow and Smith (1975, p. 154) that the role of the multifactorial model in familial disease may be as a temporary tool useful during the period of ignorance for estimating risks and for providing indicators about the relations between different diseases and the relation of diseases with measurable continuous characters. Major breakthroughs must come from more fundamental research. Our application of the methods devised for the threshold traits resulted in a satisfactory compatibility between the data and the multifactorial model. At this time we are willing to suggest that the genetic heritability of the liability for schizophrenia is about 70%, and the cultural-inheritance component accounts for about 20% of the combined liability.

It is important to understand the implications of finding that a trait such as the liability to schizophrenia has a high heritability. In the samples so far studied, it means that environmental factors were relatively unimportant as causative agents of the schizophrenias. However – and this cannot be emphasized too strongly – these data do not permit the conclusion that curative or preventive measures will be ineffective. As Falconer (1965, p. 69) has pointed out,

The environmental factors proved to be unimportant are those operating in the population sampled and these do not include special treatments or preventive measures. *No prediction can be made from a knowledge of the degree of genetic determination about the efficacy of curative or preventive treatments. All that could be said in such a case is that one will have to look outside the range of normal environments experienced by the untreated population.* (italics added)

To bolster the reasonableness of our position, we appealed to traits in other species and to other common medical genetic conditions. We believe that a weighted polygenic model offers hope that some facets of the schizophrenic phenotype will be shown to segregate simply or to have detectable biochemical or neurophysiological consequences such as those expected with genes of large effect. For their heuristic value, we offered the concepts of causal networks of minimal complexity and of a scheme for depicting the epigenesis of schizophrenia. Because even the hard science of physics requires the Heisenberg uncertainty principle, it should not be embarrassing to operate within a field – the psychiatric genetics of schizophrenia – with a necessary amount of uncertainty.

BIBLIOGRAPHY

Anderson, V. E. Genetic hypotheses in schizophrenia. In A. R. Kaplan (Ed.), *Genetic factors in "schizophrenia."* Springfield, Ill.: Charles C Thomas, 1972, pp. 490–494.

Bleuler, E. 1911. *Dementia praecox or the group of schizophrenias* (Joseph Zinkin, trans.). New York: International Universities Press, 1950. (Originally published 1911.)

Bleuler, M. *The schizophrenic disorders: Long-term patient and family studies* (Siegfried M. Clemens, trans.). New Haven: Yale University Press, 1978.

Brown, D. D. Gene expression in eukaryotes. *Science,* 1981, *211,* 667–674.

Cloninger, C. R., Reich, T., Suarez, B., Rice, J., & Gottesman, I. I. The principles of psychiatric genetics. In M. Shepherd (Ed.), *Handbook of psychiatry.* Vol. 5. *The scientific foundations of psychiatry.* Cambridge University Press, in press.

Curnow, R. N., & Smith, C. Multifactorial models for familial diseases in man. *Journal of the Royal Statistical Society, A,* 1975, *138,* 131–156.

Davison, K., & Bagley, C. R. Schizophrenia-like psychoses associated with organic disorders of the central nervous system: A review of the literature. In R. N. Herrington (Ed.), *Current problems in neuropsychiatry.* Ashford, England: Headley Brothers, 1969. (*British Journal of Psychiatry,* Special Publication #4, 113–184.)

Dobzhansky, T. *Genetics of the evolutionary process.* New York: Columbia University Press, 1970.

Edwards, J. H. Familial predisposition in man. *British Medical Bulletin,* 1969, *25,* 58–64.

Elston, R. C. Major locus analysis for quantitative traits. *American Journal of Human Genetics,* 1979, *31,* 655–661.

Elston, R. C., Namboodiri, K. K., Glueck, C. J., Fallat, R., Tsang, R., & Leuba, V. Study of the genetic transmission of hypercholesterolemia and hypertriglyceridemia in a 195 member kindred. *Annals of Human Genetics,* 1975, *39,* 67–87.

Falconer, D. S. The inheritance of liability to certain diseases estimated from the incidence among relatives. *Annals of Human Genetics,* 1965, *29,* 51–76.

Falconer, D. S. The inheritance of liability to diseases with variable age of onset, with particular reference to diabetes mellitus. *Annals of Human Genetics,* 1967, *31,* 1–20.

Farkas, T., Reivich, M., Alavi, A., Greenberg, J. H., Fowler, J. S., MacGregor, R. R., Christman, D. R., & Wolf, A. P. The applications of [^{18}F]2-deoxy-2-fluoro-D-glucose and positron emission tomography in the study of psychiatric conditions. In J. Passonneau, R. Hawkins, W. D. Lust, & F. A. Welsh (Eds.), *Cerebral metabolism and neural function.* Baltimore: Williams & Wilkins, 1980, pp. 403–408.

Fraser, F. C. Evolution of a palatable multifactorial threshold model. *American Journal of Human Genetics,* 1980, *32,* 796–813.

Fraser, G. R., & Friedman, A. I. *The causes of blindness in childhood.* Baltimore: Johns Hopkins University Press, 1967.

Gottesman, I. I., & Shields, J. A polygenic theory of schizophrenia. *Proceedings of the National Academy of Sciences,* 1967, *58,* 199–205.

Gottesman, I. I., & Shields, J. *Schizophrenia and genetics: A twin study vantage point.* New York: Academic Press, 1972.

Grüneberg, H. Genetical studies on the skeleton of the mouse. IV. Quasi-continuous variations. *Journal of Genetics,* 1952, *51,* 95–114.

Hanson, D. R., & Gottesman, I. I. Genetic concepts for psychopathology. In H. M. vanPraag, M. H. Lader, O. J. Rafaelsen, & E. J. Sachar (Eds.), *Handbook of biological psychiatry* (Vol. 1). New York: Dekker, 1979, pp. 273–301.

Heston, L. L. The genetics of schizophrenic and schizoid disease. *Science,* 1970, *167,* 249–256.

Huxley, J. A., Mayr, E., Osmond, H., & Hoffer, A. Schizophrenia as a genetic morphism. *Nature,* 1964, *204,* 220–221.

Jarett, L. Pathophysiology of the insulin receptor. *Human Pathology,* 1979, *10,* 301–311.

Kay, D. W., & Roth, M. Environmental and hereditary factors in the schizophrenias of old age ("late paraphrenia") and their bearing on the general problem of causation in schizophrenia. *Journal of Mental Science,* 1961, *107,* 649–686.

Leonhard, K. *The classification of endogenous psychoses* (5th ed.). New York: Irvington, 1979.

Lerner, I. M. *The genetic basis of natural selection.* New York: Wiley, 1958.

Li, C. C. *Path analysis: A primer.* Pacific Grove, Calif.: Boxwood Press, 1975.

Matthysse, S., & Kidd, K. K. Estimating the genetic contribution to schizophrenia. *American Journal of Psychiatry,* 1976, *133,* 185–191.

Matthysse, S., Lange, K., & Wagener, D. K. Continuous variation caused by genes with graduated effects. *Proceedings of the National Academy of Sciences,* 1979, *76,* 2862–2865.

McGuffin, P. Is schizophrenia an HLA-associated disease? *Psychological Medicine,* 1979, *9,* 721–728.

McKusick, V. *Mendelian inheritance in man* (5th ed.). Baltimore: Johns Hopkins University Press, 1978.

Meehl, P. E. Schizotaxia, schizotypy, schizophrenia. *American Psychologist,* 1962, *17,* 827–838.

Meehl, P. E. Specific genetic etiology, psychodynamics, and therapeutic nihilism. *International Journal of Mental Health,* 1972, *1,* 10–27.

Meehl, P. E. *Psychodiagnosis: Selected papers.* Minneapolis: University of Minnesota Press, 1973.

Meltzer, H. Y. Biology of schizophrenic subtypes: A review and proposal for methods of study. *Schizophrenia Bulletin,* 1979, *5,* 460–479.

Morton, N. E., Gulbrandsen, C. L., Rhoads, G. G., Kagan, A., & Lew, R. Major loci for lipoprotein concentrations. *American Journal of Human Genetics,* 1978, *30,* 583–589.

Morton, N. E., & MacLean, C. J. Analysis of family resemblance. III. Complex segregation of quantitative traits. *American Journal of Human Genetics,* 1974, *26,* 489–503.

Murphy, E. A. One cause? Many causes? The argument from the bimodal distribution. *Journal of Chronic Diseases,* 1964, *17,* 301–324.

Neel, J. V., & Schull, W. J. *Human heredity.* Chicago: University of Chicago Press, 1954.

Notkins, A. L. The causes of diabetes. *Scientific American,* 1979, *241,* 62–73.

O'Rourke, D. H., Gottesman, I. I., Suarez, B. K., Rice, J., & Reich, T. Refutation of the general single locus model for the etiology of schizophrenia. *American Journal of Human Genetics,* in press.

Passonneau, J., Hawkins, R., Lust, W. D., & Welsh, F. A. (Eds.). *Cerebral metabolism and neural function.* Baltimore: Williams & Wilkins, 1980.

Penrose, L. S. *The biology of mental defect* (3rd ed.). New York: Grune & Stratton, 1963.

Rao, D. C., Morton, N. E., Gottesman, I. I., & Lew, R. Path analysis of qualitative data on pairs of relatives: Application to schizophrenia. *Human Heredity,* in press.

Reich, T., James, J. W., & Morris, C. A. The use of multiple thresholds in determining the mode of transmission of semi-continuous traits. *Annals of Human Genetics,* 1972, *36,* 163–184.

Reich, T. Rice, J., Cloninger, C. R., Wette, R., & James, J. The use of multiple thresholds and segregation analysis in analyzing the phenotypic heterogeneity of multifactorial traits. *Annals of Human Genetics,* 1979, *42,* 371–390.

Rice, J., Cloninger, C. R., & Reich, T. Analysis of behavioral traits in the presence of cultural transmission and assortative mating: Applications to IQ and SES. *Behavior Genetics,* 1980, *10,* 73–92.

Robinson, N. M., & Robinson, H. B. *The mentally retarded child* (2nd ed.). New York: McGraw-Hill, 1976.

Rosenthal, D. (Ed.). *The Genain quadruplets.* New York: Basic Books, 1963.

Serban, G. Stress in schizophrenics and normals. *British Journal of Psychiatry,* 1975, *126,* 397–407.

Sing, C. F., & Skolnick, M. (Eds.). *The genetic analysis of common diseases: Application to predictive factors in coronary heart disease.* New York: Alan Liss, 1979.

Slater, E., & Cowie, V. *The genetics of mental disorders.* London: Oxford University Press, 1971.

Smith, C. Heritability of liability and concordance in monozygous twins. *Annals of Human Genetics,* 1970, *34,* 85–91.

Smith, C. Recurrence risks for multifactorial inheritance. *American Journal of Human Genetics,* 1971, *23,* 578–588.

Suarez, B., Hodge, S. E., & Reich, T. Is juvenile diabetes determined by a single gene closely linked to HLA? *Diabetes,* 1979, *28,* 527–532.

Suarez, B., Reich, T., & Trost, J. Limits of the general two allele single locus model with incomplete penetrance. *Annals of Human Genetics,* 1976, *40,* 231–244.

Thoday, J. M. New insights into continuous variation. In J. F. Crow & J. V. Neel (Eds.), *Proceedings of the Third International Congress of Human Genetics.* Baltimore: Johns Hopkins University Press, 1967, pp. 339–350.

Waddington, C. H. *Principles of development and differentiation.* London: Macmillan, 1966.

Woolf, C. M. Congenital cleft lip: A genetic study of 496 propositi. *Journal of Medical Genetics,* 1971, *8,* 65–83.

Wright, S. An analysis of variability in number of digits in an inbred strain of guinea pigs. *Genetics,* 1934, *19,* 506–536. (a)

Wright, S. The results of crosses between inbred strains of guinea pigs, differing in number of digits. *Genetics,* 1934, *19,* 537–551. (b)

12   Epilogue

The schizophrenia puzzle is in the process of being solved, and we are optimistic that it will be solved before the twentieth century ends. The level of research activity, the rate of schizophrenia-relevant discoveries, and the enthusiasm across the panorama of the neurobiological sciences are such as to sustain our optimism (e.g., Lipton, Dimascio, & Killam, 1978; Passonneau et al., 1980; Usdin, Sourkes, & Youdim, 1980).

Neurobiology and schizophrenia

The primal question – How does the brain work? – is more than a rhetorical one. It even appears that, in principle, it will be somewhat easier to detect how the brain malfunctions than how it functions normally. Even a superficial glance at the raw materials for the sciences of neurobiology instills awe. It has been estimated that the adult brain contains 100 billion (10^{11}) neurons (Cowan, 1979). The typical neuron has approximately 1,500 synapses for a total of 10^{14} synapses. At each synapse there are 1 million receptor molecules that permit communication with other neurons. Chemical substances called neurotransmitters provide the means by which signals are sent from one neuron to the next in a particular CNS circuit. Thirty or so such substances have been identified in one class (e.g., dopamine, serotonin, norepinephrine), and an additional 200 or so neuropeptides (e.g., opioid enkephalins, β-endorphin, and vasopressin) may also be involved as neurotransmitters with specific inhibitory and excitatory action (Iversen, 1979; Snyder, 1980).[1]

Our case for the role of genetic factors in the etiology of schizophrenia is built on clinical-population genetics data, but it implies a biochemical and/or biophysical cause for the malfunctioning of the brain that leads to the

---

[1] See references for additional readings relevant to the molecular genetics of schizophrenia that go beyond the scope of our book.

development of schizophrenia. At present there *is* a gap between the population genetics of schizophrenia and the molecular genetics of schizophrenia, with eager hands reaching across the gap from both sides. The construction of appropriate causal networks (e.g., Figures 11.1, 11.2) in each of the two main domains and then their linking by another causal network will be among the exciting discoveries that lie ahead (Comings, 1979; Garattini, Pujol, & Samanin, 1978; Reis et al., 1981).

Because we believe schizophrenia depends to a considerable extent on relatively specific genetic factors, we must compare not only patients but also their normal relatives on posited biological measures. This will be true no matter how important social, psychological, and therapeutic factors may be for the pathogenesis and the outcome of schizophrenia.

For advances to occur in the understanding of the genetic factors, what is required is a characteristic that can be reliably measured: one that is stable through different stages of the illness, including remissions, and that is distributed differently in schizophrenics, in persons with other psychiatric disorders, and in the general population. The next step would be to carry out family and twin studies to see whether the characteristic in question could be used as a genetic marker of the predisposition to schizophrenia. A good genetic marker should be present in all the identical twins of schizophrenics, whether they are currently affected, whether they have previously been affected but are now in remission, or whether they have never been affected with schizophrenia. The trait should occur to a lesser degree in the fraternal twins, siblings, and other relatives, and in a way that fits a genetic hypothesis. The trait would be useful if it proved a quantitative one for which relatives correlated in a manner consistent with a highly heritable polygenic trait. In the case of diabetes, blood sugar amount does not meet all these criteria, but it may be mentioned as a somewhat analogous example for a disorder that has some parallels with schizophrenia. It would be nice to have a relevant and ethical loading test as we have for diabetes and phenylketonuria.

Our hypothetical biological variable would be equally useful as a genetic marker if it segregated in families like a simply inherited Mendelian trait. Depending on its frequency in schizophrenics, it could then reveal itself as anything from a minor contributor (like blood group O appears to be in duodenal ulcer) to a major factor in a polygenic system on Thoday's model (cf. Chapter 11), or a distinct class of schizophrenia with a high risk for relatives as on the heterogeneity model. If all schizophrenics but only about 3% of nonschizophrenics possessed the trait, the monogene of Slater's theory could be confirmed.

There are, of course, difficulties in biochemistry that are as great as those in a soft science like psychology. Both are plagued by the problems of where to start looking; of finding a method that gives the same results in different laboratories; and of identifying a constitutional trait and not one that is an effect of the disorder itself rather than a precursor of it, and that is not influenced by drugs, diet, or emotional state.

One of a number of systems likely to prove rewarding when it comes to finding the "twisted molecules" that eventually lead to the twisted thoughts is that of neural transmission itself. We can ask where in the system and which components may be out of order. The process can be divided into three stages, one or more of which may be the candidates to study by twin and family methods. It could involve the synthesis and metabolism of one or more neurotransmitters (or transmitter modulators). It could involve the storage, release, and re-uptake of one or more transmitters. And it could involve the binding of the transmitter to postsynaptic membrane receptors and/or the subsequent response of the target tissue (Brown, 1981; Crow, Johnstone, & Owen, 1979; Nicol & Heston, 1979). We will note in passing that receptor proteins and uptake sites have only recently become subjects for biochemical analysis. The study of the neurotransmitters that may be relevant to schizophrenia is complicated by the fact that they do not cross a cell membrane but bind to a receptor on the exterior of the postsynaptic membrane and require a "second messenger" to complete the signal. Some neurons may transmit by means of more than one neurotransmitter. Some neurotransmitters (such as dopomine) may have more than one type of receptor molecule (McSwigan et al., 1980). The assembling and maintenance of receptor molecules is a very dynamic process involving continuous degradation and replacement.

In the last few years, attention has been focused for very good reasons on one particular neurotransmitter, dopamine, although other neurotransmitters, discovered and potential, continue to be of interest as well. Dopamine is clearly relevant to our understanding of schizophrenia because antischizophrenic drugs act mainly by their ability to block postsynaptic dopamine receptors. Such pharmacological evidence, however, as Iversen (1978) points out, does not necessarily imply that schizophrenia must be a dopamine disorder in which there is either too much dopamine or the receptors are supersensitive or pathologically overabundant. Various lines of evidence (Barchas, Elliott, & Berger, 1978; Bird, Spokes, & Iversen, 1979; Crow, 1980; Meltzer, 1980; Owen et al., 1981), using cerebrospinal fluid in treated schizophrenics and using postmortem brain specimens from schizophrenics who have died, suggest there is no generalized overactivity of the neurons that produce dopamine. However, the number of dopamine receptors in limbic areas of the brain is increased, even when allowance is made for treatment with antischizophrenic medication. Treatment per se with such drugs leads to an increase in receptors.

The story of dopamine and its role in schizophrenia is far from over, and the same can be said of other neurotransmitters. It is interesting, for example, that propranolol has been reported (Yorkston et al., 1977) to have led to miraculous "cures" in schizophrenics who did not respond to other treatments. This drug does not have any dopamine-blocking properties, but does block the effects of the neurotransmitter, serotonin (Iversen, 1978). Recent research (Peet, Middlemiss, & Yates, 1981) suggests a pharmacokinetic interaction that increases plasma levels of phenothiazines. Such information, after it has been replicated, adds to the excitement of biochemical research on schizophrenia. What is the role of the naturally occurring neuroanatomical asymmetries in neurotransmitter neurons (Glick, Jerussi, & Zimmersberg, 1977; Oke et al., 1978)? Pharmacological responses may help us unravel the problems of clinical heterogeneity and genetic heterogeneity (Klein et al., 1980). Progress in genetics and biochemistry need not go hand in hand as we have seen in the instances of Huntington disease where the genetics is simple, and in diabetes where a relevant substance – insulin – has been identified, but with still obscure genetics.

It is only a question of time (and it may already have been accomplished by the time this book is published) before scientists are able to radioactively label precursors of dopamine and other putative neurotransmitters[2] (both for schizophrenia and for other mental disorders treated pharmacologically with some success) and to observe their actions in the living brains of schizophrenics and other patients using the relatively noninvasive techniques of positron emission tomography. Such information will add large and perhaps critical pieces to the schizophrenia puzzle. It will be problematic whether scientists can ethically ask the healthy relatives of patients to undergo the same procedures so that we may gather information relevant to the genetics of the mental disorders. The use of identical twins, concordant and discordant for schizophrenia, in this kind of experiment is likely to hasten the acquisition of critical puzzle pieces.

Prospective high-risk studies and schizophrenia

One burgeoning and important area of schizophrenia research that we have neglected up to this point is that of the prospective longitudinal study of the children of one or of two schizophrenic parents – the so-called high-risk strategy (Erlenmeyer-Kimling et al., in press; NIMH, 1981; Watt et al., in press). Such a strategy was suggested for psychopathology in 1957 by Pearson and Kley as an economic way to observe the development of

---

[2] The neurotransmitters themselves do not cross the "blood–brain barrier."

schizophrenia. By studying schizophrenics before they become ill, it should be possible to distinguish between those aspects of neurobiological and psychological malfunction that are indicators of the genetic predisposition to developing schizophrenia and those that may be simply the consequence of a disturbance in state. Possible indicators may be detected at any age (including prenatally, say by fetoscopy), but they require confirmation by lengthy follow-up in order to see which children actually develop schizophrenia. Many promising, but no definitive, leads have been unearthed by the current contingent of high-risk investigators (cf. Garmezy, 1978; Hanson, Gottesman, & Meehl, 1977; Neale & Oltmanns, 1980; Watt et al., in press).

Follow-up information provides the ultimate test of any claim that individuals have been identified with the highest genetic risks (cf. Schulsinger, 1980), or that a genetic trait in the population has been discovered that will correlate with the predisposition to schizophrenia, or that interacting environmental factors have been identified that open the door to preventive intervention. One disadvantage, from the genetic point of view, of studying the offspring of schizophrenics prospectively is that only 10% of schizophrenics in general have schizophrenic parents. The earlier the age at which the high-risk children were ascertained, the greater the proportion exposed from an early age to environmental conditions not experienced by the vast majority of schizophrenics. It is obvious that rearing by psychotic or other sick parents can lead to childhood disturbances in behavior for strictly environmental reasons (Rutter, 1966).

That about half of all schizophrenics (Bleuler, 1978; Slater & Roth, 1969) do show evidence of abnormality, not necessarily "schizospecific," long before overt psychosis is the best evidence for the contention that prospective studies of children of schizophrenic parents will be able to discern the beginnings of schizophrenia. However, these efforts will be successful only if valid critera for schizophrenia are used to define the schizophrenic parent sample. Concentrating on severely affected families or families with many affected relatives will increase the chances of including future schizophrenics among presumed high-risk children. Even if the broad definitions of schizophrenia that encompass pseudoneurotic and pseudopsychopathic cases are valid, the relatively milder severity of these varieties reduces the yield for high-risk studies.

There are at least three important goals for high-risk research (cf. Mednick & Baert, 1981). The first is to define the range of specificity of the characteristics that precede adult schizophrenia so that they can be used in the general population. Retrospectively, some preschizophrenics appear behaviorally normal, some seem "different," and others are markedly disturbed. Childhood psychopathology is often associated with adult mental illness, but childhood symptomatology is a poor predictor of adult health or diagnosis (cf. Achenbach, 1974; Rutter & Hersov, 1977). To resolve the specificity issue, children of schizophrenic parents must be compared to children at risk for other kinds of psychopathology – for example, comparing the children of recurrent unipolar depressives and of those with chronic physical illness.

A second important goal for high-risk researchers is to quantify the relation between endophenotypic indicators–predictors and outcomes. The usefulness of predictors will, of course, be directly proportional to the accuracy of the predictions of overt schizophrenia. The predictors' false positive and false negative rates will have to be determined by extensive follow-ups, and the frequency of the predictor traits in high-risk samples will have to be compared with estimates of the population base rates (Meehl & Rosen, 1955) obtained from control samples of children born to normal parents and to parents suffering from depression and from chronic physical illness. Base rates may vary as a function of social class or other demographic characteristics, so that both matched as well as unmatched (general population) comparison groups will be necessary (Meehl, 1970).

A third goal of high-risk research is to determine whether valid childhood predictors of adult schizophrenia identify the etiological roots of schizophrenia. At least three possibilities must be considered. (1) The predictor variables might be indicators of the high-risk genotype. Such predictors should help to elucidate specific neurobiological deficits associated with the development of schizophrenia and would denote vulnerable individuals with the potential for developing a future schizophrenia, even though some (perhaps most) of these individuals will remain clinically normal throughout their lives. (2) Valid childhood predictors of adult schizophrenia might identify potentiators (Figure 11.2) or correlates of potentiators that lead to breakdown. Such potentiators might be parts of predisposed individuals' environments or general genetic backgrounds. For example, let us say school failure in high-risk children often predicts breakdown. Such a school-failure sign might be due to family pathology (or low IQ), and the family pathology (or low IQ) might be a potentiator of schizophrenia in predisposed individuals. Yet the school-failure sign is neither a consequence of the high-risk genotype nor, by itself, an early sign of schizophrenic behavior. (3) Childhood predictors might represent the earliest signs (or effects) of already potentiated schizophrenias. Such "predictors" would indicate when schizophrenic behaviors begin but would not necessarily shed light on either the genetical or environmental contributors to the development of schizophrenia.

It seems likely that at least some early-developing schizophrenics will be detected by high-risk researchers. In our own sample (Hanson, Gottesman,

& Heston, 1976), 5 out of 30 (17%) 7-year-old children of our consensus-diagnosed schizophrenic mothers and fathers were characterized by having poor motor skills, large within-individual inconsistencies in performance on cognitive tasks, and enduring "schizoidlike" patterns of withdrawal, emotional flatness, irritability, negativism, and emotional instability. None of the 30 children of consensus psychiatric controls and none of 56 children born to normals had all three indicators. The 5 children exhibited some of the behaviors found in adult schizophrenics (e.g., loose, bizarre thoughts, and extreme anxiety), but none was reported to have delusions or hallucinations, and none fitted the syndrome of adult schizophrenia when seen at age 7. Most had severely schizophrenic parents, and 2 children had a second parent with psychiatric problems. Assuming that a diathesis–stressor model of schizophrenia is valid, these 5 children appear to have a higher risk for schizophrenia than all the other children studied. It might be possible to detect some symptoms of the syndrome early in the life of predisposed individuals, but, again, any sample of high-risk children will have to be followed well into adulthood to establish the validity of proposed preschizophrenic traits. Early detection may, however, require a pharmacological stressor in a "loading test" (e.g., Janowsky et al., 1977) selected so as to be relevant to theories about the pathogenesis of schizophrenia; ethical considerations loom large in this area.

Much of the current enthusiasm for high-risk studies in schizophrenia can be traced to the imaginative and productive work of Mednick and Schulsinger (1968) in Copenhagen. Their hypothesis that potential schizophrenics have an abnormal autonomic nervous system and an abnormally fast electrodermal recovery rate that may have a genetic basis has been of heuristic value to the field. Most of these ideas were based on early results using the first 20 "sick" children identified in 1967 at an average age of 15. On the follow-up (H. Schulsinger, 1976, 1980), more overt schizophrenics were found *outside* the "sick" high-risk subsample than in it. Of 15 consensus-diagnosed schizophrenics in the reinterviewed high-risk subjects, only 4 had been identified in 1962 as being in the pathological group; a further 2 schizophrenics in the "sick" group could not be reinterviewed because of suicide.

The possibility of detecting *some* schizophrenics-to-be in childhood should not imply that *all* schizophrenia can be predicted from childhood. Schizophrenia may well be too diverse in etiology for the recognition of *a* premorbid schizophrenic personality or *a* single neurobiological characteristic that could be equated with the genotype for schizophrenia. Even if a perfect indicator of the high-risk genotype is discovered, prediction of all cases of schizophrenia will be impossible so long as the environmental contributors to schizophrenia are unspecifiable. So far, *no* specific environmental source of liability is known; the most likely environmental contributor, stress, may come from many sources and, apparently, may come during any stage of development. Prenatal or birth complications, early deprivations, broken homes, censuring parents, the death of someone close, failures in school, poor work or social relations, childbirth, a bad drug trip, as well as all kinds of *good* fortune may have effects on a predisposed individual that are obvious only in retrospect. In prospect, it will be impossible to prophesy the events themselves, let alone their effects.

A useful mental exercise for those concerned about the etiology of schizophrenia is to ask themselves the following questions about putative etiological factors: Do the factors lead to cost-effective percentages of true and false positives and true and false negatives? Is the factor "one-way pathognomonic" in that its presence rules in schizophrenia? Is it "two-way pathognomonic" in that its presence rules in schizophrenia and its absence rules out schizophrenia? The answers to these questions will suggest whether putative etiological factors have a strong influence on schizophrenia or are merely moderator variables (Meehl, 1977).

If we wanted to conjure up a futuristic – if impossible – experimental design so as to resolve most of the questions raised by the studies and strategies we have reviewed, we would need a prospective longitudinal study of identical and fraternal twins who were offspring of well-characterized (biologically and psychologically) dual-mating schizophrenics. One twin in each pair would be kept by the biological parents and the other would be adopted at birth into a good home with well-studied adoptive parents. Of course, the study would commence with the conception, monitor fetal heart-rate changes to stress, and would include a battery of serial, noninvasive biological and psychological examinations at the cutting edge of their respective subdisciplines over a 30-year period.

Reprise

Our present knowledge, despite elements of uncertainty, permits us to conclude unequivocally that genetic factors are importantly involved in the etiology of schizophrenia. Some of the factors are probably specific. By specific we mean that some genes, whatever other effects they have on other traits, contribute to the liability of developing schizophrenia rather than, or more than, they do to, say, cholesterol levels, diabetes, eye color, or anxiety neurosis. The specific schizophrenia-related genes are posited to be differentiable from the general genetic contributors to the total liability, with the latter serving as modifiers or potentiators. Regrettably, no individual schizophrenia-related gene has yet been identified let alone characterized biochemically or biophysically.

It bears repeating that both the unspecified genes and the unspecified environments are each necessary but not sufficient for developing schizophrenia. Efforts aimed at finding good endophenotypes and true genetic markers of the vulnerable genotypes are to be encouraged, as is basic research on how the brain works. We are far from a dead end.

Whatever ultimate form the solution of the schizophrenia puzzle takes, it will have to accommodate itself to the following set of large puzzle pieces:

- No environmental causes have been found that will invariably or even with moderate probability produce a genuine schizophrenia in persons who are unrelated to a schizophrenic index case.
- Schizophrenia occurs in both industrialized and undeveloped societies. In the former, the lifetime risk (with conservative diagnostic standards) is usually about 1% by age 55.
- Within large urban communities there is a marked social class gradient in the prevalence of schizophrenia, most of which can be attributed to premorbid downward social drift of predisposed persons.
- The risk of schizophrenia to the relatives of index cases increases markedly with the degree of genetic relatedness (25%, 50%, 100%) even in the absence of shared, specific environments. The observed risks, however, are not compatible with any simple Mendelian genetic models.
- The risk to the relatives of schizophrenics varies with the severity of the proband's illness, the number of other relatives already affected, and, in the case of offspring, with the status of the other parent – for example, schizophrenic × normal . . . schizophrenic × schizophrenic.
- Gender/sex is not relevant in schizophrenia except for age at onset: Paternal half siblings of index schizophrenic adoptees are as often schizophrenic as the maternal half siblings; offspring of male schizophrenics are as often schizophrenic as those of female schizophrenics; the sex ratio for schizophrenia is equal by the end of the risk period; female twin pairs are not significantly more concordant than male pairs (MZ); and opposite-sex DZ pairs are as concordant as same-sex DZ pairs in recent studies.
- The identical twin (monozygotic or MZ) concordance rates for schizophrenia are at least 3 times those of fraternal twins (dizygotic or DZ) and some 35 to 60 times the general population risk.
- More than half of the MZ pairs in recent studies are discordant for schizophrenia despite sharing all their genes in common, thereby demonstrating unequivocally the importance of environmental contributors to liability.

- MZ and DZ twins as such are not at a higher risk for schizophrenia than singletons.
- Identical twins who are clinically discordant for schizophrenia each transmit schizophrenia to their offspring at the same high rate. This fact underlines the reality of the concepts of incomplete expression and incomplete penetrance of genes.
- Identical twins reared apart from childhood (12 authenticated pairs) are concordant for schizophrenia to about the same extent as those reared together. When considering this situation, however, one should realize that raising identical twins in different homes is a very rare event yielding information that may not be generalizable.
- Children of schizophrenics placed early for nonfamilial adoption still develop schizophrenia as adults at rates considerably higher than the population rate, sometimes as high as those rates in children reared by their own schizophrenic parents.
- Adoptive relatives (step-parents, step-siblings) of schizophrenic adoptees do not have significantly elevated rates of schizophrenia compared to the biological relatives of the adoptees, who do have high rates.
- Children of normal parents ($N = 21$) cross-fostered into homes where an adoptive-parental figure later became schizophrenic do not show an increased rate of schizophrenia.
- Probands whose schizophrenialike psychoses occur after head injuries or epilepsy have first-degree relatives whose risks for schizophrenia do not differ from those of the general population. This point emphasizes the reality of nongenetic schizophreniform psychoses (phenocopies) and the necessity of accurate diagnosis, because there are many imitators of schizophrenia.
- Childhood psychoses appearing before puberty do not seem to be genetically related to schizophrenia.
- The observed risks in different classes of schizophrenics' relatives are compatible with a multifactorial-polygenic-threshold model of transmission similar to that found useful for advancing knowledge about other common genetic diseases and congenital malformations, but variants of single-major-locus theories cannot be excluded.
- Because no *corpus delicti* has yet been found that can be equated with a genotype for schizophrenia, the premorbid schizophrenic is currently not identifiable. Hence ambiguity and uncertainty haunt attempts to fit specific models of genetic transmission.

The scientific quest for the explanation and the solution of the schizophrenia puzzle is not immune from serious disruption by ideological, egoistical, and political attacks. Although we wish it could be otherwise, scientific facts, just like other facts, have been filtered through values and personalities of one kind or another. Scientists, after all, are only human. Fortunately, an unfettered science is eventually self-correcting.

We hope the flashes of excitement generated by finding puzzle pieces and fitting some of them together and the subsequent emergence of what the schizophrenia puzzle might, in part, look like have been transmitted to the reader. We challenge you to throw out the extraneous pieces, to correct the erroneous pieces, to find the missing pieces, and to help complete the schizophrenia puzzle.

BIBLIOGRAPHY

Achenbach, T. M. *Developmental psychopathology.* New York: Ronald Press, 1974.

Barchas, J. D., Elliott, G. R., & Berger, P. A. Biogenic amine hypotheses of schizophrenia. In L. Wynne, R. L. Cromwell, & S. Matthysse (Eds.), *The nature of schizophrenia: New approaches to research and treatment.* New York: Wiley, 1978, pp. 126–142.

Beloff, H. (Ed.). A balance sheet on Burt. *Bulletin of the British Psychological Society,* 1980, *33*, Suppl.

Bird, E. D., Spokes, E. G. S., & Iversen, L. L. Increased dopamine concentration in limbic areas of brain from patients dying with schizophrenia. *Brain,* 1979, *102,* 347–360.

Bleuler, M. *The schizophrenic disorders: Long-term patient and family studies* (S. M. Clemens, trans.). New Haven: Yale University Press, 1978.

Brown, M. S. *LDH receptor mutations and the genetics of familial hypercholesterolemia.* Paper presented at the meeting of the American Society for Human Genetics, Dallas, October 1981.

Comings, D. E. A search for the mutant protein in Huntington's disease and schizophrenia. In T. N. Chase, N. S. Wexler, & A. Barbeau (Eds.), *Advances in neurology* (Vol. 23). New York: Raven Press, 1979, pp. 335–359.

Cowan, W. M. The development of the brain. *Scientific American,* 1979, *241,* 112–133.

Creese, I., Burt, D. R., & Snyder, S. H. Dopamine receptor binding predicts clinical and pharmacological potencies of antischizophrenic drugs. *Science,* 1976, *192,* 481–483.

Crick, F. H. C. Thinking about the brain. *Scientific American,* 1979, *241,* 219–232.

Crow, T. J. Molecular pathology of schizophrenia: More than one disease process? *British Medical Journal,* 1980, *280,* 66–68.

Crow, T. J., Baker, H. F., Cross, A. J., Joseph, M. H., Lofthouse, R., Longden, A., Owen, F., Riley, G. J., Glover, V., & Killpack, W. S. Monoamine mechanisms in chronic schizophrenia: Post-mortem neurochemical findings. *British Journal of Psychiatry,* 1979, *134,* 249–256.

Crow, T. J., Johnstone, E. C., & Owen, F. Research on schizophrenia. In K. Granville-Grossman, (Ed.), *Recent advances in clinical psychiatry.* London: Churchill Livingstone, 1979, pp. 1–36.

Erlenmeyer-Kimling, L., Marcuse, Y., Cornblatt, B., Friedman, D., Rainer, J. D., & Rutschmann, J. The New York high-risk project. In N. F. Watt, E. J. Anthony, L. C. Wynne, & J. Rolf (Eds.), *Schizophrenia: Children at risk.* Cambridge University Press, in press.

Fish, B., & Hagin, R. Visual-motor disorders in infants at risk for schizophrenia. *Archives of General Psychiatry,* 1973, *28,* 900–904.

Garattini, S., Pujol, J. F., & Samanin, R. (Eds.). *Interactions between putative neurotransmitters.* New York: Raven Press, 1978.

Garmezy, N. Observations on high-risk research and premorbid development in schizophrenia. In L. Wynne, R. L. Cromwell, & S. Matthysse (Eds.), *The nature of schizophrenia: New approaches to research and treatment.* New York: Wiley, 1978, pp. 460–472.

Geschwind, N. Specializations of the human brain. *Scientific American,* 1979, *241,* 180–199.

Glick, S. D., Jerussi, T. P., & Zimmersberg, B. Behavioral and neuro-pharmacological correlates of nigrostriatal asymmetry in rats. In S. Harnad, R. W. Doty, L. Goldstein, J. Jaynes, & S. Krauthamer (Eds.), *Lateralization in the nervous system.* London: Academic Press, 1977, pp. 213–250.

Growdon, J. H. Neurotransmitter precursors in the diet: Their use in the treatment of brain disease. In R. J. Wurtman & J. J. Wurtman (Eds.), *Nutrition and the brain series.* Vol. 3. *Disorders of eating and nutrients in treatment of brain diseases.* New York: Raven Press, 1979, pp. 117–181.

Hanson, D., Gottesman, I. I., & Heston, L. L. Some possible childhood indicators of adult schizophrenia inferred from children of schizophrenics. *British Journal of Psychiatry,* 1976, 129, 142–154.

Hanson, D., Gottesman, I. I., & Meehl, P. E. Genetic theories and the validation of psychiatric diagnosis: Implications for the study of children of schizophrenics. *Journal of Abnormal Psychology,* 1977, *6,* 575–588.

Hartmann, E. Schizophrenia: A theory. *Psychopharmacology,* 1976, *49,* 1–15.

Iversen, L. L. Biochemical and pharmacological studies: The dopamine hypothesis. In J. K. Wing (Ed.), *Schizophrenia: Towards a new synthesis.* London: Academic Press, 1978, pp. 89–116.

Iversen, L. L. The chemistry of the brain. *Scientific American,* 1979, *241,* 134–149.

Janowsky, D. S., Huey, L., Storms, L., & Judd, L. L. Methylphenidate hydrochloride effects on psychological tests in acute schizophrenic and nonpsychotic subjects. *Archives of General Psychiatry,* 1977, *34,* 189–194.

Kety, S. S. Disorders of the human brain. *Scientific American,* 1979, *241,* 202–214.

Klein, D. F., Gittelman, R., Quitkin, F., & Rifkin, A. *Diagnosis and drug treatment of psychiatric disorders: Adults and children.* Baltimore: Williams & Wilkins, 1980.

Kornetsky, C. Hyporesponsivity of chronic schizophrenic patients to dextroamphetamine. *Archives of General Psychiatry,* 1976, *33,* 1425–1428.

Lee, T., Seeman, P., Tourtelotte, W. M., Farley, I. J., & Hornykiewicz, O. Binding of ^{3}H-apomorphine in schizophrenic brains. *Nature*, 1978, *274*, 897–900.

Lipton, M. A., Dimascio, A., & Killiam, K. F. (Eds.). *Psychopharmacology: A generation of progress.* New York: Raven Press, 1978.

Lipton, M. A., Mailman, R. B., & Nemeroff, C. B. Vitamins, megavitamin therapy, and the nervous system. In R. J. Wurtman & J. J. Wurtman (Eds.), *Nutrition and the brain series.* Vol. 3. *Disorders of eating and nutrients in treatment of brain diseases.* New York: Raven Press, 1979, pp. 183–264.

McSwigan, J., Nicol, S., Gottesman, I. I., Tuason, V., & Frey, W. Effect of dopamine on activation of rat striatal adenylate cyclase by free Mg^{2+} and guanyl nucleotide. *Journal of Neurochemistry*, 1980, *34*, 594–601.

Mednick, S. A., & Baert, A. E. (Eds.). *Prospective longitudinal research: An empirical basis for the primary prevention of psychosocial disorders.* Oxford: Oxford University Press, 1981.

Mednick, S. A., & Schulsinger, F. Some premorbid characteristics related to breakdown in children with schizophrenic mothers. In D. Rosenthal & S. Kety (Eds.), *The transmission of schizophrenia.* Oxford: Pergamon Press, 1968, pp. 267–291.

Meehl, P. E. Nuisance variables and the ex post facto design. In M. Radner & S. Winokur (Eds.), *Minnesota studies in the philosophy of science* (Vol. 4). Minneapolis: University of Minnesota Press, 1970, pp. 373–402.

Meehl, P. E. Specific etiology and other forms of strong influence: Some quantitative meanings. *Journal of Medicine and Philosophy*, 1977, *2*, 33–53.

Meehl, P., & Rosen, A. Antecedent probability and the efficiency of psychometric signs, patterns, or cutting scores. *Psychological Bulletin*, 1955, *52*, 194–216.

Meltzer, H. Y. Relevance of dopamine autoreceptors for psychiatry: Preclinical and clinical studies. *Schizophrenia Bulletin*, 1980, *3*, 456–475.

National Institute of Mental Health. Risk factor research in the major mental disorders. DHHS Publication No. (ADM)81-1068. Superintendent of Documents, U.S. Government Printing Office, Washington, D.C. 20402, 1981.

Nauta, W. J. H., & Feirtag, M. The organization of the brain. *Scientific American*, 1979, *241*, 88–111.

Neale, J. M., & Oltmanns, T. F. *Schizophrenia.* New York: Wiley, 1980.

Nicol, S. E., & Heston, L. L. The future of genetic research in schizophrenia. *Psychiatric Annals*, 1979, *9*, 14–25.

Oke, A., Keller, R., Mefford, I., & Adams, R. Lateralization of norepinephrine in human thalamus. *Science*, 1978, *200*, 1411–1433.

Owen, F., Cross, A. J., Crow, T. J., Lofthouse, R., & Poulter, M. Neurotransmitter receptors in brain in schizophrenia. *Acta Psychiatrica Scandinavica*, 1981, Suppl. 291, 20–28.

Owen, F., Cross, A. J., Crow, T. J., Longden, A., Poulter, M., & Riley, G. J. Increased dopamine-receptor sensitivity in schizophrenia. *Lancet*, July 29, 1978, pp. 223–225.

Passonneau, J., Hawkins, R., Lust, W. D., & Welsh, F. A. (Eds.). *Cerebral metabolism and neural function.* Baltimore: Williams & Wilkins, 1980.

Pearson, J. S., & Kley, I. B. On the application of genetic expectancies as age specific base rates in the study of human behavior disorders. *Psychological Bulletin*, 1957, *54*, 406–420.

Peet, M., Middlemiss, D. N., & Yates, R. A. Propranolol in schizophrenia. II. Clinical and biochemical aspects of combining propranolol with chlorpromazine. *British Journal of Psychiatry*, 1981, *139*, 112–117.

Reis, D. J., Baker, H., Fink, J. S., & Joh, T. H. A genetic control of the number of dopamine neurons in mouse brain: Its relationship to brain morphology, chemistry and behavior. In E. Gershon, S. Matthysse, X. O. Breakefield, & R. D. Ciaranello (Eds.), *Genetic research strategies in psychobiology and.psychiatry*. Pacific Grove, Calif.: Boxwood Press, 1981, pp. 215–230.

Rutter, M. Children of sick parents: An environmental and psychiatric study (Maudsley Monograph No. 16). London: Oxford University Press, 1966.

Rutter, M., & Hersov, L. (Eds.). *Child psychiatry*. Oxford: Blackwell, 1977.

Sarbin, T. R., & Mancuso, J. C. *Schizophrenia: Medical diagnosis or moral verdict?* New York: Pergamon Press, 1980.

Schulsinger, H. A ten-year follow-up of children of schizophrenic mothers: Clinical assessment. *Acta Psychiatrica Scandinavica*, 1976, *53*, 371–386.

Schulsinger, H. Clinical outcome of ten years of follow-up of children of schizophrenic mothers. In S. B. Sells, R. Crandall, M. Roff, J. Strauss, & W. Pollin (Eds.), *Human functioning in longitudinal perspective*. Baltimore: Williams & Wilkins, 1980, pp. 33–40.

Seeman, R., Lee, T., Chica-Wong, M., & Wong, K. Antipsychotic drug doses and neuroleptic/dopamine receptors. *Nature*, 1976, *261*, 717–718.

Shields, J., & Gottesman, I. I. Genetic studies of schizophrenia as signposts to biochemistry. In L. L. Iversen & S. P. R. Rose (Eds.), *Biochemistry and mental illness*. London: Biochemical Society, 1973, pp. 165–174.

Slater, E., & Roth, M. *Mayer-Gross, Slater and Roth clinical psychiatry* (3rd ed.). London: Baillère, Tindall, & Cassell, 1969.

Snyder, S. H. Brain peptides as neurotransmitters. *Science*, 1980, *29*, 976–983.

Spokes, E. G. S. An analysis of factors influencing measurements of dopamine, noradrenaline, glutamate decarboxylase and choline acetylase in human post-mortem brain tissue. *Brain*, 1979, *102*, 333–346.

Usdin, E., Sourkes, T. L., & Youdim, M. B. H. *Enzymes and neurotransmitters in mental disease: Based on a symposium held at the Technion Faculty of Medicine, Haifa, Israel, August 28–30, 1979*. Sussex, England: Wiley, 1980.

Watt, N., Anthony, E. J., Wynne, L., & Rolf, J. (Eds.). *Schizophrenia: Children at risk*. Cambridge University Press, in press.

Yorkston, N. J., Gruzelier, J. H., Zaki, S. A., Hollander, D., Pitcher, D. R., & Sergeant, H. G. S. Propranolol as an adjunct to the treatment of schizophrenia. *Lancet*, September 17, 1977, pp. 575–578.

Name index

Subject index

acute schizophrenia, 7, 90,121, 139–43,228
adoption strategies: adoptees' families, 75–7, 139–45; adoptees method, 75–7, 130–7, 242; crossfostering, 75–7, 137–9; overview, 140–1, 145–6
affective disorder: epidemiology, 17–28, 114; separation from schizophrenia, 7–13, 41, 92–3, 106, 113, 133, 240; twin studies, 106, 109
age correction, 20–2, 24–9, 46, 105, 107, 111
age of onset distribution, 26–9, 150, 158
alcoholism, 41, 74, 114, 117, 172, 219
American Psychiatric Association, 14
amphetamine, 1, 155, 202, 205, 219, 242
antischizophrenia genes, 96, 130–1
antisocial personality (criminality), 132, 136–7, 145, 187
assortative mating, 21, 87–9, 92–7, 144, 146
autism, early infantile: age of onset, 150, 156–7, 163; familial morbidity, 154–9, 162–4; genetics, 159–61, 164–5; phenomenology, 149–52, 161; prevalence, 152–4, 162; serotonin, 159–60; twin studies, 155–8, 161–3
autonomic nervous system, 241

biographical (cohort) method, 24–6
birth complications (OCs, PBCs), 120, 127, 134, 143, 153, 162–5, 174–7, 196–9, 242; see also birthweight; neuropathology
birthweight, 74, 119, 143, 175–6, 178–81, 197–9
blindness, 53, 62, 94, 164, 209
borderline schizophrenia, see schizophreniform psychosis; spectrum, schizophrenia
breeder hypothesis, see social mobility

cancer, 193–6
cardiovascular disease, 53, 63, 77, 193–4, 218, 221, 226

case history data, 2–5, 32, 88–9, 94–5, 118, 121–6, 172–4
causal networks, 211–15, 218, 236–8
childbirth, 107
cleft lip, 63, 223–4
color blindness, 53, 62, 209
communication deviance, 94–5, 138, 146, 173–4, 239
concordance, see twin strategy
cost of mental illness, 16
crossfostering, see adoption strategies
CT scan, see tomography

deafness, 93
diabetes, 195, 211–14, 221, 226, 236, 238
diagnosis, 1–15; criteria, 2, 5–7, 39–40; cross-national, 7–13, 37–40; historical aspects, 37–49; narrow vs. broad, 10–13, 90–2; reliability, 5, 115; validity, 1–2, 9–13, 120–3, 138, 145, 239
discordant MZ twins, 46, 72–5, 115–23, 172, 175, 238; offspring of, 108–9, 228–9
divorce, 186–91, 201
DNA, 54–6, 58, 209
dominance-submissiveness, 74, 119–23, 177–81, 213
drift hypothesis see social mobility
DSM-III, 2, 6–7, 92
dual matings of schizophrenics, 48–9, 85–6, 92–7, 242

effective genotype, 56–8, 63–9, 116
Einheitspsychose, 92
emigration, 17, 23, 25, 30–3, 108
environmentability, 180, 225
environmental factors in combination, 177–81, 227–9, 241–2
epidemiology, 16–35; admissions/discharge, 18–19; historical trends, 17, 21–2; incidence, 18–29; prevalence, 18, 23–5, 44, 110, 142, 240; treated vs. true, 22–5
epigenesis, 55–8, 169, 210, 227–30

NO